My prayer is that God will use this book to both motivate and equip you to help your kids develop convictions about their faith.

From the foreword by Sean McDowell, PhD, Biola University professor, speaker, and author of more than eighteen books, including *A New Kind of Apologist*

I can't think of a more relevant or more needed book for parents raising kids in today's culture. This book on apologetics will lead parents in critical conversations that will help grow and guide kids to be lifelong followers of Christ.

Kristen Welch, author of *Raising Grateful Kids in an Entitled World*

Hey parents: Do you want to reduce the chances that your child will follow the crowd to the point of rejecting Christ and the values and truths you hold so dearly? Then you need to have the conversations that Natasha Crain so brilliantly describes in this book. Prevent heartbreak later by reading and heeding this book now!

Frank Turek, PhD, president of CrossExamined.org and author of *I Don't Have Enough Faith to Be an Atheist* and *Stealing from God*

Here's my suggestion for this smart, funny, honest, and *practical* book: read each chapter carefully. Then read it again (they're short). Then pray that your kids ask questions about God. If within five minutes they do not, ask them the questions listed at the end of each chapter. May this book lead to thousands more moms and dads engaging with their kids through an intelligent faith. And may there be tens of thousands more kids who feel loved because the adults in their lives take their questions seriously.

Jeff Myers, PhD, president, Summit Ministries

I am a veteran of dinner-table and long-car-ride conversations with my kids about key issues in theology, philosophy, and apologetics.

I'm a huge fan of doing this. I've seen how it can cause anti-Christian arguments from skeptics to roll off my kids because they have already heard some of the best arguments for Christianity. It is a lost art, but not lost on Natasha Crain. She is my go-to person on how to train parents and engage kids on these topics of eternal importance. Buy a case of her books and pass them around to other parents and grandparents you know. Then, put it all into practice and watch what God does. It might be the most important thing you can do with your kids in a wildly skeptical age. It turns out that Christianity is true, and our arguments are solid. We and our kids need to be equipped. Thank you, Natasha, for giving us such a wonderful resource to help us all to do the job.

Craig Hazen, PhD, founder and director of the apologetics program at Biola University, author of *Five Sacred Crossings*

Talking with Your Kids about God is the most important Christian parenting book you will buy this year. Natasha Crain has masterfully crafted a practical, engaging resource that will give you the confidence and knowledge you need to have meaningful conversations with your kids. Have you ever felt like you aren't ready to navigate difficult questions about God with your kids? This book will change that. Natasha has written a smart, accessible, and winsome guide for parents who are eager to lead their kids to the truth. Get it *now*, and don't miss the next books in this important series.

J. Warner Wallace, cold-case detective, senior fellow at the Colson Center for Christian Worldview, and author of *Cold-Case Christianity*, *God's Crime Scene*, *Forensic Faith*, and the accompanying children's books

As an evangelist who spends much of my time talking with those who have doubts and questions about God—and as the father of two young children—I highly recommend *Talking with Your*

Kids about God. Not least because the questions kids ask are often some of the deepest and most honest, but also because if we don't answer their questions, they're going to conclude there are no answers and walk away at the first opportunity. Natasha has written a fantastic tool to equip parents to talk honestly with their kids, to listen properly, to ask good questions, and to help them see that there's only one good reason to be a Christian—not because mum or dad believe it, but because it's true.

Andy Bannister, PhD, adjunct speaker, Ravi Zacharias
International Ministries

Talking with Your Kids about God is an outstanding resource for equipping parents with the techniques and knowledge they need to have effective conversations with their children about the truths of Christianity. Natasha Crain has done an extraordinary job of distilling a large body of material into readable and interesting chapters that can be tackled by topic. As a scholar in the field of science and religion, I was particularly impressed with her treatment of the scientific issues that intersect with the Christian faith. I'll be recommending her book to every parent I know.

Melissa Cain Travis, MA, author of the Young Defenders
storybook series and assistant professor of apologetics,
Houston Baptist University

If you want your kids to develop a well-reasoned, evidence-based faith that can withstand the onslaught of cultural attacks, buy this book today! Natasha Crain makes complex scientific and theological issues accessible for concerned parents like you and me. Each chapter is clear, concise, and Christ-centered, empowering parents to engage in conversations that can change the course of their children's lives. Your entire family will benefit from this important resource!

Jerusha Clark, author of twelve books, including *Your Teenager
Is Not Crazy* and *Every Piece of Me*

All across the country and around the world, I get asked the same questions over and over again: How do I talk to my kids about the tough questions they will have about God? Are there any books out there that can help me? I can now answer both questions with one answer: this book. Easy to read and easy to use, this book will help you to have the important, insightful, and intelligent conversations you need to have with your kids about God.

Michael C. Sherrard, pastor, cocreator of Ratio Christi
College Prep, and author of *Relational Apologetics*

In a world that's increasingly skeptical about Christianity, our kids need to understand what they believe and why. *Talking with Your Kids about God* is a fantastic tool to make those conversations easy and natural. As a children's pastor, I can tell you this book is one of the best investments you'll ever make in your child's faith. Every parent and children's or student pastor needs to unpack these chapters with their kids.

Jason Byerly, children's pastor and author
of *God's Big Adventure* family devotional

As a homeschooling mother, it is imperative to me that my children know what they believe and why. Rather than waiting for them to encounter the world's arguments by surprise, Natasha empowers parents to guide their children in asking crucial questions, reasoning through the answers, and taking ownership of their own faith. The curriculum-style format makes this a fantastic resource for homeschoolers, Sunday school classes, or small groups, equipping the next generation with the greatest gift we can give them: a deeply rooted faith that can withstand the storms of doubt, skepticism, and an increasingly hostile culture.

Rachel Bjorklund, homeschooling mother of four,
Classical Conversations tutor

TALKING
with YOUR KIDS
about GOD

TALKING
with YOUR KIDS
about

30 Conversations
Every Christian Parent
MUST HAVE

NATASHA CRAIN

BakerBooks
a division of Baker Publishing Group
Grand Rapids, Michigan

Published by Baker Books
a division of Baker Publishing Group
PO Box 6287, Grand Rapids, MI 49516-6287
www.bakerbooks.com

Printed in the United States of America

Library of Congress Cataloging-in-Publication Data
Names: Crain, Natasha, 1976– author.
Title: Talking with your kids about God : 30 conversations every Christian parent must have / Natasha Crain.
Description: Grand Rapids : Baker Books, 2017. | Includes bibliographical references.
Identifiers: LCCN 2017026984 | ISBN 9780801075520 (pbk.)
Subjects: LCSH: Christian education of children. | Christian education—Home training. | Apologetics.
Classification: LCC BV1475.3 .C735 2017 | DDC 248.8/45—dc23
LC record available at https://lccn.loc.gov/2017026984

Published in association with the literary agency of Mark Sweeney & Associates, Naples, Florida.

17 18 19 20 21 22 23   7 6 5 4 3 2

To my mom and grandma Elsie—
two ladies who always exemplified
what it means to love the Lord.

Contents

Foreword

Do you care about raising your kids in the Christian faith? Are you afraid that the culture might capture their hearts and minds? If these are concerns you have, as I do, then this book is for *you*. Natasha Crain is committed to helping parents equip their kids with a biblical worldview. As a parent of three young children, I thank God for her efforts.

While there are both many people who write on apologetics (myself included!) and many books on parenting, Natasha has a unique angle—*she writes about apologetics as a parent for parents*. She takes tough concepts and makes them accessible, while providing practical ways to share these truths with kids.

As parents, we have the greatest influence on our children. That's right, you and I influence our kids more than celebrities, athletes, youth pastors, teachers, and friends. So how can we best use that influence? Studies reveal that one of the most important things we can do is have conversations with our kids. Yes, simply *talking* with them about God, and other tough questions about faith, is one of the most important steps we can take (see Deut. 6:4–9).

This is why *Talking with Your Kids about God* is so critical and timely. Natasha identifies thirty of the most important questions kids need answers to today. And she equips us with not only knowledge about these issues but also practical steps on how to have fruitful conversations with our kids about them.

Please allow me to offer three suggestions and some words of encouragement for when you read this book.

First, you don't have to be the expert. This book will equip you with all you need to know to have meaningful conversations with your kids. If further questions arise along the way (which is a good thing!), then seek answers from experts together. Just being willing to have these conversations is half the battle.

Second, begin as early as possible. There's a temptation to put these questions off, but this is a big mistake! Kids who have wrestled with tough questions *before* they are challenged are much more likely to maintain a vibrant faith than those caught off guard.

Third, just do what you can. Having *some* of these conversations is better than none at all. Ideally, you want to get through all these questions (and more), but simply beginning the process and doing what you can have tremendous value.

As parents, it is easy to feel overwhelmed by all the voices vying for the hearts and minds of our children. But don't be discouraged. We can make a difference. My parents had conversations with me about God, and it made a big difference in my faith. And this is what I try to do with my own kids.

I hope you will get a copy of *Talking with Your Kids about God* and begin these conversations today. My prayer is that God will use this book to both motivate and equip you to help your kids develop convictions about their faith. Go for it!

Sean McDowell, PhD,
Biola University

Acknowledgments

First and foremost, I thank God for unexpectedly leading me into this journey of writing and speaking about apologetics. I had no idea when I started my blog that it would lead to this, but I'm so glad God had better plans than what I envisioned.

I want to thank my husband, Bryan, for being extraordinarily supportive of the time needed for me to write books and for always being my first set of editorial eyes. I am so grateful for your love and can't imagine life without you.

Thank you to Rebekah Guzman, Chad Allen, and the whole Baker team for their professionalism and their passion to publish this book, and to Liz Heaney for her editorial prowess. It has been a pleasure working with each of you.

My sincerest thanks to Sean McDowell for his willingness to write a foreword for the book and to each of the endorsers for their kind words. Your support means a lot to me.

Many thanks to my calm and wise literary agent, Mark Sweeney, for his work in placing the book and for his continued guidance.

I doubt I would be an author at all if not for my first editor, Steve Miller, who saw something in my blog writing that led him to reach out to me about writing books. He has believed in my abilities as a writer and in the importance of parents learning apologetics since we first met. Thank you, Steve, for your amazing support and encouragement.

Jim Wallace has been an unbelievably helpful mentor in all things writing and speaking. Jim, it's a privilege to know and learn from you.

Last but not least, I greatly appreciate those who agreed to read early drafts of the book and provide valuable feedback: Jason Byerly, Troy Caya, Alisa Childers, Ray Ciervo, and Dick DiTullio. Your time and willingness to help meant a lot to me. A special thank you to Doug Beaumont for lending his keen philosophical and theological insights to the project. The book benefited greatly from your review!

Introduction

My backyard is where plants go to die.

Each year when spring rolls around, I think I can grow a few potted plants outside and enthusiastically head down to the local nursery. I buy plants with beautiful green leaves, already starting to produce fruit, and drive home ready to take on the world one homegrown tomato at a time.

Within a month, my plants die . . . every single time.

I can't pretend I don't know why—I'm the world's laziest waterer. I start off strong but soon fail to water the plants until they're almost dead. Feeling guilty, I then drench them with buckets of water one last time, but it's too late. They can't recover, and soon they're in the trash.

Last year I was determined to do things differently. With my characteristic spring enthusiasm, I picked out pepper, tomato, and basil plants. I meticulously watered them *every* day. But despite my discipline, the tomato plant soon turned yellow, the basil plant was burnt by the sun, and the pepper plant was devoured by caterpillars.

Not knowing what to make of all this, I finally purchased a gardening book to learn more about keeping plants alive. I couldn't believe how much there was to consider! I thought gardening was simple—dirt, seeds, and water. In reality, it's a lot more complex.

- *Each plant has unique needs.* Even if I remembered to water each day, my discipline wasn't going to keep my plants thriving, because different plants have different needs. The tomato plant turned yellow because I watered it *too* much.
- *Plants need more than one ingredient and in the right amounts.* I had assumed that plants simply need water to grow. I hadn't considered the amount of sunlight each one needs, nor the type of soil or fertilizer. The basil plant died from too much sun.
- *The environment plays a major role.* Not only did I need to proactively give my plants what they require, but I also needed to proactively protect them from predators. Caterpillars were able to eat my pepper plant because I hadn't warded against them.

One afternoon as I thought about my failure as a gardener, I was struck by the resemblance between what plants need for physical growth and what kids need for spiritual growth.

But how much more important is the care of our children's souls?

If I really cared about growing plants, I would have educated myself on gardening much sooner. It just wasn't a priority. But as parents called to the all-important role of leading our kids to know Jesus, we can't afford to just "give it our best shot" and see what happens, with a possible do-over next spring. Too much is at stake, and good intentions are not enough. We have to know what we're doing.

We need both *direction*—the knowledge of what to do—and *discipline*—the commitment to doing it.

Discipline and Direction: A Key Relationship

To better understand the importance of discipline and direction for Christian parenting, consider these three scenarios:

1. *When we have* no discipline *and* no direction, *we're leaving our kids to wilt spiritually.* This happens when we're inconsistent in "watering" their spiritual lives (no discipline) and when we don't understand all that they need to thrive (no direction). It's an easy trap to fall into when we're busy. Our spiritual training ends up being a mealtime prayer here and there, a wishy-washy commitment to church, and occasional references to the Bible thrown in for good measure (especially when someone's behaving badly). If guilt takes over, we may "drench" our kids with more church activities or devotionals for a while, but for many kids, it's too little, too late.

2. *When we have* discipline *but no direction,* *we're working hard but not necessarily doing the work our kids need most.* I had this problem when I faithfully watered my plants each day, not realizing how many other factors were involved in helping them grow. Despite my intentions, the plants still didn't have what they needed to survive. Similarly, some parents are very disciplined, in that they're consistently mindful of their kids' spiritual development, but they're not knowledgeable of the many "ingredients" that go into a strong faith or the "environmental factors" that will challenge their efforts today. *Research has shown repeatedly that at least 60 percent of kids from Christian homes turn away from faith by their early twenties.*[1] Clearly, the hard work of many well-intentioned Christian parents is not resulting in thriving spiritual lives for their kids as adults. Discipline without direction can be dangerous.

3. *When we have* discipline *and* direction, *we're confident.* We know we're doing what we should to help our kids develop a deeply rooted faith. We're setting aside time each week for our family to grow together spiritually and weaving faith throughout our daily lives based on our knowledge of what our kids need. We know we'll never be perfect parents and that, ultimately, God is sovereign, but we rest in the comfort of knowing we're being as faithful as we can be to our calling.

I think it's clear which scenario we should want for our homes.

This book will help get you there.

It won't give you discipline—you're the only one who can prioritize your kids' spiritual development—but it will give you direction.

What Kind of Direction?

When I started my Christian parenting blog, NatashaCrain.com, in 2011, I was a *discipline without direction* parent. I was committed to raising my young kids in a Christ-centered home, but I wasn't sure what I should be doing. I started the blog simply thinking I would meet like-minded parents and exchange ideas about raising faithful kids.

But as my readership grew and people started sharing my articles with friends online, something unexpected happened: my blog began attracting a stream of challenging comments from skeptics of Christianity—comments I had no idea how to answer.

There were challenges about how I knew God existed.

About the relationship between science and the Bible.

About God's actions in the Old Testament.

About the plausibility of miracles.

About the amount of evil and suffering in the world.

About contradictions in the Gospels.

About the reasonableness of hell.

About everything you can imagine.

Despite having been a lifelong Christian, and despite having spent hundreds of hours in church and Sunday school, I was not prepared for this onslaught. I realized that my kids were growing up in a very different world than the one in which I grew up. Teaching them about Christianity wasn't going to be as simple as "dirt, seeds, and water." My kids were going to need a lot more from me, and I had to find out what that was.

It was time to become a more educated gardener.

I launched into an in-depth study of Christian apologetics—how to make a case for and defend the Christian faith—and over time transformed my website into a place where I help equip other parents with the same knowledge. It's become my passion, and today more than 250,000 people each year read my blog.

Eventually, I had the opportunity to write an apologetics book specifically for parents: *Keeping Your Kids on God's Side: 40 Conversations to Help Them Build a Lasting Faith.*[2] It covers conversations across the major subject areas of God, truth and worldviews, Jesus, the Bible, and science. To follow *Keeping Your Kids on God's Side*, I wanted to write books that dig into one of these major subject areas at a time, delving into many more questions than was possible in a book covering multiple areas.

That's what *Talking with Your Kids about God* does. This book is a resource for Christian parents on thirty of the most important subjects kids need to understand about God in light of challenges from our secular world. Whether you've read *Keeping Your Kids on God's Side* and are looking for the next step in your learning or want to jump directly into this in-depth resource on the subject of God specifically, you'll find the direction you need to have thirty important faith conversations that will benefit your kids for a lifetime.

How to Use This Book

First and foremost, *Talking with Your Kids about God* is designed to equip you, the adult, with the knowledge you need to have these conversations with your children. In other words, don't hand this book directly to your kids—it's not written for them! This is *your* guide.

That said, it can be intimidating to figure out how to talk to kids about tough subjects even when you understand those subjects yourself. It helps to have guidance on how to break down the content into manageable pieces of conversation centered on the most important points—so that's exactly what I've provided at the end of every chapter.

Each "Conversation Guide" has three sections: "Open the Conversation," "Advance the Conversation," and "Apply the Conversation."

In "Open the Conversation," you'll find one or two questions intended to get your kids thinking about the subject. Resist the temptation to dump a chapter's worth of knowledge on them at that point. Instead, listen to your kids' answers and ask follow-up questions to learn more about their thoughts.

In "Advance the Conversation," you'll find two or more questions to help you probe the key ideas from the chapter. These questions will not cover every detail you read. They'll give you the opportunity to highlight the most important points, then it will be up to you to decide how deep to take the conversation. Discussion tips are offered with most of these questions.

In "Apply the Conversation," you'll find a quote from a skeptic of Christianity that pertains to the subject. Most are taken from conversations between Christians and skeptics online. They're the kinds of comments your kids are most likely to run into on their own eventually. After reading the quote together, ask them to respond to it based on what they learned from the chapter.

Don't shy away from doing this, no matter how old your kids are. If you help your kids apply their learning by responding to these quotes, I have no doubt you'll find this activity to be one of the most valuable parts of this book.

Are you ready to become a more fruitful gardener and help your kids thrive spiritually? I know you are. "Plant" yourself in a comfortable chair, and let's dive in.

PART 1

The Existence *of* God

Overview

A couple of years ago, my husband and I were invited to a dinner party with a few other new parents from our kids' Christian elementary school. After we worked our way through appetizers and the requisite small talk, the conversation turned to our respective faith backgrounds. One of the moms confessed that, as much as she loved the Lord, she struggled with how to share her faith with her son—so she had enrolled him at a Christian school where others might be able to do a "better job."

Another mom replied, "Well, I don't worry too much about it. I just tell my daughter that believing in God is like believing in Santa Claus. Some people believe, and some don't. It's a matter of faith."

I glanced over at the mom who said that, ready to laugh *with* her at the idea of placing God and Santa in the same category.

But she wasn't laughing.

She had just matter-of-factly shared what she honestly thought was a helpful way of explaining belief in God's existence to her daughter, and other parents around the table nodded approvingly. I continued poking at my salad, contemplating just how annoying I would be if I suggested we stop to define the biblical notion of faith and evaluate the differences between faith in Santa and faith in God. I concluded I didn't want to rain on the remaining festivities, so I just kept eating—something I still regret.

If an atheist had overheard our dinner party conversation, they would have delighted in my friend's comparison of God and Santa because that's precisely how atheists want us to think:

God and Santa: two entities with no evidence to demonstrate their existence.

God and Santa: childish beliefs people should outgrow once they understand there's no evidence to demonstrate their existence.

Philosopher Daniel Dennett is one of many atheists who have made this comparison, saying, "The kindly God who lovingly fashioned each and every one of us and sprinkled the sky with shining stars for our delight—that God is, like Santa Claus, a myth of childhood, not anything a sane, undeluded adult could literally believe in."[1]

Here's the good news: atheists talk about God's existence (or lack thereof) in specific, predictable ways. That means we have the reference point for how to prepare our kids accordingly. We don't have to fumble around, hoping that what we've taught our children about God's existence will somehow be enough to ground their faith. In fact, if we do just fumble around, speaking about God in whatever terms feel most comfortable to *us*—like comparing God and Santa—we may unintentionally set our kids up for spiritual vulnerability.

Knowing that atheists consistently claim there's "no evidence" for God, we need to raise kids who understand what, exactly, that means and how to think critically about such claims. Part 1 of this book is designed to help you do just that. In these chapters, we'll explore the evidence for God's existence in nature and how that relates to the claims of skeptics.

If thinking about God's existence in these ways is new to you, please don't feel alone. While most Christians are prepared to speak to God's existence based on their personal experiences, few have studied the *objective* evidence for God's existence in nature. This independent evidence, however, is critical to understand because people can have contradictory personal experiences. For example, atheists may believe God doesn't exist based on what *they've* experienced. By teaching our kids about the objective evidence for God's existence in nature, we're preparing them for a world that wants them to believe their personal experiences with God are no different from a child's personal "experience" with Santa and that they'll find no more evidence for God outside themselves than they'll find for Santa at the North Pole.

Three Keys to Impactful Conversations about the Existence of God

1. *Introduce these discussions by explaining why it's so important to learn about the evidence for God's existence in nature.* Most kids will identify that they can know about God from the Bible and from their own experiences, but, like most adults, they've probably never had the opportunity to engage with the evidence for God's existence in nature. To get kids thinking about the subjects in part 1, ask, "How do you know God exists?" Be sure to affirm that personal experience is important in the life of a Christian, but explain why it's also important to understand the objective evidence God has given us in nature.

2. *Clarify terms.* The nuanced meaning of certain words is important for these discussions, so be sure to clarify up front what they mean (and, remember, younger kids may have never heard these words before). Key terms in this section include *atheist, agnostic, skeptic,* and *theist.* An atheist, as we'll use the term, is someone who believes there is no God.[2]

31

An agnostic is someone who believes nothing is known or can be known about the existence or nature of God. A skeptic is a broader catchall category of people who reject the claims of Christianity (note that skepticism in general can have many meanings, but this is what it will mean in the context of this book). A theist is someone who believes in a God who interacts with his creation (for example, Judaism, Christianity, and Islam are all theistic faiths).

3. *Help kids remember the evidence by teaching them to memorize the "big three" questions covered by chapters 2, 3, and 4: Where did the universe come from? Where did life come from? and Where did our moral understanding come from?* While many other subjects could be discussed with respect to the evidence for God's existence, these are three of the most important and frequently debated in today's world. Even if kids don't remember all the chapter details, the questions themselves can serve as a "mental directory" for key concepts in the future.

1. What Can We Learn about God from Nature?

One afternoon my three kids came running into the house. My five-year-old proudly revealed a large Spiderman bouncy ball that had made its way into our backyard.

"Mommy, look! We have a new ball! It was just sitting by the barbeque!"

Rest assured, we have plenty of other balls rolling around our backyard. But, of course, the novelty of one that had suddenly appeared was very exciting.

"It probably belongs to Mason. Just throw it back over the fence," I told them. Mason lived next door.

"But, Mommy," my older daughter pleaded, "we don't *know* it's his, so we shouldn't assume that and just give it to him. It could belong to anyone."

My daughter was technically right; we didn't *know* it was his. Unless he showed up and proved his ownership, we couldn't be sure. Still, I pushed my daughter on her logic.

"You're right. We don't *know* it's his. There are millions of *possible* explanations for how it got here. I heard some kids visiting our other neighbors this weekend. Maybe it's theirs. Or maybe the wind blew it over from a house farther away. Or maybe it fell from an airplane or an alien put it there or maybe it popped into existence all by itself!"

My kids looked at me, unamused, and impatiently awaited the point they knew was coming.

"While there are tons of possible places the ball could have come from, by far the most *likely* place is Mason's house. He's the only kid in a neighboring house who regularly plays in the backyard, we know he loves Spiderman, and balls from his yard have landed in our yard before. Throw it back."

With that, they threw it over the fence and announced they were now "totally" bored. (Without this incredible new ball, of course, there was suddenly nothing to do.)

Like the Spiderman bouncy ball, the universe doesn't verbalize where it came from, why it's here, and what we should do with it. But that doesn't mean we can't evaluate all the information we do have in nature to draw reasonable conclusions about these things.

In this and the next five chapters, we'll be looking at the universe, life, and our innate moral knowledge—the "balls" in our backyard— to learn how nature powerfully points to the existence of God. But before we do, we need to clarify what these pieces of evidence can and cannot tell us. That's the subject for our first chapter.

General Revelation: God's "Word" in Nature

As Christians, we believe God has revealed himself in the inspired words of the Bible's authors. Indeed, the Bible is our most extensive source of knowledge about him. But Christians often overlook the natural world as another important source of God's "Word" to us.

The knowledge about God that we obtain through the observation of nature is called general revelation. Psalm 19:1–2 says, "The heavens declare the glory of God; the skies proclaim the work of his hands. Day after day they pour forth speech; night after night they reveal knowledge." The apostle Paul says there is no excuse for not believing in God because he has so clearly revealed himself in nature:

> The wrath of God is being revealed from heaven against all the godlessness and wickedness of people, who suppress the truth by their wickedness, since what may be known about God is plain to them, because God has made it plain to them. For since the creation of the world God's invisible qualities—his eternal power and divine nature—have been clearly seen, being understood from what has been made, so that people are without excuse. (Rom. 1:18–20)

Paul goes on to say that God has also given humans an innate knowledge of right and wrong—a moral conscience:

> (Indeed, when Gentiles, who do not have the law, do by nature things required by the law, they are a law for themselves, even though they do not have the law. They show that the requirements of the law are written on their hearts, their consciences also bearing witness, and their thoughts sometimes accusing them and at other times even defending them.) This will take place on the day when God judges people's secrets through Jesus Christ, as my gospel declares. (Rom. 2:14–16)

It's clear that the Bible confirms God has revealed himself in the natural world and that we should expect to find evidence for him there. But what specifically can we learn?

What Nature Reveals about God

When we study the natural world, we see there's good reason to believe God exists given what we observe. For example, when we study the origin of the universe in chapter 2, we'll learn that science points to the universe having a beginning. It hasn't been around forever. But things don't pop into existence on their own.

Something or someone causes them to exist. The something or someone that caused the universe to come into existence had to have been *super*natural—beyond nature—since it created nature. As such, that supernatural thing or person would have to be (among other things) spaceless, timeless, immaterial, and uncaused. This description is clearly consistent with the Christian concept of God.

Similarly, we'll see in chapter 3 that evidence from physics and biology strongly points to the conclusion that life is the product of a purposeful intelligence. In chapter 4, we'll learn how our innate understanding of morality points to a moral lawgiver with authority over our lives. Nature doesn't tell us everything that the Bible tells us about God, but it provides good reason to believe that a Being consistent with whom we call God exists. In a secular world that's quick to reject the Bible with little consideration, the evidence for God's existence in nature can be the one thing that opens the door to discussing the truth of Christianity with nonbelievers. And, for Christians, this evidence can embolden our confidence in what we believe.

That brings us to this important question: If the evidence we'll be looking at is so compelling, why doesn't everyone agree it points to God?

Why People Disagree about the Evidence for God in Nature

If you ask an atheist how much evidence there is for God in the world, they will likely say there is *no* evidence for the existence of God. Meanwhile, if you ask a Christian the same question, they will likely say there's *extensive* evidence for the existence of God.

So what's going on here? How can people draw such vastly different conclusions? To answer that, we need to understand four key points about the nature of any evidence that doesn't literally speak for itself.

1. *Evidence is a body of facts that require human interpretation.* Evidence itself doesn't say anything. All evidence must be interpreted. Think about the Spiderman ball in our backyard. The ball itself didn't verbalize anything. It was my kids and I who offered explanations for its appearance. We all looked at the same evidence—the ball—and yet came to different conclusions due to our varied assumptions, the available information, our life experiences, and our motivations. For similar reasons, people look at the evidence in the natural world and inevitably draw different conclusions. That doesn't make the evidence any less valuable for consideration. It's simply the nature of *any* evidence.

2. *Because evidence requires human interpretation, there will always be multiple possible explanations for it.* An atheist once told me that he wasn't impressed by the "supposed evidence for God" because there are plenty of possible naturalistic (non-God) explanations for what we see in the world. But that's a poor reason to reject any *one* of those explanations. I offered alien involvement as a possible explanation for the ball in our backyard, but that didn't make it any less likely that the ball belonged to Mason. The relevant question is not how *many* possible explanations there are but rather which is the most *likely* explanation given the evidence.

3. *If we rule out certain possible explanations before considering the evidence, we won't ever conclude that the evidence points to those explanations.* Many people presuppose that God doesn't exist and will consider only naturalistic explanations for what they see in the universe. But if we rule out God before we even consider the evidence, *of course* we will conclude there's no evidence that points to God! This would have been like my kids telling me the ball couldn't be Mason's because . . . they know it could never be Mason's, regardless of the evidence.

4. *The best explanation for a body of evidence is often debatable and rarely certain.* It's easy to rule out certain possible explanations for evidence once we determine they're unlikely to account for what we see. For example, it wouldn't have been difficult to decide it almost certainly wasn't an airplane that dropped the ball into our backyard. But what if we had *two* neighbors with young boys who often played in the backyard with balls? We still might have had better reason to believe the ball was Mason's, but that conclusion would have been far less certain. When studying the natural world, the possible explanations for evidence are far more complex, and it's often not so easy to determine what is more or less likely. We may determine a *best* explanation, but even best explanations aren't certain.

With this chapter's context in mind, we're now ready to start looking at the evidence itself. We'll begin in the next chapter with the origin of the universe.

KEY POINTS

- While the Bible is God's most extensive revelation, he's revealed himself in nature as well (this is called general revelation).
- Evidence from nature—such as the universe, life, and our innate moral knowledge—provides good reason to believe that a Being consistent with whom we call God exists.
- There are four key reasons why not everyone agrees that the evidence in nature points to God:

  1. Evidence is a body of facts that require human interpretation.
  2. Because evidence requires human interpretation, there will always be multiple possible explanations for it.

3. If we rule out certain possible explanations before considering the evidence, we won't ever conclude that the evidence points to those explanations.

4. The best explanation for a body of evidence is often debatable and rarely certain.

CONVERSATION GUIDE

Open the Conversation

- Imagine that you grew up without hearing anything that's in the Bible. What, if anything, do you think you would be able to know about God from looking at the world around you?

Advance the Conversation

- Read Psalm 19:1–2; Romans 1:18–20; 2:14–16. What does each passage say the natural world can tell us about God? *(Be sure to introduce the term* general revelation.*)*

- Most of what we know about God comes from the Bible, but, as we just saw, nature also gives us many good reasons to believe God exists. Why do you think evidence for God's existence outside the Bible and our personal experiences is important—for both Christians and nonbelievers? *(It gives Christians more confidence in their faith and can open the door for discussion with those who reject the truth of the Bible.)*

- *(Share the ball story from the beginning of this chapter.)* Like the parent and the kids in this story, people can draw very different conclusions about the meaning of any evidence depending on their assumptions, life experiences, and motivations. What are some ways those things might impact whether people believe the evidence in the natural world points to God? *(Discuss your child's answer, then walk through the four reasons why people disagree about evidence.)*

Apply the Conversation

- Atheist author Dan Barker says, "I am an atheist because there is no evidence for the existence of God. That should be all that needs to be said about it: no evidence, no belief."[1] Based on what you learned in this chapter, when someone says there's "no evidence" for God (or anything else), what questions could you ask to clarify what that person means?

2. Where Did the Universe Come From?

If you ask most churchgoing kids, "Where did the universe come from?" they'll almost certainly answer, "God!" And if you ask them how they know that, many will point you to the Bible's famous first verse, "In the beginning, God created the heavens and the earth" (Gen. 1:1).

We've heard this verse so many times, however, that it's easy to take for granted that it makes two enormously significant claims: (1) the universe had a beginning, and (2) God was the cause of that beginning. There are many things the Bible doesn't tell us, but where the universe came from isn't one of them.

That said, what can we learn from nature itself about where the universe came from? That's the subject of this chapter. We'll frame our discussion by questioning the two hotly debated claims from Genesis 1:1: (1) Did the universe have a beginning? and (2) What could have caused the universe to begin?

Did the Universe Have a Beginning?

The first question, Did the universe have a beginning?, is both simple and profoundly important. It's simple because the universe either had a beginning or it did not. It's profoundly important because, if it did, the theological implications are glaring: something or someone had to have *caused* it to begin. If, however, the universe is eternal—it's just always existed—there's no logical need for a Creator. The universe wasn't created.

For that reason, an eternal universe is a philosophically comfortable resting place for atheists. And for hundreds of years, they were able to kick back in that easy chair because most scientists believed the universe was, indeed, eternal. An atheist's answer to the question "Where did the universe come from?" would have been, "It didn't 'come' from anywhere; it's always been here!" Everything started changing, however, in the early 1900s. Scientific evidence began to mount that the universe *couldn't* have existed forever and that, instead, it began to exist at a specific point in the past. Today, many scientists agree with respected cosmologist Alexander Vilenkin, who says, "With the proof now in place, cosmologists can no longer hide behind the possibility of a past-eternal universe. There is no escape, they have to face the problem of a cosmic beginning."[1]

A detailed discussion of the evidence that led scientists such as Vilenkin to such a conclusion is beyond the scope of this chapter. However, we're going to look at three of the most important findings to date: the expansion of the universe, cosmic background radiation, and the second law of thermodynamics (these terms may sound complicated, but don't worry—we'll break them down).

The Expansion of the Universe

By 1917, Albert Einstein had created a cosmological model of the entire universe. But there was a "problem." His equation predicted that the universe couldn't be static—it had to be either expanding or contracting. Since the prevailing belief at the time was that the universe *was* static, Einstein added a constant to his equation that forced it to continue supporting this idea.[2] Why was he so committed to a static, unchanging universe? He and other scientists understood that an *expanding* universe would imply a beginning (rewinding the process of expansion must always take you back to a beginning point for that expansion). And beginnings require a cause—an implication Einstein clearly understood.

A few years later, in the 1920s, astronomer Edwin Hubble found direct observational evidence that the universe was, indeed, expanding. Using the world's largest telescope at the time, Hubble detected that galaxies are moving away from us, like spots on an inflating balloon. Based on this and other mounting evidence from the same time period, Einstein eventually retracted the "fudge factor" he had used to forcefully support a static universe. An expanding universe—one implying that dreaded beginning point—was well on its way to becoming a widely accepted scientific fact.

Cosmic Background Radiation

When the idea of an expanding universe started catching on, scientists also developed theories to describe the nature of that expansion. The predominant theory (both then and now) was that the universe started out much hotter and denser than it is today and expanded and cooled over time. In the 1940s, scientists predicted that if the universe did emerge from such conditions—and hadn't always existed in an eternal, steady state—there would be lasting effects in the form of cosmic background radiation (residual heat in the universe). In 1965, that prediction was confirmed through an accidental discovery by radio astronomers Arno Penzias and Robert Wilson. Penzias and Wilson eventually won a Nobel Prize for discovering this supporting evidence that the universe *began* in an extremely hot, dense state.[3]

The Second Law of Thermodynamics

The second law of thermodynamics says that the *amount* of energy within a closed system (such as the universe) will always stay the same, but the amount of *usable* energy in a system will continually decrease. Usable energy is utilized for things such as productivity, growth, and repair. In these processes, usable energy is permanently converted into unusable energy. Since the universe is a closed system, with no new energy being infused into it from the outside, it's ultimately "running down" as available energy is used. Here's the big takeaway: there's still plenty of usable energy in the universe today, so that implies the universe hasn't been around forever. If the universe were eternal, there would be no usable energy left.

Despite the strong scientific evidence that points to the universe having a beginning, the case isn't closed for everyone. Remember what we discussed in chapter 1: there will always be multiple interpretations of the evidence. Perhaps the most popular alternative theory is that our universe is just one of a vast number of other universes that together make up a "multiverse." The corresponding claim is that the multiverse could be eternal, even if our own universe isn't. That possibility has been vigorously challenged, however, by scientists who have shown that if our universe is expanding—as all observational evidence suggests—eternal multiverse models are mathematically impossible.[4] And if we're in a multiverse that itself had a beginning, we would be right back to asking the same question: Where did the multiverse come from?

As you can see, it's hard to ignore the evidence that supports the claim that the universe had a beginning. It's time to look more closely at the implications of that beginning.

What Could Have Caused the Universe to Begin?

If the universe did have a beginning, we must then ask, What could have *caused* the universe to begin? The possibilities are limited: (1) the universe came into existence from nothing, unlike any known thing *within* the universe, or (2) something or someone caused the universe to exist.

This is tricky ground for atheists who accept that the universe had a beginning. Will they claim that the universe defied the law of cause and effect, popping into existence from nothing? Or will they accept that something or someone must have caused the universe to exist, opening the door to the possibility of a Creator God?

Philosopher Quentin Smith is an example of an atheist who maintains that the universe really did pop into existence from nothing. He says, "We came from nothing, by nothing, and for nothing."[5] Similarly, the American Humanist Association's "Humanist Manifesto" states that they regard the universe as "self-existing and not created."[6] Others have been more specific about the nature of "nothing." Physicist Stephen Hawking, for example, says, "Because there is a law such as gravity, the universe can and will create itself from nothing. . . . It is not necessary to invoke God to light the blue touch paper and set the universe going."[7] It's a bold assertion but one with an obvious flaw. Where did the law of gravity come from? It too must have come from somewhere. Furthermore, laws themselves don't create anything. They simply describe what happens under certain conditions.[8] So even if a law could exist without cause, that still wouldn't explain how the universe emerged. Another physicist who has tried to redefine the word *nothing* is Lawrence Krauss. In his book *A Universe from Nothing: Why There Is Something Rather than Nothing*, Krauss's "nothing" turns out to be empty space ruled by the laws of quantum physics.[9] Krauss clearly has the same problem Hawking does: his nothing is something.

In short, no one has successfully demonstrated how the universe could have emerged from true nothingness because there is no known mechanism for that in the natural world. Aside from asserting that the universe began to exist without cause (as Smith does) or redefining the word *nothing* (as Hawking and Krauss do), we are left with a single logical conclusion: if the universe began to exist, something or someone *super*natural—beyond nature—must have made that happen. We can infer some other things about this supernatural cause as well: in order to create space, time, and matter, the cause would have to be spaceless, timeless, immaterial, and uncaused itself . . . as well as enormously powerful. While none of this tells us that the supernatural cause is synonymous with the God of the Bible, it's certainly consistent with him. The existence of a universe with a beginning is significant evidence for a Creator who acted just as Genesis 1:1 says.

KEY POINTS

- In its first verse, the Bible boldly states that the universe had a beginning and that God brought it into existence.
- For hundreds of years, scientists believed the universe was eternal. This changed in the 1900s, when scientific evidence started to mount that the universe had a beginning. Today, this is a widely accepted scientific fact.
- This leads to the question of what or who could have *caused* the universe to begin. Nothing in the universe comes into existence on its own, so it defies our experience to suppose that the universe itself did.
- Something or someone *super*natural must have caused the universe to exist. In order to create space, time, and matter, the cause would have to be spaceless, timeless, immaterial, and uncaused itself. This doesn't tell us that the supernatural cause is synonymous with the God of the Bible, but it's certainly consistent with him.

CONVERSATION GUIDE

Open the Conversation

- Read Genesis 1:1. What two important things does the Bible's first verse tell us about the universe? *(It had a beginning, and the cause was God.)*

Advance the Conversation

- It's not only the Bible that tells us the universe had a beginning and hasn't just always existed. Scientific findings point to the fact that the universe had a beginning as well. *(Discuss the scientific findings from this chapter as appropriate for your child's understanding.)* Why do you think the question of whether the universe had a beginning is important in the discussion of the evidence for God's existence? *(If the universe were eternal, there would be no logical need for a Creator.)*

- If something begins to exist in the world, something else *caused* it to exist. We've never seen something come into existence by itself! For example, think about a car, a flower, and a puddle of water. What was the cause of each one that brought it into existence? *(Have your child trace the causes all the way back to the beginning.)*

- If we know the universe had a beginning, and everything that begins to exist was caused to exist by something else, what do you think could have caused the universe to exist? To answer the question, think about what the cause would have to be like in order to be able to create everything in the world. *(Discuss the fact that in order to create time, space, and matter, the cause itself would have to be spaceless, timeless, and immaterial. Explain that the Bible tells us much more about God but that this is consistent, supporting evidence for his existence.)*

47

Apply the Conversation

- In an online forum, a person asked how atheists can argue that the universe came from nothing. An atheist replied, "Personally I do not claim that the universe 'came from' anything at all and it did not 'appear.' The universe just is . . . it needs no creation story."[10] Based on what you learned from this chapter, how would you respond to this person?

3. Where Did Life Come From?

One afternoon my husband decided to buy the kids an ant farm. Having promised me that it would be both "fun and educational" to have dozens of ants take up residence in a small container within our home, he placed the order and the kids eagerly awaited the shipment.

When the ants arrived, we funneled them into their new living arrangement, filled with a blue gel that the instructions questionably assured us would provide for the ants' every need. For the next couple of days, the ant farm turned out to be a great learning experience as my kids observed the ants' various tunneling activities. I thought, *Maybe this wasn't such a bad idea after all.*

But the thrill turned to disappointment when later in the week we awoke to piles of dead ants inside the supposedly ant-friendly habitat. Not knowing how to separate the dead ants from the live ones, we uncomfortably left the ant farm untouched in the corner of the room. After one more day, the ant farm had turned into an ant cemetery. When no one was looking, I took the sad sight out to the trash.

The moral of the story: never buy an ant farm. Just kidding (kind of). But there's a more relevant point to be made. When we talk about where life on Earth came from, two key questions emerge. First, what are the necessary conditions for life to exist and flourish? Like the ants, we can't live just anywhere. Life as we know it has some very specific requirements.[1] Second, where did life itself come from? Even if the ant farm company had provided us with a perfect ant habitat, ants would not have appeared there out of necessity. We had to funnel them in. Similarly, just because the universe met the right requirements for life doesn't mean life had to develop. Much is required for life to flourish even given a suitable "home."

Let's look more closely at these two questions and see how the answers point us toward the existence of God.

What Are the Necessary Conditions for Life?

In the previous chapter, we looked at how the mere existence of a universe with a beginning points to the existence of God. But the *kind* of universe and planet we have is further evidence for God's existence. It "just so happens" that our universal home is precisely structured in the way necessary for us to be here. This phenomenon is called the fine-tuning of the universe.

Fine-tuning can be seen in two ways. First, the constants of nature have extremely precise values. If they were just slightly different, life as we know it couldn't exist. Consider, for example, the force of gravity. If the gravitational force was too weak, it wouldn't be able to hold stars together, and stars (of the kind like our sun) are a necessary source of energy for living things. If the gravitational force was too strong, stars could hold together, but they would burn out too quickly to support life. As another example, consider the relationship between the strong nuclear and electromagnetic forces (two of nature's four fundamental forces). Carbon is the central element necessary for life, but it couldn't exist as needed if the strengths of the strong nuclear and electromagnetic forces weren't so finely balanced. There are dozens of such facts, and even most skeptics acknowledge the *apparent* fine-tuning of the constants of nature.[2]

Fine-tuning is also seen at the level of our planet and solar system. For example, the Earth orbits the sun within a narrow range of distance where liquid water—a necessity for life—can exist (known as a habitable zone). If we were slightly closer to the sun, water would evaporate. If we were slightly farther from the sun, water would turn to ice. But it's not just the distance to a star and its energy output that determine a planet's habitability. The atmosphere of a planet is also a critical factor. Venus and Mars are both within our solar system's habitable zone, but neither has the necessary atmosphere to allow for life. Venus's thick atmosphere traps too much energy from the sun, making it too hot for life. Mars's thin atmosphere traps too little energy, making it too cold for life. Earth, on the other hand, has an atmosphere with just the right mix of oxygen and nitrogen to allow for life to flourish.

This is just a tiny sampling of some of the (easier-to-understand) ways the Earth seems to be finely tuned to support life. Astrophysicist Hugh Ross has cataloged over 150 parameters of a planet, its planetary companions, its moon, its star, and its galaxy that must have values falling within narrowly defined ranges for physical life of any kind to exist—things like galaxy size, galaxy mass distribution, galaxy type, galaxy location, mass of other planets, and mass of the sun.[3] Ross has estimated that there is less than 1 chance in 10^{282} that even one life-supporting body would occur anywhere in the universe.[4] Of course, probabilities are subject to all kinds of assumptions, but regardless of the calculated value, the point remains the same: it's extraordinarily improbable that all these factors would line up just right for life to exist and flourish by chance. *A more reasonable explanation for such delicate fine-tuning is that life is the product of a purposeful intelligence beyond nature.*

Skeptics, of course, disagree. Some say the universe is this way by chance and that if it hadn't been this way, we just wouldn't be here to notice it.[5] While it's theoretically possible that fine-tuning just happened by chance, we have to remember the difference between *possible* and *likely* explanations, which we discussed in the first chapter. The existence of a supernatural intellect capable of purposefully designing the universe in this way is a far more plausible explanation for what we observe than is simple chance.

Other skeptics embrace the idea of a possible multiverse (see chap. 2) and say that if infinite other universes exist, it shouldn't be surprising that *one* would happen to have the precise conditions needed for life. But even if a multiverse exists (something highly debatable), there's no reason to expect that an unguided process would naturally produce universes that have all possible values of the physical parameters. There's no reason to assume that even *one* would inevitably be structured in the way our universe is. We have no idea how all those hypothetical universes might look.

Still other skeptics say that things are this way by necessity—that yet-to-be-discovered laws made our universe's structure inevitable. Aside from the fact that such laws have not been discovered, the existence of a hypothetical "super law" only moves the problem back one level: Where did the super law that finely tuned the other laws come from?

Based on all the information we have, we can reasonably conclude that our life-supporting universe is the result of a purposeful intelligence beyond nature.

Let's now consider where life itself came from.

Where Did Life Come From?

Origin-of-life scientists study ways in which life could have originated from nonliving matter via natural processes—a hypothetical development called abiogenesis. How abiogenesis could have
occurred has baffled scientists for decades because the emergence
of even the simplest living cell would have required an incredibly
improbable series of events to occur naturally.

While this is an extremely complex subject, we can begin to appreciate the nature of these difficulties by considering what would
be required to build just *one* functioning protein (a minimally
complex cell would require at least one hundred such proteins
working together).[6]

Proteins are built from a chain of amino acids—compounds
made of carbon, hydrogen, oxygen, nitrogen, and sometimes sulfur.
One of the most challenging questions facing origin-of-life researchers is how these amino acids first formed. Researchers believe the
conditions of the early Earth and its atmosphere were very different
from conditions today and that those conditions would have been
extremely hostile to the natural formation of amino acids. Extensive research has been done over the last sixty years to determine
how these vital protein building blocks could have first emerged in
such conditions, but no viable pathway has yet been discovered.[7]

Clearly, this is a major problem—we can't make a protein chain
if we don't have amino acids to link together. But for the sake of
our example, let's assume we have the necessary amino acids in
hand. It's time to create a protein. Once again, this is no easy task.
Philosopher of science Stephen C. Meyer has explained the proba-
bilistic difficulty of attaining a single short, functioning protein
composed of just one hundred amino acids:[8]

- All the amino acids must link together using a chemical
  bond called a peptide bond. But, in nature, there are many

other types of chemical bonds possible between amino acids. The probability of building a chain of one hundred amino acids in which all linkages involve peptide bonds is roughly 1 chance in 10^{30}.

- Every amino acid has a mirror image of itself—both a "left-handed" and a "right-handed" form. Functioning proteins use only the left-handed ones, yet the two versions occur in nature with roughly equal frequency. This compounds the improbability of a functioning protein developing. The probability of randomly attaining only left-handed amino acids in a peptide chain one hundred amino acids long is, again, roughly 1 chance in 10^{30}.

- The left-handed amino acids must also bond together in the correct sequence for the protein to function properly (just as letters must be correctly sequenced to form a meaningful sentence). There are twenty different amino acids used in proteins. Given that each position in the sequence can be held by any one of these twenty, the probability of this hypothetical chain forming naturally is roughly 1 chance in 10^{65}.

Translation: the chance formation of even a single protein—a key component of life—is extraordinarily improbable. And proteins are just *one* component of a minimally complex cell. Other important cellular-level building blocks of life include DNA and RNA—highly complex nucleic acids that hold and utilize the information needed for a living organism to exist and function. DNA and RNA work together to *make* proteins. But there's a problem. They can't do that without the *help* of certain proteins. So which came first—DNA and RNA (which make proteins) or the proteins necessary to help DNA and RNA make proteins?

These are just some of the many origin-of-life conundrums researchers face because the cell is such a well-oiled, intricate system. Finding plausible ways the various parts could have (1) developed (given the assumed conditions of the early Earth) and then (2) eventually come together in the ways needed to create the first living organism has proven elusive. Meyer concludes, "For this reason, quantitative assessments of cellular complexity have simply reinforced an opinion that has prevailed since the mid-1960s within origin-of-life biology: chance is not an adequate explanation for the origin of biological complexity and specificity."[9]

As we continue to acknowledge, this doesn't mean it's not *possible* that these things all happened by chance in a purely naturalistic world. But when we look at the intricate nature of how living things work, we find good reason to believe they're the purposeful product of intelligence.

KEY POINTS

- When we talk about where life on Earth came from, two key questions emerge: (1) What are the necessary conditions for life to exist and flourish? and (2) Where did life itself come from?
- Our universal home is precisely structured in the way necessary for us to be here—a phenomenon called the fine-tuning of the universe.
- We observe fine-tuning in both the values of the constants of nature (such as the force of gravity) and the parameters of our planet and solar system (such as Earth's distance from the sun).
- Much is required for life to exist even given a suitable "home." How the first life could have emerged from nonliving matter via natural processes has baffled scientists for decades because the cell is such an intricate system of extraordinarily complex components such as proteins, DNA, and RNA.

- Given the fine-tuning of the universe and the intricate nature of life, we have good reason to believe both were the purposeful product of intelligence—not blind chance.

CONVERSATION GUIDE

Open the Conversation

- Imagine that you bought an ant habitat, which was filled with a blue gel. A few days after you put ants in the habitat, they died. What would you conclude about that ant habitat? *(Use this as an opportunity to discuss the fact that living things require some specific living conditions to exist and flourish.)*

Advance the Conversation

- We humans have certain things we need in order to live, just like ants. What are some examples of our own habitat requirements? *(Explain how the universe is structured in just the right way to provide the things your child mentions and introduce the term* fine-tuning. *Give examples from this chapter, such as gravity and the Earth's distance from the sun.)*
- For many years, scientists have been trying to determine how the first life could have formed on Earth from natural processes (meaning, without involvement from God). But the development of even the simplest cell would have required a series of extremely unlikely things to happen. That would be like expecting LEGO pieces to (1) form on their own from things around the house, then (2) make themselves into a functioning car, all by chance! What are some reasons why you wouldn't expect LEGOs to form on their own or to make themselves into a car without a person being involved?

(Explain what a cell is, if necessary, then walk through what it takes to make one protein, if age appropriate.)

- Given how the universe is structured to allow life to exist and how much is required for life to develop, what do you think is a more reasonable explanation for the way things are: these things happened by chance, or they were designed that way by an intelligent Being like God? Why? *(If your child is young, take time to explain the terms* reasonable, chance, *and* intelligent Being.*)*

Apply the Conversation

- A person commenting on an online article said, "Had [fine-tuning] not occurred . . . life here would either not exist or it would be different. That doesn't mean there's some big fairy who made it happen. Just because we survived on this planet does not mean a god made the planet for us."[10] How would you respond?

4. Where Did Our Moral Understanding Come From?

A teenage girl came across my blog one afternoon and left the following comment:

> I have a totally different view on the value of Christianity. Do we really need religion in this day and age? If you know the difference between right and wrong, why do you need religion? If you can show respect, why do you need religion? If you can make a positive difference in someone's life, why do you need religion? What matters is how you treat someone. Put a smile on their faces. It's that easy.

I've received many similar comments over the years. People often believe that Christianity is simply a system of moral rules (it's not, but that's another subject) and subsequently claim they don't need that system because they already know the difference between right and wrong. Who needs a teacher when the subject has already been mastered?

Ironically, this claim proves too much. The fact that almost everyone recognizes that they innately know what's right and wrong is a significant piece of evidence *for* God's existence. This is called the moral argument. The moral argument makes the case that (1) objective moral values exist (that is, there are things that are right or wrong for all people, regardless of anyone's personal opinion) and that (2) the existence of these objective moral values implies the existence of a moral authority (such as God). In other words, if there are certain moral "laws" that apply to all people—such as you shouldn't kill someone for fun—then there must be a moral law*giver* with the authority to create those laws.

In this chapter, we'll consider the two key questions addressed by the moral argument: (1) Do objective moral values exist? and (2) Where would objective moral values come from?

Do Objective Moral Values Exist?

Like the commenter on my blog post, most people assume there are things we all *know* are right or wrong. When a child is kidnapped or an innocent person is killed by gang violence, no one asks a friend, "Hey, what's your opinion on what happened? Do you think that was a good thing or a bad thing?" We don't ask because we assume others would make the same value judgment: these things are wrong.

If there are things that are indeed right or wrong, regardless of anyone's opinion, then objective moral values exist. They are as much facts about reality as statements like "humans breathe air." But is it possible that, despite what may seem self-evident, there is no objective morality? That actions such as kidnapping are actually neither right nor wrong, as much as it may make us cringe to admit it? That's exactly what some people claim—that seemingly "objective" moral truths are simply an illusion. They believe we're just so accustomed to our societal norms that we incorrectly assume objective moral values must exist.

Skeptics commonly point to two things to make the case that morality is *subjective* (relative to individual opinion) rather than *objective*. First, they say that cultures differ in what they consider moral. For example, some cultures have practiced senicide—the authorized killing of elderly community members. In other cultures, this would be considered immoral. Doesn't that suggest that objective moral values, like "murder is bad," must not exist? Not at all. Oftentimes, apparent moral differences between cultures reflect a difference in their evaluation of *circumstances*, not a difference in underlying values. Every culture agrees, for instance, that the intentional, unjustified killing (murder) of other humans is wrong. Cultures sometimes differ, however, on what *justifies* killing someone. In the case of senicide, cultures may justify killing their sick elderly as a loving act of mercy—something very different to them than murder. Many supposed moral differences between cultures are not actually differences in underlying moral values at all.[1]

For the sake of argument, however, let's say we could find a culture that truly believes killing people at any time is acceptable. Would *that* prove objective moral values don't exist? Again, not at all. Some people may insist that two plus two equals five, but that doesn't mean there isn't an objectively right answer. Even if examples of true moral disagreement could be found, that doesn't outweigh the fact that a core set of moral values runs throughout almost all cultures—evidence that strongly suggests objective moral values do exist.

The second way skeptics make a case against the existence of objective moral values is by attempting to demonstrate that our sense of right and wrong is just a by-product of evolution. This claim is one our kids are especially likely to encounter because they'll hear it in biology classes. I experienced this recently when I taught an apologetics class at a nearby church. After the first meeting, in which we discussed objective morality, a teenage girl approached me to talk about her biology class. She said she had learned that evolution drives animals to cooperate and help one another because, ultimately, doing so aids in the survival of their species. If, for example, an elephant sees another elephant in distress, it may self-sacrificially come to the elephant's assistance because doing so will help the group survive overall. The girl asked, "Doesn't that explain why we *think* morality is objective? Aren't we just conditioned to see certain things as right or wrong because those things have helped our species survive for millions of years?"

There are two things to understand about the claim that evolution explains our sense of morality. First, it assumes evolutionary theory is true. A discussion of the evidence for and against evolution is beyond the scope of this chapter, but it's enough for our current purpose to say that the accuracy of evolutionary theory is not a foregone conclusion. And if evolutionary theory isn't accurate, then neither is this claim. (For a discussion of what evolution is and the evidence for and against it, see part 5 of *Keeping Your Kids on God's Side*.)

Second, it's highly questionable to describe animal behavior in terms of morality. Dolphins, for example, are known for "random acts of kindness." They've saved swimmers from sharks and have even guided stranded whales back to sea. But morality, as humans intuitively understand it, is not merely a description of what's good and bad. It's also a *prescription* of what we should or shouldn't do. We don't just say that murder is bad, for example; we say we shouldn't do it. There's a moral obligation attached. If we apply this same understanding to the animal world, we would have to say that dolphins *should* be kind to others. But no one applies moral obligations to animals. We see their actions as facts of their existence, not something appropriate for moral judgment (is there ever moral outrage when animals kill each other—or, for that matter, when animals do anything?). Even if evolutionary theory accurately explained how certain behaviors evolved to aid survival, it wouldn't explain the jump to our human sense of moral obligation.

So can we prove that objective moral values exist? No. However, the weight of the evidence, based on our deepest human intuition and cultural observation, is that certain objective moral values transcend human opinion and are binding on all people.

Where Would Objective Moral Values Come From?

If objective moral values do exist, as we have good reason to believe, we must then ask ourselves where those objective moral values come from. In other words, to what or to whom do we have a moral obligation based on those values? Universal moral laws would logically require a moral law*giver* who has the proper authority to make such laws. As ethicist Richard Taylor explains, "A duty is something that is owed . . . but something can be owed only to some person or persons. There can be no such thing as a duty in isolation. . . . The concept of moral obligation [is] unintelligible apart from the idea of God."[2]

This necessary relationship between the existence of objective moral values and a moral lawgiver is so clear that most atheists deny the existence of objective moral values in the first place. Interestingly, however, a few atheists do believe objective morality exists without God. Atheist neuroscientist and author Sam Harris argues, for example, that moral questions do have objectively right and wrong answers but that the source of those answers is science. In his book *The Moral Landscape: How Science Can Determine Human Values*, Harris says, "Questions about values—about meaning, morality, and life's larger purpose—are really questions about the well-being of conscious creatures. Values, therefore, translate into facts that can be scientifically understood."[3] Some atheists point to Harris's work to validate the idea that even *if* a case can be made that objective moral values exist, it doesn't necessarily imply a moral lawgiver.

But let's look more closely at what, exactly, Harris is saying. He defines morality as the "well-being of conscious creatures" and then says that science can tell us which behaviors are good and which are bad based on how those behaviors impact well-being. *This is a redefinition of morality.* Harris isn't talking about what we normally call morality at all. He's talking about what leads to creatures having the "best"—most comfortable—lives possible (and, of course, science can answer some of those questions).[4] This is wordplay—not a case for the existence of objective moral values in the absence of a moral authority. Even many high-profile atheists have recognized the problems with Harris's thesis and have publicly critiqued its multiple issues.[5]

If objective moral values exist, it's extremely difficult to avoid the natural conclusion that the best explanation for those values is a Being consistent with whom we call God.

KEY POINTS

- Our most basic human intuition tells us that some things are right or wrong for all people and are not subject to a person's individual judgment. If this is true, then objective moral values and duties exist.

- Some people challenge the reality of objective morality because cultures sometimes appear to differ on what is considered moral. However, this is often a disagreement on circumstances rather than on underlying moral values.

- Other people claim that evolutionary theory explains the development of our moral understanding and that it's only an illusion that objective moral values exist. But labeling animal behavior in terms of human morality is problematic because no one believes animals have moral *obligations*— a key part of what we normally associate with human morality.

- We cannot prove that objective moral values exist, but the weight of the evidence, based on cultural observation and our deepest human intuition, is that certain values and duties transcend human opinion and are binding on all people— moral "laws."
- If moral laws exist, the best explanation for those laws is the existence of a moral lawgiver.

CONVERSATION GUIDE

Open the Conversation

- Imagine that someone you know broke into your house and stole everything in your room. When you confronted the person, they shrugged and said, "I think stealing is fine. I had fun wiping out your room." How would you respond? Why? *(Introduce and explain the term objective moral values.)*

Advance the Conversation

- Think of something you assume people all over the world believe is wrong to do. *(Give time to consider examples.)* If you discovered that there were people somewhere who don't think these things are wrong to do, would that mean the rightness or wrongness of those actions is really just a matter of opinion? Why or why not?
- Animals often help each other or humans. For example, an elephant may save another elephant in danger, or a dolphin may save a swimmer from a shark. When animals act in such ways, would you say it's the "right" thing for them to do? Why or why not? *(Use your child's answers to this and the previous question to explain why the two most common objections to the existence of objective morality fail.)*

- If objective moral values really do exist, what are some explanations for where they might have come from? *(Discuss your child's answers and why it's most reasonable to conclude that objective moral laws come from a moral lawgiver.)*

Apply the Conversation

- Read the comment from the beginning of this chapter. Using what you just learned, how would you respond to the person's core question, "If you know the difference between right and wrong, why do you need religion?"

5. What Is the Difference between God and a Flying Spaghetti Monster?

If you've never heard of the Flying Spaghetti Monster, the title of this chapter may seem weird. Why should we bother talking about the differences between God and a Flying Spaghetti Monster? How could that be relevant to a discussion about God's existence?

As it turns out, the Flying Spaghetti Monster isn't just a random fictional creature. No, no. We wouldn't spend time on that. It's a specific fictional creature that skeptics use to actively promote the idea that belief in God is silly and unwarranted.

The Flying Spaghetti Monster gained its celebrity status in 2005, when twenty-four-year-old Bobby Henderson wrote a satirical letter to the Kansas State Board of Education protesting their decision to allow intelligent design to be taught as an alternative to evolution in public schools. Henderson claimed that the universe was created by a Flying Spaghetti Monster and that the "overwhelming scientific evidence pointing toward evolutionary processes is nothing but a coincidence, put in place by Him."[1]

Henderson went on to describe a silly set of beliefs—for example, that teachers must wear full pirate regalia to teach kids about his religion—and insisted that these beliefs be given equal class time with intelligent design and evolution.

The point Henderson wanted to make, of course, was that there's no evidence for the existence of God, so there should be no reason to favor teaching intelligent design over any other "unjustified" idea—like the one that a Flying Spaghetti Monster created the universe.[2] His letter became a cultural phenomenon, and today the Church of the Flying Spaghetti Monster has tens of thousands of "members" all over the world, offers certificates of ordination, sells trinkets and bumper stickers, and encourages people to send in reports of Flying Spaghetti Monster sightings. The Flying Spaghetti Monster may have started out as a statement specifically about the supposed irrelevance of intelligent design theory, but it's taken on a broader identity in popular culture. It now symbolizes the pervasive idea that there's no evidence for God's existence and that belief in God is, therefore, ridiculous.

Given what we've learned in the first four chapters, it's a perfect time to "noodle" on this comparison of flying pasta and God. (Sorry! I can't help myself when there's a pun begging to be used.)

No Evidence for God or a Flying Spaghetti Monster?

Underlying the Flying Spaghetti Monster idea is the claim that there is no evidence for God's existence, just as there is no evidence for the Flying Spaghetti Monster's existence. To evaluate this comparison, let's revisit what we learned in chapter 1.

Recall that evidence itself doesn't say anything—people must *interpret* the evidence. So when we say there's evidence for or against something, it's shorthand for talking about evidence that people are *interpreting* as being for or against something. But what if there's no evidence at all to interpret? That's what the fans of the Flying Spaghetti Monster (Pastafarians, as they call themselves) are saying.

To illustrate the problems with this claim, imagine that I'm at your house and I tell you and a friend that I may or may not have put something in the closed room next to you. There are no clues—no evidence—to help you determine what, if anything, it is. Let's say you guess I put a dog in the room and your friend guesses a toy. With absolutely nothing to go on, the two guesses would be equally valid. I could have put any one of a million things in the room or nothing at all. If your friend continues to insist, however, that it *has* to be a toy, you'd probably think such a claim is ridiculous. This is the kind of situation Pastafarians believe we're in—one in which a claim that God exists is as valid as a claim that a Flying Spaghetti Monster exists because they're both assertions made in the absence of any relevant evidence. And if they're right, we should agree it's foolish to insist that God exists. We don't want to devote our lives to the belief that there's a toy (or a dog) in the other room when there's no reason to do so.

But what if it turns out there *is* some evidence to consider? Let's say that before you guess what's inside the room, you investigate the area around it. You notice what looks to be dog hair nearby, even though you've never had a dog in the house. Then you notice what looks like paw prints just inside your front door. A few minutes later, you hear sounds coming from within the room, as if something is alive and scratching around inside. With this evidence in mind, you tell your friend you're confident there's a dog in the room and explain your reasoning. Your friend replies, "That's crazy! Those things have nothing to do with what's in the room. That hair is probably from my dog and just came off my shirt. Those so-called paw prints? They could be tracks from someone's shoes. And the sounds? Just the air conditioner rattling.

We have no way of knowing what, if anything, is in that room since there's no evidence."

In many ways, this discussion is similar to the debate between theists and atheists. Theists say that the origin of the universe, the origin and the development of life, and the nature of our moral understanding are best explained by the existence of a creating, designing, and moral-lawgiving Being consistent with whom we call God. Atheists say that none of these things have anything to do with God. They believe they're best explained by a yet unknown natural mechanism (in the case of the origin of the universe) or by evolutionary theory (in the case of life and our moral understanding).

In reality, atheists and theists are looking at and trying to explain the same set of facts about the universe. Contrary to the way atheists make it sound by asserting there is "no evidence," theists are not blindly guessing that God exists. Theists are looking at a set of facts about the universe—again, the same facts at which atheists are looking—and are asserting that the existence of God is the best explanation for those facts. Atheists can make their own assertions about what best explains the facts, but it's disingenuous to claim that theists aren't basing their beliefs on any evidence at all.

So what does it mean when atheists say there's no evidence for God? It means there are no facts about the universe that they believe are best explained by the existence of a deity. This is a fine distinction but an important one for kids to understand. It's the difference between them thinking their belief in God is completely untethered to evidence for his existence . . . and understanding that there are important facts about the universe that atheists and theists explain *differently*. With the knowledge that there *is* evidence to consider, and an understanding of why there's good reason to believe God is the best explanation for that evidence, our kids will be significantly better prepared to engage with the claims of a secular world.

Before we conclude, let's not miss the fact that the existence of a Flying Spaghetti Monster would explain *nothing*. There's literally no evidence that would be best explained by the existence of airborne wheat. Comparisons between God and a Flying Spaghetti Monster are absurd and intellectually shallow. As Christian philosopher William Lane Craig has said:

> The real lesson to be learned from the case of the Flying Spaghetti Monster is that it shows how completely out of touch our popular culture is with the great tradition of natural theology. . . . That people could think that belief in God is anything like the groundless belief in a fantasy monster shows how utterly ignorant they are of the works of [famous philosophers], past and present. . . . Given the revival of natural theology in our day over the last half century, we have no excuse for such lame caricatures of theistic belief as belief in the Flying Spaghetti Monster.[3]

KEY POINTS

- The Flying Spaghetti Monster symbolizes the pervasive idea that there's no evidence for God's existence and that belief in God is, therefore, ridiculous.
- Theists, however, are not blindly guessing that God exists. Theists are looking at a set of facts about the universe and are asserting that the best explanation for those facts is the existence of God.
- Atheists are looking at the same set of facts and are asserting that there are better *natural* explanations for those facts.
- Atheists and theists can legitimately disagree over the interpretation of the evidence, but it's disingenuous for atheists to claim that theists aren't basing their beliefs on any evidence at all.

CONVERSATION GUIDE

Open the Conversation

- Imagine that I told you and a friend I may or may not have put something in your bedroom and closed the door. You look around and see no clues—no evidence—to help you figure out what, if anything, I put in your room. You guess I put a toy inside, and your friend guesses a pillow. Is one guess better than the other guess? Why or why not? *(Explain that neither guess can be better when there's absolutely no evidence to consider.)*

Advance the Conversation

- Now imagine that I told you a Flying Spaghetti Monster created the world and everything in it. If what I said were true, what kind of evidence for the Flying Spaghetti Monster's existence do you think you'd find in the universe? Be creative! There are no right or wrong answers. *(At the conclusion of your discussion, establish that there's no evidence that a Flying Spaghetti Monster exists.)*

- Some people say that believing in God is like believing in a Flying Spaghetti Monster because there's no evidence that either exists. Based on what you learned in chapters 2–4, do you think this is a good or bad comparison? Why? *(Recap the evidence and clarify the difference between no evidence and different interpretations of evidence.)*

Apply the Conversation

- In his book *The God Delusion*, atheist Richard Dawkins says, "I have found it an amusing strategy, when asked whether I am an atheist, to point out that the questioner is also an atheist when considering Zeus, Apollo, Amon Ra, Mithras,

Baal, Thor, Wotan, the Golden Calf and the Flying Spaghetti Monster. I just go one god further."[4] Why do you think Dawkins is comparing God to these fictional deities? How would you respond to his comparison?

6. How Much Evidence Do We Need to Be Confident God Exists?

Ratio Christi is an organization that is making a major impact for Christ on college campuses—one of the most challenging environments for young Christians today. Their mission is to "equip university students and faculty to give historical, philosophical, and scientific reasons for following Jesus Christ."[1] Ratio Christi does so by planting collegiate chapters that facilitate conversations on these subjects.

Eric Chabot is the founder and director of the Ratio Christi chapter at Ohio State University, where he's been engaging with students on the truth of Christianity since 2004. Chabot says that in all the years he's been involved in campus outreach, he's heard one objection to God's existence more than any other:

Why won't God show me a direct sign that he exists?

In other words, students feel that despite whatever evidence there is that theoretically points to God's existence, *it's not enough.*

Having read the last few chapters, you may think these students aren't aware of the compelling evidence for God's existence in nature. And that's undoubtedly true for many. But for others, the key problem is the *amount* and *type* of evidence. They want more in order to believe.

An example of this is an agnostic student Chabot video interviewed for his blog. Chabot asked the student, "What would be compelling reasons to believe that the God of the Bible exists?" The student replied:

> I would have to say unambiguous, direct evidence. . . . Some people will use their explanation for God existing as things we don't know . . . [like] the arguments [that] everything is so fine-tuned, but that doesn't do much for me. I would very much prefer to have actual, direct evidence of somebody saying, "This directly points to God Himself coming down and speaking." And at that point I'd have to verify with someone that I'm not hallucinating. . . . It has to be some direct evidence of God, not an extrapolation of evidence from something else.[2]

The claim that there's not enough evidence to prove God's existence is nothing new, of course. People have always desired more. Famous atheist philosopher Bertrand Russell was once asked what he would say if someday he ended up standing before God and God asked him why he never believed. Russell said he would reply, "Sir, why did you not give me *better* evidence?"[3]

We'll conclude part 1 by addressing the claim that the evidence we have just isn't enough for a person to confidently believe God exists.

What We Want versus What We Have

In order to determine whether this common challenge has merit, we first need to establish an important fact: the kind of evidence we would *like* to have has no bearing on the best explanation for the kind of evidence we *do* have. The student Chabot interviewed said he "preferred" certain kinds of evidence, but personal preferences are beside the point. It's often the case that when skeptics raise the challenge that there's not enough evidence, they're not evaluating the strength of the evidence we have —they're simply asserting that they personally require a different kind of evidence in order to believe in God.

To see why such an assertion is futile, think for a moment about the work detectives do. Every day detectives investigate crime scenes and evaluate evidence in order to identify suspects and, ultimately, solve crimes. But a suspect rarely leaves behind a note that says, "I, John Doe, did it. You can reach me at 555–1212." Would detectives prefer that kind of evidence? Of course! But without it, do they throw their hands in the air and say they won't, therefore, ever be persuaded to believe that any given individual committed the crime? Of course not. Detectives understand that the question is not what evidence they wish they had but how best to explain the evidence they do have. Similarly, we can sit around all day and talk about the nature of the evidence we wish God would give us, but that's neither here nor there. We aren't absolved from the need to draw conclusions about the existing evidence just because we wish the evidence were different.

The appropriate question to address, therefore, is specifically about the evidence we *have*: Is that evidence enough for us to be confident God exists?

Is the Evidence We Have Enough?

To answer this question, we have to define the word *enough*. What might be enough for one person to believe in God might not be enough for another person. Enough is a highly subjective quantity. For example, here's what one atheist blogger says would be "enough" for her:

> If I saw an unambiguous message from God, I would be persuaded of his existence. If I saw writing suddenly appear in the sky, in letters a hundred feet high, saying "I Am God, I Exist, Here Is What I Want You To Do"—and if that writing were seen by every human being, written in whatever language they understand, comprehended in the same way by everyone who saw it—I would be persuaded that God existed.[4]

If this blogger applied a similar criterion to anything else in life, there is very little she would be able to say she knows. "Enough" for her is nothing short of *undeniable* evidence that God exists, though we lack that kind of evidence for the existence of many things (for example, do we have undeniable evidence that George Washington existed?). Clearly, this is an inconsistent standard of proof. That said, even if we don't have such certain evidence for anything else, why *wouldn't* a perfectly loving and good God make the fact of his existence undeniable?

There's a reasonable answer to that question: God wants us to use our free will to seek him. Some amount of free will is necessary for us to genuinely love God. Otherwise, we would be like robots whose affections are forced, and a forced love is no love at all. If God revealed himself completely, he would effectively be removing our freedom to seek and love him.

The seventeenth-century Christian philosopher Blaise Pascal put it this way:

> Willing to appear openly to those who seek him with all their heart, and to be hidden from those who flee from him with all their heart, God so regulates the knowledge of himself that he has given indications of himself, which are visible to those who seek him and not to those who do not seek him. There is enough light

for those to see who only desire to see, and enough obscurity for those who have a contrary disposition.[5]

Though many atheists claim to need undeniable evidence for God's existence, it's important to understand that there's good reason to believe God wouldn't give us such evidence. So let's push this one step further. Short of certainty, do we have enough evidence to be *confident* God exists (at a level that would make us confident of most other beliefs we hold)? To answer that question, let's recap what we've seen:

- *The universe* (chap. 2). We have a universe that began to exist, so it must have had a cause beyond itself capable of creating everything *in* the universe—a cause that is spaceless, timeless, immaterial, and enormously powerful.
- *The fine-tuning of the universe* (chap. 3). The universe appears to be finely tuned to support the existence of life, both in the constants of nature and in the parameters of our Earth and solar system. This strongly suggests that the universe is the product of purposeful intelligence.
- *The origin of life* (chap. 3). Chance does not seem to be an adequate explanation for the origin of biological complexity and specificity. When we look at the intricate nature of how living things work, there's good reason to believe they are the purposeful product of intelligence.
- *The innate human understanding of objective morality* (chap. 4). Humans have a near-universal sense that certain things are right or wrong, regardless of personal opinion. If there are objective moral "laws," it's reasonable to conclude they come from a moral lawgiver with higher than human authority.

Any one of these pieces of evidence may not be compelling enough for a person to feel they can confidently believe in God.

But it's the collective evidence, all pointing in the same direction, that makes the case for God so powerful. J. Warner Wallace is a cold-case homicide detective and former atheist who became a Christian after investigating this evidence from a detective's perspective. In his excellent book, *God's Crime Scene: A Cold-Case Detective Examines the Evidence for a Divinely Created Universe*, he explains how he could no longer ignore where the cumulative evidence pointed:

> As an atheist, I was very comfortable as the captain of my own ship. . . . I am not a theist today because I was raised by believers—I wasn't. I am not a believer because I was hoping for heaven or afraid of hell—I had no sense of value for either. I am not a theist because I was trying to fill a "void" or satisfy a "need"—I felt none. I believe God exists because the evidence leaves me no reasonable alternative. The evidence points to a very specific "suspect."[6]

Can people always come up with other explanations for each piece of evidence? Sure. We established that back in chapter 1. But we also established that the number of possible explanations has nothing to do with which explanation is best. In this case, we have multiple pieces of evidence (and many more not addressed in this book) that can all be explained by the same "suspect."[7] Even if we don't have enough evidence for certainty (and, as we saw, there's good reason for that), we clearly have enough for confidence.

KEY POINTS

- People often say there's not enough evidence to believe God exists—that God should make himself known in other ways. But the evidence we would like to have has no bearing on the best explanation for the kind of evidence we do have.

- The more appropriate question to ask is about the amount of evidence we *have*: Is *that* evidence enough for us to be confident God exists?
- While many people answer no to that question unless they have certainty, there's good reason to believe God wouldn't reveal himself in such an undeniable way: he would effectively be removing our freedom to seek and love him.
- Short of certainty, do we have enough evidence to be confident God exists (at a level that would make us confident of most other beliefs we hold)? Absolutely. The many pieces of evidence we have are powerfully explained by the same "suspect"—God.

CONVERSATION GUIDE

Open the Conversation

- If you could pick any way for God to make himself more known to you—for example, popping up in your living room or writing a big message in the sky—what would you pick? Why?

Advance the Conversation

- Since God hasn't revealed himself in the way you just described, does that make you doubt he exists? Why or why not? *(Clarify the difference between evaluating what we have and what we would like to have.)*
- Many people wish God would make himself known in an undeniable way, like showing up in every person's living room. Can you think of any reasons God wouldn't do that? *(Talk about the importance of having free will in order to be able to truly love God.)*

- Think about the evidence in nature we've been studying—the origin of the universe, the origin and the development of life, and our moral understanding. When you look at all the evidence together, do you think there's enough evidence in nature to be confident God exists? Why or why not? *(Discuss the importance of looking at all the evidence together and read the quote from J. Warner Wallace. Talk about the importance of all the evidence pointing to the same "suspect.")*

Apply the Conversation

- Read the quote from the interview of the agnostic student at the beginning of the chapter. How would you respond to what he said? If you could have a conversation with him, what are some questions you would ask to better understand what he believes and why he believes it?

PART 2
Science
and
God

Overview

The American Humanist Association (AHA) is an organization that actively promotes the worldview that "reason and science are the best ways to understand the world around us, and that dignity and compassion should be the basis for how you act toward someone else."[1] With hundreds of local chapters, over six hundred thousand social media followers, extensive political activism, and ad campaigns on TV, radio, billboards, and buses, the AHA is highly influential.

One initiative of the AHA, a website called Kids Without God (kidswithoutgod.com), welcomes young visitors to its home page, saying, "Welcome to Kids Without God, a site for the millions of young people around the world who have embraced science, rejected superstition, and are dedicated to being Good Without A God!" Young kids can read a short online book called *Meet Darwin*, watch a handful of science videos, and get instructions for a variety of simple science experiments. The statement is obvious: kids "without God" are kids who believe in science rather than in God.

A brief overview of *Meet Darwin* will help you more fully appreciate how the AHA wants kids (and everyone else) to see the relationship between science and God. The text introduces kids to a fun little dog named Darwin who loves to learn about the world through science experiments. The reader then learns that Darwin also enjoys stories from a "long, long time ago." He acknowledges that some people still believe those stories, but he knows they aren't real. Instead of believing in ancient books about gods, Darwin is a humanist who believes in being a good person. The book concludes, "Darwin loves using his imagination, but he only believes in things he can see in the real world. Things like friendship, and being nice, and learning."

Apparently, Darwin the Dog doesn't believe he can know *anything* from history, since he can't presently see those things in the "real world." And he's barking up the wrong tree of knowledge if he automatically rejects the truth of a document just because it was written long ago. But then again, he's a dog, so we'll give him some grace on his lack of critical thinking.

We humans, however, need to understand the poverty in the overarching idea that a person must choose between science and belief in God—a false dichotomy that's becoming a given in the public mind today. It's especially important for parents to know that the belief that Christianity is anti-science has become a leading reason why many young adults are walking away from faith. Researchers at the Barna Group have found that 29 percent of eighteen- to twenty-nine-year-olds with a Christian background say churches are "out of step with the scientific world we live in," and 25 percent say "Christianity is anti-science."[2] The fact that more than a quarter of kids from a Christian background have accepted this harmful and false secular narrative should raise a giant red flag of concern for us as Christian parents. (As a side note, the Barna Group's research has also found that only 1 percent of youth pastors address any issue related to science in a given year. Don't be tempted to think you can pass this subject off to your church to handle on your behalf.[3])

So how should we tackle this seemingly huge science versus God debate with our kids? That's what part 2 is about. In part 1, we discussed some specific scientific findings and their relevance to the question of God's existence, but in part 2, we're addressing broader philosophical questions about the *relationship* between God and science. By the end of this section, you'll be well on your way to being able to explain to Darwin the Dog why he needs to think more deeply about the relationship between science and God before he stars in his next book. More importantly, you'll be ready to have these discussions with your kids.

Three Keys to Impactful Conversations about Science and God

1. *Discuss these subjects with kids starting in elementary school.* You may think only older kids can understand these questions or be interested in them. Please know this is not the case. With the increasing number of atheist adults in America, there is an increasing number of kids growing up hearing that God and science are opposed, even if they don't understand what that means.[4] Just recently, the eight-year-old son of a friend of mine came home from school and said his friend told him she doesn't believe in God—she "believes in science" like her dad. So don't skip this section because you assume it will be over your child's head. Instead, tailor your discussions to your child's age. As you'll see in the conversation guides, there are many ways to have age-relevant discussions on these topics.

2. *Emphasize that people often use the same words to mean different things, so answers to big questions aren't necessarily obvious.* One of the most difficult aspects of having the following conversations with your kids is that they require some nuanced thought. While it's tempting to want to give our kids black-and-white answers ("Of course God and science aren't

85

opposed!"), they need more thoughtful guidance to engage with today's world ("What do you *mean* by God? What do you *mean* by science?"). Throughout your conversations, continue to point out the importance of thinking at this deeper level.

3. *Charitably acknowledge where Christians have varying views on science-related issues.* Even Christians disagree on some questions about the relationship between God and science. In particular, the subjects discussed in chapter 8 ("Do Science and Religion Contradict Each Other?") can lead to heated debates among believers. This book does not take a position on these disagreements but rather explains why the disagreements exist so you can have an informed discussion with your kids about the scriptural and scientific considerations involved. It's critical for kids to understand the issues that divide atheists and theists, but it's also important for them to know where Christians disagree.

7. Can Science Prove or Disprove God's Existence?

With the growing number of atheist adults in America, there's a growing demand for programs that cater to atheist children. One such program is a summer camp called Camp Quest, which has fifteen locations throughout the United States. Campers ages eight to seventeen participate in various traditional camp offerings along with an important core of so-called freethought activities designed to bolster kids' understanding of an atheistic worldview.[1]

One of the popular freethought activities is the Invisible Unicorn Challenge. Campers are told there are two invisible unicorns that live at Camp Quest but cannot be seen, heard, tasted, smelled, or touched. An ancient book handed down over countless generations contains the only proof of their existence. The challenge? Try to disprove their existence. (Campers learn they can't.)

Obviously, these kids are supposed to think the unicorns are like God—that we can't disprove the idea that there are invisible unicorns around us just as we can't disprove the idea that there's an invisible God. But just because Camp Quest acknowledges that

God can't technically be disproven doesn't mean this is an act of goodwill toward a theistic worldview. Camp Quest uses the Invisible Unicorn Challenge to implicitly say, "Hey, anyone can come up with an idea that something invisible and undetectable (like God) exists. It's not your job to disprove it, because you can't. Instead, use science to find out real stuff about the world!" While Camp Quest's stated point of the challenge is to teach kids to "think critically and rationally," it's clear given the context of the camp's purposes that they intend for kids to make the connection to the question of God.[2]

For reasons we'll discuss in this chapter, most atheists, if given the context of the Invisible Unicorn Challenge, would agree that science similarly can't disprove the existence of God. Nonetheless, there is a major cultural misunderstanding on this topic because people use the words *science*, *God*, and *prove/disprove* in many different senses, and an ongoing stream of popular discourse makes it *sound* as though it's an accepted fact that science disproves God. As mathematician Amir Aczel said in his book *Why Science Does Not Disprove God*:

> Without a shred of evidence on their side, [popular atheist writers] declare: "Science proves there is no God! Respond!"—and a public that may not be steeped in all the nuances and technicalities of science is left flummoxed, and hence vulnerable to [those writers'] overconfident pronouncements.[3]

As Christian parents, we don't want our kids to be perplexed by such claims, so it's important for us to understand the nuances of this topic and to discuss them with our kids accordingly. To do so, we need to consider two questions: (1) What do we mean by science? and (2) What do we mean by God? While this chapter focuses on the claim that science can disprove God's existence, we'll also briefly consider the opposite claim that science can prove God's existence.

What Do We Mean by *Science*?

Broadly speaking, science is what we call the systematic study of the structure and behavior of the natural world through observation and experimentation. Within science, there are many areas of study—for example, biology, chemistry, and physics. Sometimes people use the broader word *science* even when they're technically referring to one of these specific branches of science. This distinction will become important in the next chapter. But here's the key takeaway for now: the nature of scientific study is such that it *never* leads to absolutely certain knowledge—strict proof or disproof. At best, science can offer a high degree of confidence in various conclusions based on the weight of the evidence. Biologist and vocal atheist Jerry Coyne explains:

> Scientific truth is never absolute, but provisional: there is no bell that rings when you're doing science to let you know that you've finally reached the absolute and unchangeable truth and need to go no further. Absolute and unalterable truth is for mathematics and logic, not empirically based science. As the philosopher Walter Kaufmann explained, "What distinguishes knowledge is not certainty but evidence."[4]

Can science prove or disprove God's existence? The quick (and scientifically accurate) answer to the question is no, because the nature of science isn't to prove or disprove *anything* with absolute certainty.

Sometimes when people claim that science disproves God's existence, they simply don't understand this nature of scientific inquiry. Oftentimes, however, people use this wording colloquially to mean something more like science "strongly suggests" God doesn't exist. We should understand this implied meaning as well and not just dismiss a person's (perhaps poorly stated) claim based on technicalities. To take *that* discussion further, we now need to consider various usages of the word *God*.

What Do We Mean by *God*?

As Christians, we think of God in a specific way based on our knowledge of him from the Bible. It's easy to forget that the word *God* can mean different things to different people, however. Two uses of the word *God* are particularly pertinent to this discussion:

- *Meaning 1: a supernatural being who may or may not exist.* When people talk about God in this broadest sense, they're not addressing any one religion's specific concept of God. They're simply talking about a supernatural being who may or may not exist and who may or may not have created the world.

- *Meaning 2: a given religion's concept of God.* People sometimes use the word *God* as shorthand for the beliefs of a given religion. For example, a person may say they could never believe in "God" while specifically meaning the God of the Bible and corresponding Christian beliefs.

Now that we've distinguished between these meanings, we're ready to answer the question of whether science "strongly suggests" God doesn't exist.

Does Science Strongly Suggest God Doesn't Exist?

We'll break down our answer according to the two meanings of God we just discussed.

Meaning 1: A Supernatural Being Who May or May Not Exist

Recall from our earlier discussion that science has a particular scope: it explains the mechanics of the natural world. If by God we simply mean a being who may or may not exist beyond that natural world, it follows that the possible existence of such a being is beyond the scope of what science can investigate. This is the kind of God that the Invisible Unicorn Challenge implicitly makes a statement about. And most atheists would agree, given this definition, that science says nothing about God.

However, this question is not at the heart of the debate. The heart of the debate is where we talk about God using the second meaning.

Meaning 2: A Given Religion's Concept of God

Evolutionary biologist and bestselling atheist author Richard Dawkins is known for making some of the strongest statements about how science supposedly shows God doesn't exist. While Dawkins acknowledges that science can't strictly disprove God's existence, he says that science can show "there almost certainly is no God."[5] Many nonbelieving scientists have criticized Dawkins for going beyond what is "within the scope of science to deny," but when scientists speak in terms of *scope*, that's a signal that they're primarily talking about the first meaning of God.[6] Dawkins, on the other hand, primarily talks about the second meaning—God as conceived of specifically by Christianity and other major world religions.

In his various anti-theistic writings, Dawkins attacks the idea of God by questioning religion-specific claims, such as direct creation (as opposed to evolution), the nature of God in the Old Testament, the plausibility of miracles, the reality of objective morality (see chap. 4), and so on. Dawkins says that science can weigh in on these ideas because they make claims that intersect with the natural world and can therefore be investigated by normal scientific methods. He emphasizes, "The fact that we can neither prove nor disprove the existence of something does not put existence and non-existence on an even footing."[7] Dawkins concludes that the evidence adds up to *near* certainty that God doesn't exist.

Other examples abound of scientists and laypeople claiming that science strongly suggests God doesn't exist because scientific findings allegedly contradict religious claims. It's critical to remember that most of these same people readily acknowledge that science can't literally disprove anything and that science can say nothing about a hypothetical being who may exist beyond nature—but, again, that's not where the debate really lies. The debate, regardless of the terminology used at a given time, is over the relationship between science and *religion*—and, more specifically, between the findings of a given *branch* of science (such as evolutionary biology) and a particular *claim* of a religion (such as God's direct creation of life).

So are those in Dawkins's camp correct? Do scientific and religious claims contradict each other, leading to the conclusion that God almost certainly doesn't exist? We'll look at this more narrowly defined question in the next chapter.

KEY POINTS

- Scientific study *never* leads to absolute certainty—strict proof or disproof. Science can't prove or disprove God's existence because the nature of science isn't to prove or disprove *anything* with absolute certainty.

- Oftentimes, people claim that science disproves God's existence when they mean something more like science "strongly suggests" God doesn't exist.

- The key to better understanding such a claim is clarifying what a person means by God. Is this person talking about (1) a supernatural being who may or may not exist or (2) a given religion's concept of God?

- Using the first meaning, even most atheists would agree that such a being is beyond the scope of science to investigate. The true debate lies in the second meaning, when we're talking about the relationship between scientific findings and the claims of a given religion.

CONVERSATION GUIDE

Open the Conversation

- Imagine that I told you there are two invisible unicorns in our town, but they cannot be seen, heard, or touched. The only proof of their existence is contained in a book handed down over many generations. Can you think of a way to disprove the unicorns' existence? Why or why not?
- Do you think God is like an invisible unicorn? Why or why not? *(Use this as an opportunity to recall what was learned in part I about evidence.)*

Advance the Conversation

- Some people talk about science as something that can prove or disprove God's existence. To understand what they mean, and whether that's correct, we have to understand what is meant by the word *science* and what is meant by the word *God*. How would you define these two words? *(Let your child define them, then explore the meanings from this chapter—emphasizing the two meanings for the word God. Explain that science can give us a high degree of confidence but not proof or disproof. This applies to God as well.)*
- Most atheists agree that science can't tell us anything about God's existence if, by God, we only mean a supernatural being who may have created the world. Why do you think even atheists agree on that? *(Revisit the definition of science as*

*the study of the natural world and explain how this means it doesn't
address what may be beyond nature.)*

- Much of the time when people say that science disproves
  God's existence, what they mean is that they believe certain
  scientific findings disprove certain claims of a religion—for
  example, they believe scientific evidence contradicts something the Bible says is true. What is an example of one thing
  in the Bible that science could say something about, and what
  is one thing science could not say something about? *(A good
  example of the former is a historical claim that archaeology could
  weigh in on. A good example of the latter is whether Jesus was
  resurrected. The resurrection was a miracle. If God exists, he's not
  tied to working within the natural laws investigated by science.)*

Apply the Conversation

- On a debate website, a person said, "I believe that science
  has the ability to disprove that a God exists. My aunt is currently taking an anthropology class in college and it basically
  disproves everything in the Bible."[8] Which meaning of God is
  this person using? How would you respond to what they said?

8. Do Science and Religion Contradict Each Other?

Like many moms, I'm concerned about what foods my kids eat. Not only do I want them to make healthy choices (fruit, not sugar cookies), I also want them to consider the ingredients that go into the food they eat (all-natural bread, not bread with fifty ingredients).

One of our local grocery stores has a private label brand that caters to shoppers like me. The packaging proudly states that each product is "free from 101 artificial additives, preservatives, and ingredients." Since I always look at ingredient lists directly, I had never thought about this strange brand promise until my son commented on it one day.

I was pulling one of the brand's cereal boxes off the shelf when he asked, "What about all the *other* artificial additives, preservatives, and ingredients? This cereal is free from only 101 of them."

He was serious, but I had to laugh at his astute observation of marketing gone awry. Such a claim *sounds* good, but it brings up the question of what the product is *not* free from! For all we know, it could be free from 101 bad ingredients but filled with 12 others that are even more toxic.

Similarly, we sometimes try to make Christianity seem more palatable to nonbelievers (or even our kids) by focusing on noncontroversial teachings, such as the importance of loving others—a Christianity "free from 101 conflicts with the secular world." When we do so, not only are we not being faithful to the whole of Christian truth, but we are also missing the opportunity to address the challenges skeptics pose head-on, and it's certain science-related challenges that skeptics commonly find so "toxic" to the truth status of Christianity. We can't shy away from addressing these subjects with our kids. If there *are* apparent conflicts between the mainstream scientific consensus and what the Bible says, we should acknowledge them and discuss why they exist.

Note that certain truth claims of other religions have their own possible conflicts with science, but this chapter is focused on Christianity specifically.[1] I've narrowed the discussion to the two most important subjects today: the age of the Earth and evolution. These topics account for the vast majority of science versus religion debates in America.[2]

The Age of the Earth: Thousands or Billions of Years Old?

The mainstream scientific consensus is that the Earth is 4.5 billion years old. This is widely accepted as scientific fact, and many fields of study—astronomy, geology, paleontology, biology, and archaeology to name a few—take it as a given. Many Christians, however, believe the Earth is six to ten thousand years old (this view is commonly called young-Earth creationism, and those who hold it are called young-Earth creationists).[3] Clearly, there is a conflict between the mainstream scientific consensus and the view of young-Earth creationists: the Earth cannot be both 4.5 billion and six to ten thousand years old.

There are two key things we should understand about this conflict. First, even Christians have varying views on the age of the Earth. The conflict here, therefore, is more specifically between the mainstream scientific consensus and a specific Christian view of what the Bible says on the subject. The Bible never explicitly gives a year when God created the world, so Christians are divided on whether we can and should make a conclusion about the Earth's age from Scripture. Young-Earth creationists believe various biblical passages on genealogies and historical time spans should be combined to arrive at a biblically authoritative age of the Earth.[4] Other Christians believe the mainstream scientific interpretation of data is reliable and that the appropriate interpretation of Scripture doesn't *tell* us how old the Earth is. (In *Keeping Your Kids on God's Side*, I explain in detail how the two sides arrive at their conclusions.)

Second, young-Earth creationists believe there is scientific evidence for their view. Organizations such as Answers in Genesis, the Institute for Creation Research, and Creation Ministries International devote significant resources to scientific research supporting young-Earth creationism; they don't disregard the importance of science.

In short, there *is* a conflict between the mainstream scientific consensus and the young-Earth creationist view. Young-Earth creationists acknowledge this tension while emphasizing the priority of the young-Earth interpretation of Scripture.

Life on Earth: A Result of God's Direct Creation or Evolution?

The word *evolution*, in its most basic sense, means a species has undergone genetic change over time (a species is a group of organisms capable of interbreeding—for example, humans are a species).

This isn't controversial. Everyone agrees this kind of change can be documented within a human lifetime.

Evolutionary theory, however, encompasses much more than that (and this is what I'll refer to as evolution for the remainder of the chapter). The theory of evolution is a group of propositions that seeks to explain how all life on Earth evolved from a single primitive species that lived roughly 3.5 billion years ago. This is where the controversy lies: Can the same mechanisms that facilitate genetic change within a species actually create new species—and, more specifically, every species on Earth? Most biological scientists say yes, the process is one and the same. Many Christians say no, species change, but variation has limits.

As with the age of the Earth, Christians have varying views on this. Research shows that 32 percent of Americans believe humans did, in fact, evolve . . . with God guiding that evolution. This view is called theistic evolution and is in contrast with the mainstream scientific view that evolution occurs via purely natural, unguided processes (this view is called naturalistic evolution). Why do most scientists work from the assumption that evolution is *unguided?* Some say there's no evidence of guidance, while others say evolutionary theory, as it's currently understood, is not even *compatible* with the idea of divine guidance.[5] This means that even for Christians who accept evolution, there remains a fundamental conflict with mainstream scientists over whether there's an intelligence *behind* evolution.[6]

For Christians who reject evolutionary theory, the conflict between the scientific consensus and religious belief is even more significant. As explained previously, young-Earth creationists reject both the ancient age of the Earth required for evolution and evolution itself as a method of creation. Other Christians (called old-Earth creationists) accept the ancient age of the Earth but believe God was actively involved in the direct creation of life (to what degree, how, and when are matters of debate).[7]

So why do many Christians continue to reject evolution? While that answer varies greatly by individual, there are two main reasons. First, many Christians believe the Bible itself leaves no room for an evolutionary interpretation. They believe Genesis is clear that God directly created humans and that there are no hints of an evolutionary process. In addition, the historicity of Adam and Eve is a significant related issue. Most evolutionists don't believe Adam and Eve were historical people. However, if a historical first couple did not exist, the important questions of how and when sin entered the world are left unanswered. Without a clear biblical explanation of how the problem of sin arose, the need for the solution of Jesus can be diminished. Theistic evolutionists acknowledge the importance of these questions and offer a variety of responses.[8] The most common one is that God directly created the human *soul* and that the *soul* is the central issue, not how God prepared material bodies for those souls.

Second, many Christians reject evolution because they believe there isn't sufficient scientific evidence for it. In some cases, Christians reject current evolutionary theory (the explanation of how evolution theoretically works) but accept the idea of common descent (the idea that all life descends from the same organism).[9] In other cases, Christians reject both common descent and current evolutionary theory, believing that scientific evidence for both is lacking.

Concerning both the age of the Earth and evolution, it's important to remember that the accurate interpretation of scientific data and the accurate interpretation of the Bible will never be in true conflict. If apparent conflicts arise, (at least) one interpretation is wrong. When we're convicted of the accuracy of our interpretation of Scripture, we shouldn't be afraid to acknowledge when the Bible conflicts with scientific consensus. Scientists can be wrong. On the other hand, when there *is* an apparent conflict, we should be willing to thoughtfully consider the scientific data. Our biblical interpretation can also be wrong.[10]

KEY POINTS

- The age of the Earth and evolution account for the vast majority of science versus religion debates in America.
- Mainstream scientists today believe the Earth is 4.5 billion years old, while some Christians believe the Earth is less than ten thousand years old (a view called young-Earth creationism). This is a tension that young-Earth creationists acknowledge while emphasizing the priority of starting from the young-Earth interpretation of Scripture.
- Christians have varying views on evolution. Even for Christians who accept evolution, a fundamental conflict with the mainstream scientific consensus remains over whether there's an intelligence *behind* evolution.
- For the majority of Christians who reject evolutionary theory (in favor of the understanding that God created life directly), the conflict between the scientific consensus and religious belief is even more significant.
- The accurate interpretation of scientific data and the accurate interpretation of the Bible will never be in true conflict. When apparent conflicts arise, (at least) one interpretation is wrong. Which interpretation is wrong is a matter of debate even among Christians.

CONVERSATION GUIDE

Open the Conversation

- The two most important subjects in which some people say there's a conflict between scientific findings and what Christians believe are the age of the Earth and evolution. If a friend asked you how old the Earth is and what evolution is, what would you say? *(Use your child's answer as an opportunity to correct any misunderstandings or to define terms for the first time with younger kids.)*

Advance the Conversation

- Most scientists have interpreted scientific data to mean the Earth is 4.5 billion years old. The Bible doesn't tell us exactly when God created the world, but some Christians interpret certain Bible verses to mean the Earth is six to ten thousand years old. The Earth can't be both of these ages, so what does this tell us about at least one of these interpretations? *(At least one must be in error. Emphasize the point that the accurate interpretation of scientific data and the accurate interpretation of the Bible will never be in true conflict. Explain that Christians interpret the Bible differently on this subject.)*

- Based on what you know about evolution, why do you think many Christians reject it? *(Talk through the two key reasons raised in this chapter.)*

- Some Christians, called theistic evolutionists, accept evolution and believe it doesn't conflict with the Bible. They believe evolution was *guided* by God. How would this view be different from an atheist's view of evolution? *(Atheists don't believe in God, so they necessarily believe all life on Earth was created by unguided, natural processes. This is a good time to discuss the evidence for and against evolution with older kids. See chapters 37–40 in* Keeping Your Kids on God's Side *for key points.)*

Apply the Conversation

- A blogger wrote, "When it comes to science, so many Christians are quick to point out how scientists don't know everything or how science gets it all wrong. . . . They just seem to hate science."[11] If you asked questions and found out this person was talking about the age of the Earth and/or evolution (something likely to be the case), how would you respond based on what you learned in this chapter?

9. Do Science and Religion Complement Each Other?

One of the reasons why the age of the Earth and evolution dominate conversations about the relationship between science and Christianity is because these subjects cause such heated debate. The problem is that when most of what the public hears about science and Christianity concerns the conflicts, it creates a skewed perception of the fuller picture—a fuller picture that includes much harmony. It's as if a large group of children are playing beautifully together, except for two kids who keep screaming at each other. Who gets all the attention? The loud ones. Science and Christianity "play beautifully together" in many important ways, but we don't hear as much about that because of the "screaming children"—the areas of alleged conflict. As a result, it's up to us, as parents, to paint a more thorough picture for our kids of the many ways science and Christianity are complementary.

In part 1, we already saw some of these ways. For example, the Bible tells us the universe had a beginning; scientific findings reveal the same (see chap. 2). The Bible also tells us God purposefully created human life; scientific findings reveal that the universe appears to be finely tuned for life and that living things have a highly intricate nature—two facts consistent with purposeful design.

Now we're going to look at three more examples of how science and Christianity play beautifully together. As noted previously, different religions make different claims about reality, so the answer to this chapter's question depends on which religion is being considered. In the interest of space, we're focusing our discussion on Christianity specifically, but some of these points apply to other theistic religions as well.

The Rational Intelligibility of the Universe

The goal of science, broadly, is to discover the order of the universe. But the feasibility of that goal depends on the assumption that the workings of the natural world *can* be discovered. We take this for granted, but we shouldn't.

The universe is both understandable and logical—something mathematician and philosopher John Lennox calls the "rational intelligibility of the universe."[1] These characteristics allow us to do science in the first place. If the universe was just a hodgepodge of chaotic events ungoverned by structured laws, science would be a hopeless task. But *why* is the world intelligible rather than chaotic? If the universe is truly the product of unguided evolutionary forces, as atheists claim, there's no reason to expect that an elegant ordering of nature would have happened on its own. But if the universe is the product of intelligence, as Christians and other theists claim, we would *expect* it to be orderly—a reflection of its rational designer.

Physicist and agnostic Paul Davies acknowledged this in his Templeton Prize address called "Physics and the Mind of God":

> In the [last] three hundred years, the theological dimension of science has faded. People take it for granted that the physical world is

both ordered and intelligible. The underlying order in nature—the laws of physics—are simply accepted as given, as brute facts. Nobody asks where they came from; at least they do not do so in polite company. However, even the most atheistic scientist accepts as an act of faith that the universe is not absurd, that there is a rational basis to physical existence manifested as a lawlike order in nature that is at least partly comprehensible to us. So science can proceed only if the scientist adopts an essentially theological worldview.[2]

In short, theism makes sense of the rational intelligibility of the universe in a way that atheism does not. That doesn't prove God exists, but it's a powerful example of how science and Christianity complement each other.

The Reliability of Human Reason

As we just saw, scientists couldn't do their work without an orderly universe to work on. But scientists also couldn't do their work without the human ability to reason in a reliable way. This ability is another example of something we take for granted but shouldn't.

Atheists believe our mental processes are fully determined by atoms moving around in our brains, the product of billions of years of unguided evolution. But if that's the case, there's no reason to assume any of our beliefs are true—they would simply be the result of various physical laws acting upon us. Some atheists, such as philosopher Thomas Nagel, have acknowledged the uncomfortable implications of this fact. Nagel admits, "Evolutionary naturalism provides an account of our capacities that undermines their reliability, and in doing so undermines itself."[3]

Most of us intuitively believe, however, that we can trust in the reliability of our reasoning and that our thoughts are not just atoms colliding. This assumption is most consistent with a theistic worldview like Christianity, which claims that humans are made in the image of God. While theologians debate what the image of God encompasses, almost all agree that it includes a capacity for understanding and rational thought. This capacity, among other things, uniquely enables us to have a relationship with our Creator.

Christian apologist and author Frank Turek explains it this way in his book *Stealing from God: Why Atheists Need God to Make Their Case*:

> If we are open-minded enough—meaning we haven't ruled God out in advance by blindly putting our faith in the ideology of materialism—then we can see that our minds work because they are made in the image of the Great Mind. That is, our minds can apprehend truth and can reason about reality because they were built by the source of truth, reason, and reality. Our minds were designed by God to know God and His creation.[4]

Once again, theism makes sense of what we observe in the world in a way that atheism does not. This is one more example of how science and Christianity are complementary. In a Christian worldview, we would expect that scientists are able to do their work because we believe the human mind was *designed* with the ability to understand and discover truth.

Complementary Sources of Knowledge

The other day I noticed my daughter had used a green marker to write words all over her right hand. I couldn't make out the words, except for the one that was scrawled in uppercase letters across her thumb: DIE. Finding that a bit disconcerting, I asked her, "Why does your thumb say, 'DIE'?"

She replied, "Because I wrote it there."

So helpful.

My daughter's answer was technically accurate. She was just addressing a different kind of why than I was. She was talking about the mechanics of the ink being there rather than her purpose in putting it there.

There's a similar distinction when we consider the types of questions that science and Christianity can answer. Science explains the mechanics of the universe at a level of detail far beyond what God has revealed to us in the Bible. In this way, science complements our knowledge of God because it reveals the workings of the world he created. But science can say nothing about the ultimate meaning or purpose of the universe. To answer those questions, we need the input of the One who created it in the first place. In this way, the Bible complements science. (Of course, this assumes the Bible is true—there's no value in answering questions of meaning and purpose inaccurately. But that's another question. For now, we're simply considering the ways that science and the *claims* of Christianity are complementary.)

Note that a clear line does not always exist between the domains of science and the Bible. The Bible, for example, makes historical claims that archaeological sciences can investigate. But as we've seen, some questions are outside the scope of each to answer on its own, making science and the Bible important complementary sources of knowledge about the nature of reality.

KEY POINTS

- Although the alleged conflicts between science and religion get most of the attention in public discourse, science and religion complement each other in many important ways.
- We saw some examples already in part 1, but in this chapter, we looked at three more: the rational intelligibility of the universe, the reliability of human reason, and science and religion as complementary sources of knowledge.

- The rational intelligibility of the universe refers to the fact that the universe is both understandable and logical, characteristics that allow us to do science. We would only *expect* that if the universe is the product of a mind.

- Scientists couldn't investigate this rationally intelligible world without the human ability to reason, and to reason in a reliable way. Once again, we would only *expect* our minds to be reliable if they are the *product* of a mind.

- Science and the Bible are complementary sources of knowledge about the nature of reality because some questions are outside the scope of each to answer on its own.

CONVERSATION GUIDE

Open the Conversation

- If someone asked you, "Do science and religion support each other?" what important clarifying question would you need to ask before answering? *(You would need to know which religion, since different religions make different claims about what's true.)*

Advance the Conversation

- Imagine a world in which you could never predict how long it takes for a baseball to fall to the ground—sometimes it happens instantly, sometimes it takes twenty-three minutes, sometimes it takes an hour, and so on. In other words, there's no law of gravity—things just happen in a random way. If the world were unstructured like that, with no underlying laws, do you think it would be easier or harder to do science? Why? *(Explain that science is possible only because the world is understandable and logical. But only in a theistic worldview like Christianity do we expect the universe to be ordered in this way.)*

- The Bible tells us that God created humans in his image (Gen. 1:27). In part, this means he designed us to be able to think logically about the world around us. Why is this ability important for doing science? *(Scientists are only able to do their jobs if they're able to reason well. Explain why this is an important example of how science and Christianity are complementary.)*

- What kinds of information do we learn from scientific discoveries that we don't learn from the Bible? And what kinds of information do we learn from the Bible that we could never learn from scientific discoveries? *(Discuss how science and the Bible are complementary sources of knowledge and that there are limits to what each tells us. Be sure to acknowledge that there are areas of overlap as well.)*

Apply the Conversation

- Someone created a picture to share online that says, "Science doesn't need religion to answer anything. We don't know yet is an acceptable answer. Scientists work every day to answer those questions."[5] How would you respond to this person?

10. Is God Just an Explanation for What Science Doesn't Yet Know?

I'm an only child, my mom is an only child, and my dad is an only child. That means I have no siblings, aunts, uncles, or cousins; we have a very tiny family! Because I didn't grow up with other kids, certain aspects of having three children of my own baffle me—like the constant squabbling between siblings. I just can't relate to how siblings find joy in bothering each other for the sake of bothering each other.

For a long time, a primary source of ongoing sibling angst between our two girls was that our older daughter blamed her sister for everything. Our younger daughter, whom we'll call Junior, could be one thousand miles away, but if our older daughter couldn't find her socks, Junior must have hidden them.

A single candy went missing from the candy bowl? Junior must have eaten it.

A stray pen mark was found on our older daughter's artwork? Junior must have done it.

Something fell off a half-built LEGO creation that had been sitting in the living room for five months? Surely, Junior had suddenly stepped on it.

In time, we could no longer believe our older daughter when she said her sister did something. We had to launch a full-scale parental investigation to determine if there was good reason to believe Junior was responsible or if it was just another case of what we might call "Junior of the gaps"—assigning responsibility to Junior whenever there was a gap in the knowledge of what had actually happened.

Similarly, this is what many skeptics think theists are doing when they assert that scientific evidence points to the existence of God. They claim theists use God as an explanation whenever there's a scientific gap in knowledge—a so-called God of the gaps approach—and promptly wave off any discussion. Furthermore, some skeptics compare this to how ancient people invented gods to explain natural phenomena, asserting that theists today hastily assume parts of the natural world can't be explained without God's direct involvement.

Upon a closer look, however, these are two very different God of the gaps issues, and it's important to understand why. Let's look at both challenges and consider their relevance to today's questions of God and science.

Issue 1: Gods Were Invented Because an Explanation Was Needed

Atheist ex-pastor and author Dan Barker once remarked on the problem with God of the gaps reasoning during a University of Florida debate:

> All through human history, we've had these questions. What causes thunder? What causes the lightning? I don't know, there must be

a big Thor [Norse God] up there that does it. But now, now we've learned about electricity. Now we don't need that Thor anymore. We've erased that God, right? And as the line moves up, answering more and more questions, the Gods disappear. We still have a lot more questions up here and we no longer put a God down here. . . . He's living in gaps, [and] the gaps are getting smaller.[1]

In general, Barker is right. Throughout history, people hypothesized the existence of many gods at least partly because natural phenomena needed explanations. The ancient Greeks believed lightning was a weapon of the god Zeus. They didn't know lightning is actually static electricity on a large scale. The Maori people of New Zealand believed earthquakes happened when the god Ruamoko walked around. They didn't know earthquakes happen because tectonic plates shift under the Earth. Many cultures believed pregnancy was the result of a fertility goddess's good pleasure. They didn't know fertility is the result of natural reproductive functions. These gods existed in people's minds because they were needed to explain natural phenomena before scientific explanations were available. It was science *or* the gods—no need (or room) for both.

So what does that have to do with the Christian God? Absolutely nothing. And that's the problem. Skeptics like Barker lump the Christian God in with these other gods and declare that the Christian God too is bound for irrelevancy as scientific progress marches on. But this claim makes the poor assumption that the idea of the Christian God also came into existence because people needed an explanation for natural phenomena. A basic reading of the Bible demonstrates this is not the case. Biblical writers believed God existed because he appeared to people, made covenants with them, personally gave their leaders direction, gifted certain people with accurate prophetic knowledge, and did many historical miracles to confirm his existence—as just a few examples. The Bible is undoubtedly intended to be understood as history. A skeptic may not believe the Bible is *accurate* history, but it's hardly debatable that people claimed to believe in the biblical God for reasons other than needing an explanation for natural phenomena.

Given this fact, it's meaningless to say that scientific progress will squeeze the Christian God out of his need for existence. That's like saying that if our older daughter found out I was the one who took the candy from the bowl, that knowledge would squeeze *Junior* out of her need for existence. That wouldn't happen because our older daughter had never based her belief in Junior's existence on the missing candy. Instead, she had hypothesized Junior's involvement because she *already knew* Junior existed.

That leads us to the second issue. Given a prior belief in the existence of God, when is it scientifically appropriate to assert his direct involvement in the workings of the natural world?

Issue 2: Hastily Assuming Parts of the Natural World Can't Be Explained without God's Direct Involvement

Isaac Newton was a prominent mathematician and physicist, famous for discovering several laws and theories that forever changed our understanding of science. He also believed at one point that planets could stay on their orbital courses only if God occasionally stepped in to nudge them back into place. We now know that natural laws fully account for planetary motions and that God doesn't need to directly intervene. Newton's premature speculation is an example of the second kind of God of the gaps problem: hastily assuming certain natural workings of the world can't be explained without invoking God's direct involvement.

It's important to clarify how this second God of the gaps issue is different from the first, because skeptics often conflate the two. Newton didn't believe God existed *because* he needed to account for planets staying on course (that would be like the first issue). He *already* believed in the existence of God and was speculating on one way God may interact with his creation. As we saw previously, if a phenomenon can be explained naturally, there's no reason for God's existence to be in question. But a valid concern raised by skeptics is whether God's direct involvement is the *right* explanation for a given phenomenon. In the case of Newton's divine prodding of planets, it was not.

Newton's reasoning exemplifies speculation based on a gap in knowledge—jumping to conclusions based on what he *didn't* know. Ideally, we want to draw conclusions based on what we *do* know. Christians and skeptics agree on that! But just because people have used God of the gaps reasoning in the past doesn't necessarily mean that's what Christians are doing today when they talk about scientific evidence for God's existence. Logically speaking, each instance would have to be evaluated on a case-by-case basis. So let's conclude by briefly looking back at the evidence for God's existence from part 1 to determine if it should legitimately be subject to the God of the gaps criticism.

Revisiting Three Pieces of Evidence for God's Existence

If theists were simply using God of the gaps reasoning to arrive at the evidence for God's existence in part 1, it would sound like this:

- We don't know where the universe came from, therefore God must have created it!
- We don't know where life came from, therefore God must have put it here!
- We can't fully explain our innate moral understanding, therefore God must have given it to us!

Such reasoning would be problematic—speculating on God's existence and activities based on a gap in our knowledge. But that is a gross misunderstanding of what these arguments say. Consider why:

114

- *The origin of the universe*: In chapter 2, we established that (1) the universe began to exist, (2) everything that begins to exist has a cause, and (3) this means the universe had a cause—a cause that is timeless, spaceless, immaterial, and enormously powerful. This is reasoning based on what we know, not on what we don't know.

- *The origin of life*: In chapter 3, we established that it is extraordinarily unlikely that the fine-tuning of the universe and the intricate nature of how living things work developed by unguided processes—they require a level of precision far more consistent with the existence of a purposeful intelligence beyond nature. This is reasoning based on what we know, not on what we don't know.

- *Our innate moral understanding*: In chapter 4, we established that there's a near-universal understanding of right and wrong, and this corresponds to a sense of moral obligation. But a duty can be owed only to a person—an authority. If moral laws exist, as we intuitively sense, the best explanation for those laws is the existence of a moral lawgiver. This is reasoning based on what we know, not on what we don't know.

In each of these cases, a supernatural intelligence is the best explanation for the information we *have*—not a blind guess based on information we *don't* have. A God of the gaps criticism is clearly unwarranted in this context.

KEY POINTS

- Throughout history, people hypothesized the existence of many gods because natural phenomena needed explanations (so-called God of the gaps reasoning). There was no need for both belief in a given god and a scientific explanation—they were competing *alternatives*.

- Because the Christian God was never an alternative to science, it's meaningless to say that scientific progress will somehow squeeze him out of his need for existence.

- A second and potentially more valid question about God of the gaps reasoning is whether God's direct involvement is the right explanation for a given natural phenomenon. This has to be evaluated on a case-by-case basis.

- In the cases of the evidence presented in part 1, a supernatural intelligence is the best explanation for the information we have—not a blind guess based on information we don't have.

CONVERSATION GUIDE

Open the Conversation

- The ancient Greeks believed lightning was a weapon of the god Zeus. Why do you think they came to that conclusion? What do you think would have changed their minds? *(People hypothesized the existence and activity of gods when they didn't have scientific explanations. Introduce the term God of the gaps reasoning. Explain that a given god and a scientific explanation were competing alternatives.)*

Advance the Conversation

- What are some reasons why the writers of the Bible believed God exists? *(If needed, give some examples from this chapter to get your child thinking.)* Are those reasons similar to or different from the reasons people believed in gods like Zeus? Why?

- When scientists discover new facts about the world, do those facts make God's existence less likely? Why or why not? *(No.*

Unlike ancient gods, the Christian God is not in competition with scientific explanations. People believe in him for different reasons.)

- Sometimes when people mention God of the gaps reasoning, they're talking about another kind of issue. *(Tell the story of Isaac Newton believing God was nudging planets into place.)* Why do you think this type of reasoning is not a good thing? *(We want to make conclusions based on what we know, not on what we don't know.)*

- Sometimes people suggest that the evidence for God's existence we talked about in part 1 is a similar example of God of the gaps reasoning. For example, they think Christians are saying, "We don't know where the universe came from, therefore God must have created it!" Based on what you learned in chapter 2 about the evidence for God's existence from the origin of the universe, do you agree Christians are using God of the gaps reasoning? Why or why not? *(Revisit the key points from chapter 2, if necessary, and establish that this is an argument based on what is known, not on what is unknown. Walk through the evidence from chapters 3 and 4 to demonstrate the same conclusion.)*

Apply the Conversation

- A teenager made the following claims on a website: "Science is based off cold hard facts, while the Bible is nothing [more] than an explanation that was created by an ancient people with no knowledge of modern science. . . . In the days of religions' creation, modern science (or almost any science) was not present because science had to progress from less complex roots. . . . Religion is nothing more than an uneducated way of explaining the unknown from the past. (By the way, I am fifteen and I just proved thousands of years of religion worthless.)"[2] How would you reply to this statement?

11. Can Science Explain Why People Believe in God?

In chapter 7, we talked about how the increased demand for resources serving atheist kids has led to programs like Camp Quest. Similarly, there's a growing demand for books that purport to explain to atheist children why *other* people believe in God—and why *they* don't need to.

One such book, *The Belief Book* by David McAfee and Chuck Harrison, says this about why people are religious:

> You see, for a lot of people all over the world, religion makes them feel better when they face what we don't really understand about the world, the universe, and pretty much everything. For a believer, their religion is like a nightlight that keeps the monster in the closet or under the bed away. It makes them feel safe and secure. But when we search for answers to our questions, we gain something called knowledge.[1]

There's much more to McAfee and Harrison's explanations, but the general idea is this: we can explain why people believe in God, and because we can explain it, that means God is nothing more than a figment of our collective imagination. A number of high-profile atheist philosophers and scientists have developed and promoted this idea in the last few years, and it's now a given in many skeptical circles.

The basis for the claim that we can explain why people believe in God is that scientific evidence has suggested humans are born with certain predispositions and mental tools that may make it natural for us to form religious beliefs. In this chapter, we'll look at those findings, consider why they might be the case, and evaluate the implications of the research.

Is Believing in God Part of Human Nature?

When our kids are babies, it's easy to look at them as blank slates— little eating and pooping machines just waiting for our developmental guidance. But scientists have discovered there's a lot more to tiny humans than dirty diapers. Many now believe we're born with predispositions toward certain kinds of beliefs (for example, that objects can't move through other objects) as well as cognitive processors that help us interpret information gathered through our senses (for example, an "agency detection device" that leads us to attribute various motions and sounds around us to some*one* rather than to some*thing*).[2]

Cognitive science is the interdisciplinary field that studies how the mind works. In the early 1990s, cognitive scientists started applying their findings to the question of why religious thoughts and actions are so common across cultures—perhaps humans have predispositions that make it natural for us to believe in God. That's not to say such predispositions can't be overridden by cultural and educational factors but rather that they may be an important biological basis influencing later belief development. This specific area of study is now called the cognitive science of religion.

The question of which predispositions and cognitive processors may facilitate religious beliefs is a matter of debate among researchers. The primary candidates, however, are the mental systems we use to understand intentional agents, minds, and features of the natural world.[3] One of the most widely held views is that the previously mentioned "agency detection device" leads us to believe there are invisible agents controlling the forces of nature. If we attribute things like motions and sounds to some*one* rather than to some*thing*, it's not a big step to attribute all of nature to a some*one*. Furthermore, there's strong evidence that children are predisposed to interpret features of the natural world as having purpose—something called intuitive theism.[4] Studies have shown, for example, that young kids believe things such as animals, plants, rocks, and rivers are there for a reason.[5] The connection between attributing natural events to an intelligent agent and seeing purpose in the objects of the natural world is just one way we may be born with a conceptual space for believing in a Creator or a Designer.

Christians are sometimes suspicious of this kind of research because they believe it implies humans are only material beings, reducible to chemical activities (which would be a strictly atheistic view). However, this is not a necessary implication of the science. Justin Barrett, a Christian and pioneer in the field of the cognitive science of religion, explains:

> Even if one believes in an immaterial soul that is somehow instantiated in a body, the body (and brain) matters a lot. Since this premise is common ground, explanation-building will tend to see how far it can go just resting on this shared foundation. It does not follow, however, that all [cognitive science of religion] scholars reject the existence of non-material realities such as gods or even non-material human minds or souls. The science simply does not make use of such possibilities.[6]

In other words, there's no more reason to be skeptical of the descriptive research on how our minds work than there is to be skeptical of research on how our kidneys work.

With that said, let's now turn to the independent question of *why* a natural predisposition toward religious beliefs might exist, a subject that *can* raise concerns from a Christian perspective.

Why Would Humans Be Predisposed to Religious Beliefs?

For Christians who reject evolution as the process through which human beings developed, the answer to this question is straightforward: God directly created us this way. Based on what the Bible tells us, we should *expect* to find that we are "wired" to believe in God. Ecclesiastes 3:11 says God has "set eternity in the human heart," and Romans 1:20 says God's eternal power and divine nature have been clearly seen since the creation of the world. We shouldn't be surprised, therefore, to find a biological foundation for these truths.

For those who accept an evolutionary history for humans, the question is more complex: Which evolutionary processes would have led to the development of religious beliefs? Furthermore, what does the answer imply about the *truth* of those beliefs?

Generally speaking, there are two groups of theories on how religious beliefs arose through evolutionary processes.[7] The first group suggests that religious beliefs developed because they offered some kind of evolutionary advantage by producing behaviors that aided in survival and reproduction. Researchers have varied ideas on what those evolutionary advantages may have been, but most think religious beliefs helped sustain cooperation between individuals in societal groups.

The second group of theories suggests that religious beliefs developed as a by-product of mechanisms that offered evolutionary advantages (but that the religious beliefs themselves did not offer an advantage). The most popular by-product theory is that the agency detection device originally developed as a survival mechanism; it's better to run away thinking the movement in the bushes is something like a tiger than to assume it's just the wind—just in case you're about to get eaten.[8] Researchers suggest that religious ideas may have developed as a by-product of this advantageous survival mechanism as people started assigning supernatural agency to the broader scope of nature. While scientists are far from reaching a consensus on which theory is best supported by the evidence, this "hyperactive" agency detection device tends to receive the most attention.

With this context in mind, we can now ask, "What should we make of these theories?"

Christians who reject evolution can accept the descriptive findings of cognitive science without accepting the evolutionary theories on their origins. It's important to understand this distinction and to know where the line can be drawn.

Perhaps less obvious is that there's nothing inherent in these evolutionary theories that suggests God doesn't actually exist. While those who are committed to an atheistic worldview often interpret the evolutionary theories to mean that our religious beliefs are nothing more than a fluke development of nature, the theories themselves say nothing about whether the beliefs we have formed are *true*. Philosopher Michael J. Murray puts it this way:

> These models [that are now used to explain religion], if correct, show *not one thing more* than that we have certain mental tools [regardless of how we acquired them] which under certain conditions give rise to the belief in the existence of entities which tend to rally religious commitments. But pointing that out does nothing, all by itself, to tell us about whether those religious beliefs are *justified* or not. . . . The mere fact that we have beliefs that spring from mental tools selected for by [evolutionary processes] is, all by itself, totally irrelevant to the justification of beliefs that spring from them.[9]

Even if we set aside questions about the accuracy of evolutionary theory in general, it's clear that evolutionary explanations of religious beliefs do not require the atheistic conclusions people commonly assume.

KEY POINTS

- Evidence from the field of cognitive science suggests that humans are born with cognitive processors and predispositions toward certain kinds of beliefs. The study of how these things make it natural for us to believe in *God* is called the cognitive science of religion.
- The question of which predispositions and processors may facilitate religious beliefs is a matter of debate. The primary candidates, however, are the mental systems we use to understand intentional agents, minds, and features of the natural world.
- As Christians, it shouldn't surprise us to find a biological foundation for belief in God, as the Bible tells us that knowledge of God is innate (see Eccles. 3:11; Rom. 1:20).
- While theories that explain the origin of religious beliefs from an evolutionary perspective are often interpreted through the lens of atheism, these explanations do not require the atheistic conclusions people commonly assume.

CONVERSATION GUIDE

Open the Conversation

- Scientific research has led to all kinds of findings on how our minds work. Do you think scientists will ever be able to explain why most people believe in God? Why or why not? *(This conversation could go in many directions, but use it simply to get your child thinking about the subject.)*

Advance the Conversation

- A lot of scientific evidence shows we aren't born with blank minds just waiting to be written on by our parents. You might say we come "preloaded" with some great apps that prepare us to live in the world! Researchers believe some of those "apps" make it natural and easy for humans to believe in God. If this research is correct, would that surprise you? Why or why not? *(Read the verses mentioned in this chapter—Ecclesiastes 3:11 and Romans 1:20—and explain that we shouldn't be surprised to find a biological foundation for these truths. If your child is old enough to understand the specifics, discuss the scientific findings on our predispositions and cognitive processors.)*

- Some people say that if we can explain why humans tend to believe in God, it probably means God doesn't exist. Why do you think they say that? *(They're assuming that if we can explain something scientifically, there's nothing more to it. If your child is old enough for a discussion of evolutionary theories and the related points raised in this chapter, go on to have that conversation now.)*

Apply the Conversation

- Read the quote from *The Belief Book* at the beginning of this chapter. The authors suggest that people believe in God because doing so brings them comfort. How would you respond to this statement, assuming it's part of an argument that God doesn't actually exist?

12. What Do Scientists Believe about God?

In 1998, a study came out showing that 93 percent of the members of the National Academy of Sciences (one of the most elite scientific organizations in the United States) do not believe in God. The finding caught the media's attention, and it's been a well-publicized statistic ever since.

Atheist neuroscientist and popular author Sam Harris (whom we met in chapter 4) is one of many skeptics who have referenced this data to bolster the claim that science and belief in God are inherently in conflict. Harris says:

> Although it is possible to be a scientist and still believe in God—as some scientists seem to manage it—there is no question that an engagement with scientific thinking tends to erode, rather than support, religious faith. Taking the U.S. population as an example: Most polls show that about 90% of the general public believes in a personal God; yet 93% of the members of the National Academy of Sciences do not. This suggests that there are few modes of thinking less congenial to religious faith than science is.[1]

We all know that truth isn't determined by vote, but statistics certainly get people's attention, especially when they seem to suggest that those whom society sees as the brightest among us are almost all atheists. Young people especially trust "expert opinion," so it's well worth our time as parents to explore the question of what scientists believe about God and what implications the answer has for us as Christians.

What Does Research Say about Scientists' Belief in God?

For more context, let's look at what research other than the 1998 study has shown. (Stay with me through the details. We'll circle back to the big-picture findings at the end.)

James Leuba Study (1914) with Edward Larson and Larry Witham Follow-Up (1996–98)

In 1914, psychologist James Leuba conducted the first major study of the religious views of scientists.[2] Leuba surveyed one thousand American scientists and found that 42 percent believed in a personal God.[3] He additionally segmented the results by looking at the four hundred "greater" scientists in his sample (those deemed to be *leading* scientists). In this subset, those who believed in a personal God dropped to 28 percent.

In 1996—eighty-two years later—University of Georgia researchers Edward Larson and Larry Witham repeated Leuba's survey, using the same questions, to determine how the scientific developments of the twentieth century may have changed the religious views of scientists. To many people's surprise, the overall results were almost identical: 40 percent said they believed in a personal God.[4]

Larson and Witham also wanted to repeat Leuba's attempt to look at beliefs specifically among *leading* scientists. To do so, they surveyed the National Academy of Sciences in 1998.[5] In that group, belief in a personal God dropped to 7 percent. *This is the study so often referenced to demonstrate that scientists don't believe in God.* (We'll discuss this particular finding further after considering the remaining studies.)

Religion among Academic Scientists Study (2005–8)

From 2005 to 2008, Rice University sociologist Elaine Howard Ecklund surveyed nearly seventeen hundred natural and social scientists at twenty-one elite universities on their views of religion and science. She found that nearly 50 percent of scientists identified with a religious label, and nearly one in five was actively involved in a place of worship (attending services more than once per month).[6]

In addition, Ecklund conducted statistical analyses to identify which factors were the most significant *predictors* of those beliefs and behaviors. Ecklund found that the strongest predictor of religious adherence among this group was childhood religiosity. Scientists raised as Protestants were more likely to have retained religious beliefs and practices than those raised without a religious affiliation. Similarly, those who said that religion was important in their family when they were growing up were "less likely to say they currently do not see truth in religion, do not believe in God, and do not attend religious services."[7]

These findings become important when we compare the religious upbringing of the general population with that of scientists. *A larger proportion of scientists were raised in liberal Jewish or nonreligious homes.* Ecklund concludes:

> It is an assumption of much scholarly work that the religious beliefs of scientists are a function of their commitment to science. The findings presented here show that indeed academics in the natural and social sciences at elite research universities are less religious than many of those in the general public, at least according to

traditional indicators of religiosity. Assuming, however, that becoming a scientist *necessarily* leads to loss of religious commitments is untenable when we take into account the differential selection of scientists from certain religious backgrounds. Our results indicate that people from certain backgrounds (the non-religious, for example) disproportionately self-select into scientific professions.[8]

In other words, Ecklund's research suggests that the irreligious are simply more likely to become scientists in the first place, not that the pursuit of a scientific career turns people away from God.

Pew Research Center Study (2009)

In 2009, the Pew Research Center conducted a survey of more than 2,500 scientists who were members of the American Association for the Advancement of Science (the world's largest general scientific society, with over 120,000 members).[9] Fifty-one percent of those surveyed said they believed in some form of deity or higher power—33 percent saying they believed in God, and 18 percent saying they believed in a universal spirit or higher power. For comparison with the general public, researchers noted findings from the Pew Research Center's 2006 study: 95 percent of Americans said they believed in some form of deity or higher power (83 percent saying they believed in God, and 12 percent saying they believed in a universal spirit or higher power). These findings suggest that scientists are roughly half as likely as the general public to believe in God or a higher power.

Religious Understandings of Science Study (2012–15)

Elaine Howard Ecklund also led a broader study in which more than nine thousand Americans were surveyed about their perceptions of religion and science.[10] The sample included 574 scientists. This was an extensive survey, but the most relevant finding for our current purpose was that 36 percent of scientists said, "I know God really exists and I have no doubts about it," versus 56 percent of the overall sample. (This was the question most comparable to the measures of belief in a personal God used in the previously discussed studies.)

What Implications Do These Findings Have?

In this overview of relevant research studies, we've seen that scientists are indeed significantly less likely to believe in a personal God than the general public. The exact numbers are subject to many sample and survey variables, but a reasonable statement based on the collective studies is that scientists are *at most* half as likely to believe in a personal God than the general public, with belief significantly less than that among certain groups of distinguished scientists.

We should take away three things from these findings.

First, correlation does not equal causation. In statistics, correlation simply means that two variables tend to move in the same direction—in this case, those who are scientists tend to be less likely to believe in God. This doesn't mean, however, that being a scientist necessarily *causes* someone not to believe in God. (Think of it this way: in some parts of the world, it rains almost every Easter, but that doesn't mean Easter *causes* it to rain.) If we determined that becoming a scientist *did* cause people to drop their belief in God, we might have reason to think there is some inherent conflict between the practice of science and theism. But to the contrary, Ecklund's Religion among Academic Scientists Study showed that the irreligious are simply more likely to become scientists in the first place. The available research does not suggest that scientists become irreligious as a *consequence* of their occupation, though this is what skeptics typically assume. And if becoming irreligious is not a consequence of their occupation, then the whole topic of what scientists believe about God quickly becomes less relevant.

Second, it's not true that 93 percent of scientists don't believe in God. This frequently quoted statistic refers to just one of several available studies, and there are two good reasons we shouldn't consider it to be the representative statistic. First, it's clear from the other research that this finding was an outlier—the five other major studies on this subject suggest that 33 to 50 percent of scientists believe in a personal God, with the numbers even greater if we include those who believe more broadly in a higher power. Second, this study was conducted with a unique group—members of the National Academy of Sciences, an organization of about twenty-three hundred scientists who were elected to membership by other members. We could speculate all day about why these particular scientists are less likely to believe in a personal God, but the bottom line is that this organization is not representative of the broader scientific community. The most that can be said from this study is that 93 percent of scientists who are members of the National Academy of Sciences and responded to the survey don't believe in a personal God. It's highly inaccurate to suggest that 93 percent of all scientists are atheists.

Third, what scientists believe about God ultimately has no bearing on whether God exists. While we should explore this subject because it's often raised as a challenge to the truth of Christianity, we must remember that, ultimately, beliefs aren't true depending on who holds them. They are true because they correspond to reality. Scientists don't have any more expertise on the reality of God's existence than anyone else.

KEY POINTS

- Skeptics often claim that 93 percent of scientists don't believe in God, but this statistic is highly misleading. It comes from a single survey of a unique group of scientists who are members of the National Academy of Sciences.

- Five other major studies suggest that 33 to 50 percent of scientists believe in a personal God.

- While the more accurate percentage of scientists who believe in God is much higher than what skeptics promote, scientists are significantly less likely than the general population to believe in God. Research suggests that the most significant reason for this is that the irreligious are simply more likely to become scientists in the first place. Available research does not suggest that scientists become irreligious as a consequence of their occupation.

- It's important to remember that beliefs aren't true depending on who holds them. They are true because they correspond to reality. Scientists don't have any more expertise on the reality of God's existence than anyone else.

CONVERSATION GUIDE

Open the Conversation

- Imagine that a friend said to you, "I don't believe in God because scientists don't believe in God." What questions could you ask to better understand what your friend means and what assumptions your friend is making? *(If necessary, explain what the word assumptions means. Identify questions such as, What is the source of your information about what scientists believe? Which scientists are you talking about? And if it's true that many scientists don't believe in God, why do you assume that means God doesn't exist?)*

Advance the Conversation

- A few research studies have been conducted to ask scientists about their religious beliefs and have found that, in general, scientists are less likely to believe in God than nonscientists.

Why do you think this might be? *(If appropriate for your child's level of understanding, discuss some of the specific studies in this chapter for background knowledge.)*

- Atheists sometimes use these findings to suggest that becoming an expert in science leads a person to believe God doesn't exist. What are they assuming when they say this? *(This is a bit of a tricky question, but get your child to think. This assumes that people become atheists because they became scientists. Discuss the research that shows how irreligious people tend to be more likely to go into science in the first place and talk about the difference between correlation and causation.)*

- If the research is correct and many scientists don't believe in God, does that make *you* question God's existence? Why or why not? *(Emphasize that truth should never be determined based on what specific people believe. This is why learning the objective evidence for the truth of Christianity is so important.)*

Apply the Conversation

- A woman posed the following question online: "93% of scientists are atheist or agnostic. Tell me, how does one in a religious group explain these statistics? I am an atheist myself just trying to discover how the minds of theists work."[11] Why do you think she's asking how religious people "explain" that statistic? How would you reply?

PART 3

The Nature
of
God

Overview

The 2016 American presidential election was notable in many ways, not the least of which was the sheer volume of online articles about the candidates. After a while, the stories were so predictable—"Here's why (one candidate) will ruin America's future" and "Here's why (the other candidate) will ruin America's future"—that I became jaded and stopped caring about the latest "news." But one day I saw a headline so striking that I had to read the story. I was shocked at what I read. If true, it seemed it would end the candidate's bid for the presidency. I wondered why the story wasn't everywhere, so I did a quick Google search to learn more. It turned out the article was pure fiction, posted on what has come to be known as a "fake news" website, a site where people fabricated stories in an attempt to influence election results.

You would never have known this site was fake based on a first impression. It had a traditional name, making it sound like the site of a major newspaper. It had a weather forecast in the sidebar and menu options for sections like local, global, and sports news. The website *looked* credible. But if you clicked on anything other than that story, you got a blank page. There was nothing there other than a single, fabricated article.

After the election, many people wondered if fake news sites like this one swayed results. The concern, of course, was that people may have voted for or against a candidate based on wrong information. It's the Achilles' heel of a media-saturated era: the abundance of information theoretically requires constant discernment and verification, but no one has the time to critically evaluate every piece of information that comes his or her way. We inevitably form at least some of our opinions based on perceptions of reality developed from layers of media exposure.

This is a sobering fact when applied to how our kids form religious beliefs today.

There's a significant danger that they will either accept or reject *God* based on wrong information gathered over time. Much of the wrong information they'll encounter will have an air of credibility, like the menu options and weather forecast on the fake news site I was fooled by. If we don't proactively ground our kids in an accurate, biblically based understanding of who God is, they may easily be led astray by "information" that can look and sound plausible but is dangerously deceptive.

Now, you may think there's no harm in someone accepting God based on wrong information or understanding—after all, they're still accepting him. But when kids develop an idea about God that is inconsistent with what God himself has revealed in the Bible, it can greatly affect their long-term spiritual development. As one example, a young person shared with friends online, "I'm a Christian conservative but I think that God wants us to be happy! I don't like it when Christians put down people and judge them! It's not our job to do that. [We're] supposed to love each other! God loves you and I do too!"[1] (Yes, all those exclamation points were in the original post. I don't know if I've ever been excited enough about anything to use four exclamation points. But I digress.) This is a shallow and spiritually harmful understanding of who God is. If this young person believes God's desire for our subjective happiness trumps his desire for our righteousness, this belief will adversely affect how they live as a Christian.

Perhaps more obviously, many people also reject God based on a wrong understanding of who he is. For example, someone asked online, "Christians: Do you admit your god is an arrogant, cruel and violent god? There are only 2 possibilities of god's existence: 1. God exist[s] as an arrogant, cruel and violent god. 2. God doesn't exist."[2] This person has accepted an inaccurate characterization of God's nature and is presumably rejecting God based on some very wrong information.

Part 3 of this book is designed to help you have critically important conversations about the aspects of God's nature that are most questioned and misunderstood by skeptics and Christians alike. We'll address the key touchpoints with popular culture that require a parent's careful guidance in order to help kids avoid accepting or rejecting God based on *wrong information* that leads to *wrong understanding*. Through these conversations, your kids will learn the importance of comparing what they hear about God to what the Bible actually says.

Three Keys to Impactful Conversations about the Nature of God

1. *Introduce this section by emphasizing the Bible's importance given what we learned in parts 1 and 2.* After talking about God from a more philosophical and scientific perspective in the first twelve chapters, it's important to acknowledge that God's general revelation in nature still leaves us with a limited understanding of who he is. In other words, we may know a Creator, Designer, and Moral Lawgiver exists, but that knowledge doesn't tell us anything about how he relates to us. Fortunately, God didn't leave us in the dark. He revealed

much more about himself in the Bible. Framing part 3 in this way will help your kids better understand the importance of these subjects and put parts 1 and 2 in perspective.

2. *Take time to explore your kids' current understanding of these subjects.* Kids are more likely to have engaged with the topics in part 3 than with those in parts 1 and 2. They'll have some working knowledge as a background for your discussions—knowledge that may be right or wrong. The conversation guides in this section will encourage you to spend time exploring their current understanding so you can tailor your conversations accordingly.

3. *If your kids think these subjects are simple, help them understand how complex they can be.* Older kids may look at the chapter titles in part 3 and think they already know the material. But as we'll see, none of these are simple subjects (theologians have written millions of pages on these questions). Encourage your kids to deepen their understanding, even if they think they've already got it all down.

13. What Can We Learn about God from the Bible?

I have wonderful memories of going on RV camping trips with my grandparents when I was a kid. When I see old RVs today with all the trappings of the early 1980s, I get nostalgically excited and instinctively want to crawl into the upper bunk bed that projects over the driver's seat. My husband and I have considered buying an RV but have never been convinced we'd use it enough to justify the cost. Still, we sometimes keep an eye on the ones that show up at our local dealership.

A few weeks ago, we were driving past the dealership and noticed a new RV on the lot. It didn't look like anything special from afar, but it had a price tag of $195,000! We laughed and commented on how crazy that was—why would this RV cost so much money?

Later that day, we were returning home from the opposite direction and saw the RV from behind. The price suddenly made sense: the RV was a rare luxury brand. We didn't initially know that based on our (apparently unrefined) evaluation of its appearance, but the brand immediately identified it as something special—something made in a unique way, of a certain quality, and with superior features. Knowing the brand suddenly gave us a very different appreciation for the RV's *value*.

In parts 1 and 2, we learned how evidence from nature compellingly points to the existence of God. Knowledge of such evidence is critical, but it still leaves us with a limited understanding of who God is. It's like seeing that RV in the distance but not knowing why it's worth so much. Thankfully, God chose to reveal a lot more of himself in the Bible. And with that revelation comes human responsibility: since the Bible "brands" God in a specific way, we aren't free to conceive of him however we want.

A. W. Tozer, in *The Knowledge of the Holy*, speaks pointedly to this importance of thinking rightly about God:

> It is impossible to keep our moral practices sound and our inward attitudes right while our idea of God is erroneous or inadequate. . . . I think it might be demonstrated that almost every heresy that has afflicted the church through the years has arisen from believing about God things that are not true, or from overemphasizing certain true things so as to obscure other things equally true.[1]

In this chapter, we'll look at seven of the most important attributes of God's nature that our kids should understand in order to develop right thinking about their Creator—and to identify common distortions of those truths. Two additional attributes will have their own chapters because they are so often misunderstood by Christians and skeptics alike: God's lovingness (chap. 14) and God's justness (chap. 15). When we're able to discern truths from untruths and to apply all truths in balance, we have the right intellectual foundation for knowing God.

Seven Important Attributes of God

The following overview of God's attributes includes key Bible verses, notes on what each does and doesn't mean, and an explanation of why each one matters. I know it can be tempting to skip over references to Bible verses, but if we want to think rightly about God, we should understand where in the Bible he's revealed the specifics of his character and in what way. So go straight to the source: read each verse yourself and with your kids for the best understanding.

1. Holiness

Key verses: 1 Samuel 2:2; Isaiah 6:3; Mark 1:24; Revelation 4:8; 15:4

What it means: God is set apart from all that is sinful.

What it doesn't mean: That God is just a better version of our human selves.

Why it matters: It follows from God's holiness that he is unable to be in the presence of sin (Ps. 66:18; Isa. 59:2). This is the fundamental problem of our human existence: How can we ever be reconciled with our holy Creator when we are unable to free ourselves from the sin that separates us? The answer is in 2 Corinthians 5:21: "God made him who had no sin to be sin for us, so that in him we might become the righteousness of God." We can never be holy by nature as God is, but when we put our faith in Jesus as our Savior, God declares us innocent and sin no longer separates us. When people don't understand the severity of sin, it's often because they don't understand or acknowledge the holiness of God. God isn't just a better version of our human selves; he's truly in a class of his own.

2. Sovereignty

Key verses: Genesis 50:20; 2 Chronicles 20:6; Psalm 115:3; Isaiah 40:23; Matthew 10:29; Romans 8:28; Ephesians 1:11

What it means: All things are under God's rule and control, and nothing happens without his direction or permission.

What it doesn't mean: That if we can't understand why things happen the way they do, God must either (1) not exist or (2) not be in control.

Why it matters: God's sovereignty is a key theme that runs throughout the entirety of Scripture. That said, it's a complex theological subject, and Christians have varied views on *how* God's sovereignty relates to other biblical realities—most notably, the existence of evil and the extent of human free will. In other words, if God is both holy and sovereign, how can there be evil in his creation? And if God is ultimately in control of everything, how can humans make free choices for which they're accountable? We'll reserve a fuller discussion of these two questions for later in the book (see chaps. 26 and 29), but for now, note that the answers to both questions typically involve making a distinction between what God directs and what he permits.[2]

3. Transcendence

Key verses: 1 Kings 8:27; Psalm 97:9; Isaiah 55:8–9; Acts 17:24; Romans 11:33–36; Ephesians 4:6

What it means: God is above and independent from his creation.

What it doesn't mean: That God is distant.

Why it matters: God exists outside space and time; he does not depend in any way on his creation. This attribute conflicts with the nonbiblical idea of pantheism—that God and the material world are identical (a concept in some Eastern and New Age religions). Because God exists independently of his creation, it can be easy to see him as a distant God. However, his transcendence must be understood in conjunction with his omnipresence (see below).

4. *Omnipresence*

Key verses: Psalms 33:13–14; 139:7–10; Proverbs 15:3; Jeremiah
   23:23–24; Colossians 1:17

What it means: God is present everywhere.

What it doesn't mean: That God is physically present everywhere.

Why it matters: It's often easier to imagine that God is separate
   from creation than that he's somehow present everywhere
   throughout creation. After all, we know *we* can't be in more
   than one place at a time. But God's omnipresence doesn't
   mean he's *physically* everywhere. It means he's active in and
   aware of all points in space and time. Nothing escapes his
   attention—he doesn't somehow busy himself with remote
   activities until we call upon him in prayer. On the contrary,
   God is always present, even when he's far from our thoughts.
   We can take comfort in that reality when circumstances seemingly push God away.

5. *Omnipotence*

Key verses: Genesis 18:14; Job 42:2; Psalm 33:6; Isaiah 14:27;
   Matthew 19:26; Ephesians 1:19

What it means: God is all-powerful.

What it doesn't mean: That God can do things that are illogical
   or inconsistent with his character.

Why it matters: While it's common for people to quip, "God
   can do anything!" that statement needs some qualification.
   The Bible makes it clear that God is all-powerful but that
   there are things he cannot do. Is that a contradiction? No.
   We just have to define what the Bible means by all-powerful.
   God cannot do things that are either inconsistent with his
   character or impossible. For example, Hebrews 6:18 says

God cannot lie, and James 1:13 says God cannot be tempted by evil. Both are inconsistent with his holiness. Similarly, people sometimes challenge the plausibility of God's omnipotence by asking if he can do something like create a square circle. Such a question is nonsensical. Things that are impossible by definition do not become possible by adding God's power.

6. Faithfulness

Key verses: Deuteronomy 7:9; Psalms 33:4; 119:89–90; 1 Corinthians 10:13; 2 Thessalonians 3:3; 1 John 1:9

What it means: God is trustworthy.

What it doesn't mean: That God will deliver on his promises in our preferred time frame or ways.

Why it matters: When someone makes promises but doesn't keep them, we no longer trust that person. With God, however, this is never a concern—we can be confident he will keep *all* the promises in the Bible. We may not always understand his timing or ways of delivering on his promises, but that doesn't change the fact that God is faithful. Internalizing this truth of God's character greatly shapes our relationship with him.

7. Goodness

Key verses: Psalms 31:19; 34:8; 107:1; 119:68; Romans 8:28; James 1:17

What it means: God is the source of all goodness and the standard for what we call good.

What it doesn't mean: That God defines good and bad in the same way we'd like to.

Why it matters: We tend to think of God's goodness in terms of what he *does* (as in, "God has been so good to me!"), but first and foremost, it's who he *is*. God is the standard by which we can even call something good. As author C. S. Lewis famously said, "A man does not call a line crooked unless he has some idea of a straight line."[3] Because God is the definition of goodness, we're not free to define what is good and bad on our own terms. God has revealed what is good and bad through our consciences (Rom. 2:15) and in the Bible.

Much more, of course, could be said about each of these seven attributes. For a fuller discussion of these and several more, I recommend Tozer's classic book, *The Knowledge of the Holy* (see note 1).

KEY POINTS

- Knowledge of the evidence for God's existence in nature is important, but it still leaves us with a very limited understanding of who God is. Thankfully, God chose to reveal much more of himself in the Bible.
- Since the Bible tells us specifically who God is, we aren't free to conceive of him however we want. We have a spiritual responsibility to think rightly about God.
- Characteristics of God's nature, as revealed in Scripture, are called the attributes of God. In this chapter, we looked at seven of the most important ones to understand: God's holiness, sovereignty, transcendence, omnipresence, omnipotence, faithfulness, and goodness. Two other important (and especially misunderstood) attributes are discussed in chapters 14 and 15—God's lovingness and justness.

CONVERSATION GUIDE

Open the Conversation

- When you think of God, what words come to mind that describe him? *(Ask your child to name or write down as many descriptions as possible. Explain what an attribute is and identify which of your child's words are attributes. If any words are not correct descriptions of God, discuss why.)*

Advance the Conversation

- *(Talk through each of the seven attributes with your child. Start by naming the attribute and asking your child to define it in his or her own words, if your child has some understanding of it already. Give your child the brief definition from the chapter and look up several of the corresponding verses together. Discuss what each verse tells us about that attribute of God. Conclude by talking about what the attribute doesn't mean and read the brief paragraph on why the attribute matters. There is a lot to cover in this chapter, so consider having these conversations over multiple occasions.)*

Apply the Conversation

- Consider the following question posed by a skeptic: "Why is the God of Christians, Jews, and Muslims so arrogant? He wants full control over us and our lives."[4] Which attributes that we studied in this chapter contradict the idea that God is arrogant? How does this person's belief that God "wants full control over us" differ from what God's sovereignty actually means?

14. What Does It Mean That God Is Love?

First John 4:8 says, "God is love." If people believe in God today, they almost certainly believe these three words. We like these words. They comfort us. They're easy to accept. We *want* to believe them.

But the pervasiveness of this belief is not necessarily a good thing. Many people believe in a God who bears almost no resemblance to the God of the Bible—often a Santa-like figure who's more concerned with our happiness than our holiness.

Theologian D. A. Carson, in his book *The Difficult Doctrine of the Love of God*, says:

> [The] love of God in our culture has been purged of anything the culture finds uncomfortable. . . . [But it] has not always been so. In generations when almost everyone believed in the justice of God, people sometimes found it difficult to believe in the love of God. The preaching of the love of God came as wonderful good news. Nowadays if you tell people that God loves them, they are unlikely to be surprised. Of course God loves me; he's like that, isn't he? Besides, why shouldn't he love me? I'm kind of cute, or

at least as nice as the next person. I'm okay, you're okay, and God loves you and me.[1]

When we start thinking that everything between us and God is okay because God is love, we're on shaky ground. Depending on how far a person stretches this belief, it can even be a matter of salvation. It's not a big leap from "We're all okay because God is love" to "It doesn't matter if you believe in Jesus, because God loves everyone and is okay with however we want to come to him."

But the Bible clearly states that Jesus is the *only* path to salvation: "I am the way and the truth and the life. No one comes to the Father except through me" (John 14:6).

An accurate, multifaceted understanding of God's love is foundational for our kids' spiritual health. Carson, in *The Difficult Doctrine of the Love of God*, offers an excellent framework for this understanding by outlining five key contexts in which the Bible speaks of God's love. Let's briefly look at each one.

Five Aspects of God's Love

As you read about the following aspects of God's love, consider how our understanding of this attribute can become distorted if we assume only one meaning to the exclusion of the others.

1. The Love of the Father for the Son, and of the Son for the Father

Several Bible verses speak of how God loves Jesus (Luke 3:22; John 3:35; 5:20; Eph. 1:6) and how Jesus loves God (John 14:31). This love within the Trinity has existed since eternity past (John 17:5). Importantly, that means this relationship is the source of *all* love. As Carson says, "There has *always* been an other-orientation to the love of God. All the manifestations of the love of God emerge out of this deeper, more fundamental reality: love is bound up in the very nature of God. God is love."[2]

2. God's Providential Love for All He Has Made

While the Bible doesn't typically use the word *love* in the context of God's creation, it does depict creation as the product of a loving Creator. Jesus speaks of how beautifully God clothes the grass of the fields with flowers, saying not even King Solomon was dressed so well (Matt. 6:28–30). He points out that birds don't sow or reap or store food in barns, yet they are fed by God (Matt. 6:26). He assures us that not one sparrow falls to the ground outside of God's care (Matt. 10:29). In each case, Jesus is teaching that we can trust God to provide for us because he has so caringly provided for his broader creation. It's important to understand, however, that this kind of love only sustains—it doesn't save. A saving love is something more.

3. God's Salvific Stance toward His Fallen World (How He Has Provided a Path to Salvation)[3]

The Bible's most famous verse speaks to God's *saving* love: "For God so loved the world that he gave his one and only Son, that whoever believes in him shall not perish but have eternal life" (John 3:16). As sinners, we have done nothing to deserve God's love (Rom. 5:8), but God has chosen to love us anyway. The ultimate demonstration of this love was the act of sending his own Son, Jesus, to die on the cross so we could be saved. Still, we must accept the gift he offers us in order to have that salvation. The fact that God loves us does not mean God will save everyone. If we focus only on the words "God so loved the world that he gave his one and only Son," we'll miss the necessity of our response—"*whoever believes in him* shall not perish but have eternal life" (emphasis mine).

4. God's Particular, Effective, Selecting Love toward His Elect

In theology, the word *elect* refers to God's chosen ones. Depending on the context, the elect could refer to the nation of Israel, the church as a whole, or individuals. Christians have varying views on *how* God's election relates to individuals, but there's no question the Bible speaks of God loving his chosen ones—however defined—in a way he does not love others. Such passages can be difficult to understand unless we recognize the multifaceted nature of God's love. Consider, for example, what Deuteronomy 7:7–8 says about Israel as an elect nation (see also Deut. 10:15):

> The LORD did not set his affection on you and choose you because you were more numerous than other peoples, for you were the fewest of all peoples. But it was because the LORD loved you and kept the oath he swore to your ancestors that he brought you out with a mighty hand and redeemed you from the land of slavery, from the power of Pharaoh king of Egypt.

These verses make clear that God *chose* to love Israel in a special way; Israel did not earn God's love. We see throughout the Bible that God has a special relationship with Israel that he does not have with any other nation. This doesn't mean he's unloving toward other nations but that he loves Israel in a particular way.

5. God's Love as Conditioned on Obedience

Several Bible verses at first seem to suggest that we can earn or fall out of God's love. Consider, for example, the following:

- "As the Father has loved me, so have I loved you. Now remain in my love. If you keep my commands, you will remain in my love, just as I have kept my Father's commands and remain in his love" (John 15:9–10).

- "Keep yourselves in God's love as you wait for the mercy of our Lord Jesus Christ to bring you to eternal life" (Jude 21).

The key to understanding such verses is recognizing that they refer to our relationship with God *once we know him* (see also Exod. 20:5–6). As parents, we know all too well how the closeness of our relationships with our kids can vary based on their behavior. When they're obedient, we're able to have a deeper level of intimacy. When they're in rebellion, we still love them, but we're unable to manifest that love in the closeness we would like. In the same way, these verses speak of the quality of our relationship with God, as influenced by our obedience.

Note that this contradicts the popular idea that God's love implies a moral permissiveness in which he turns a blind eye to our behavior. God has revealed his moral requirements in the Bible, and his love for us must be understood within that context. The fact that God is loving in no way means he indiscriminately approves of all our actions. (We'll discuss this more in the next chapter.)

Putting the Picture Together

When we take all of this into consideration, we see how far off course we can go in our understanding of God's love if we look at just one aspect of it—or if we don't look at the Bible at all. If we think of God's love only in terms of how he lovingly cares for creation, we'll miss the importance of what he's lovingly done to offer us salvation. If we think of God's love only in terms of salvation, we'll miss the importance of maintaining a close and obedient relationship with him after we're saved. And if we think of God's love only as conditional on obedience, we'll misunderstand that God lovingly *chose* to offer salvation and that it's not based on any merit of our own. We could go on, but the point remains the same: a biblical view of God's love requires us to acknowledge all these aspects at the same time.

KEY POINTS

- Most people who believe in God agree that he's loving, but loving can mean different things to different people. It's crucial that we define God's love based on what the Bible says.

- In this chapter, we looked at five major contexts in which the Bible speaks of God's love: (1) the love of the Father for the Son, and of the Son for the Father, (2) God's providential love for all he has made, (3) God's salvific stance toward his fallen world, (4) God's particular, effective, selecting love toward his elect, and (5) God's love as conditioned on obedience.

- When we take all these aspects of God's love into consideration, we can see how far off course we can go in our understanding of God's love if we look at just one aspect of it. God's love is necessarily multifaceted.

CONVERSATION GUIDE

Open the Conversation

- We use the word *love* in many ways. We might say, for example, that we love our parents, that we love going to the park, or that we love a song. When you hear that God is love, what does that mean to you? *(Emphasize that it's not up to us to define the meaning—we need to read what God has revealed about his nature in the Bible. Explain that God's love means different things in different contexts.)*

Advance the Conversation

- *(Note that these questions cover only three of the five contexts discussed in this chapter. For a deeper discussion with older kids, introduce the other two contexts as well.)*

- Read Matthew 6:26, 28–30; 10:29. What do these verses tell us about God's relationship to his creation? *(He lovingly cares for it and keeps it going. All people, regardless of their relationship with God, benefit from this care of creation.)*
- Read John 3:16; Romans 5:8. What do these verses tell us about God's love for humans specifically? *(He loves us so much that he was willing to send his Son to die for us so we could be saved. This love was not based on anything we did to earn it.)* How is this a different kind of love than his love for creation as a whole? *(His care for creation keeps the world going, but it doesn't save anyone.)*
- How does John 3:16 say we must respond to God's love in order to be saved? *(We must trust in Jesus—it's not enough simply to acknowledge that God loves us.)*
- Read John 15:9–10; Jude 21. How do these verses speak of God's love in a way that's different from what most people expect? What do you think these verses mean? *(Explain that these verses refer to the quality of our relationship with God once we know him and give the example from this chapter of the relationships between parents and kids.)*

Apply the Conversation

- The following statement appears on a church website: "Our belief is that God loves everyone—no matter your background, beliefs, [or] religion. . . . Our desire is that everyone feels accepted, encouraged and hopefully begin to discover how much God loves all of us and is for us."[4] Which aspect of God's love does this statement focus on presenting to prospective members? How could this single view of God's love potentially give someone a wrong idea of what it means to be a Christian?

15. What Does It Mean That God Is Just?

In the last twenty-four hours, my six-year-old daughter concluded, tears pouring down her face, that I must not love her. In fact, not only must I not love her, I'm also very mean.

Where did I go so wrong as a parent? Let me divulge the depths of my failure.

My daughter had just received a musical recorder for her birthday and proudly came to show me that she had learned to play a song. Though she had mastered it in private, she couldn't get the notes right when standing in front of me. Embarrassed, she threw the recorder at her brother, screamed, and said it was all my fault. I explained it wasn't okay to treat me or her brother in that way and told her to go to her room. She then stomped her foot so hard that she jammed her toe and dramatically fell to the ground.

I told her she still had to go to her room.

She sobbed, "You don't even care about my toe! You must not even love me! You are just so mean. If you were nice, you would feel bad about my toe and not make me go to my room!" She huffed off, slamming her bedroom door behind her.

Almost every parent has been accused of being mean or unloving in the midst of issuing consequences for their kids' bad behavior. Children seem to be born without the ability to understand simultaneously that we love them and that we must deal appropriately with their actions. In their young minds, love equals letting them do whatever they want. But from a parent's much broader perspective, rules—and consequences for breaking rules—are necessary *because* we love our kids.

Similarly, God has given us moral rules, and the backdrop is his love—as well as his holiness and goodness. If, like children, we don't recognize this backdrop, we'll grossly misunderstand God's character when we read verses such as these:

- "See, the Lord is coming out of his dwelling to punish the people of the earth for their sins. The earth will disclose the blood shed on it" (Isa. 26:21).
- "The Lord is a jealous and avenging God; the Lord takes vengeance and is filled with wrath. . . . The Lord is slow to anger but great in power; the Lord will not leave the guilty unpunished" (Nah. 1:2–3).
- "But because of your stubbornness and your unrepentant heart, you are storing up wrath against yourself for the day of God's wrath, when his righteous judgment will be revealed" (Rom. 2:5).

I'm sure that if my six-year-old read these verses, she would conclude that God too is very mean (at least I'd be in good company). She wouldn't be the only one to do so. Skeptics commonly claim that God, particularly in the Old Testament, is cruel and arbitrarily vengeful—a Being wholly inconsistent with the "God of love" Christians say they believe in.

In this chapter, we'll look at what it means for God to be *just*, as this attribute of his character sheds light on verses like those above.

God's Justness Defined

The fact that God is just means he can, should, and will judge perfectly between right and wrong and dispense justice accordingly. The Bible tells us of God's just nature in many places. For example:

- "He is the Rock, his works are perfect, and all his ways are just. A faithful God who does no wrong, upright and just is he" (Deut. 32:4).
- "The LORD reigns forever; he has established his throne for judgment. He rules the world in righteousness and judges the peoples with equity" (Ps. 9:7–8).
- "For I, the LORD, love justice; I hate robbery and wrongdoing. In my faithfulness I will reward my people and make an everlasting covenant with them" (Isa. 61:8).

Notice that God's justness is framed in terms of his righteousness. This is the key to understanding what justness is all about. God must do something about sin—the breaking of his laws—because he is holy and good. A God who didn't care about the difference between right and wrong wouldn't *be* holy and good. It's easy to understand this when we think of how we'd view an earthly judge who set every lawbreaker free. We'd have a lot of words to describe him or her, but *good* and *loving* wouldn't be two of them.

God's holiness, goodness, lovingness, and justness must go hand in hand.

We should understand two especially important applications of this truth. First, the Bible is an account of God's actions in history, so we should *expect* some of those actions to reflect the outworking of his just nature—the Bible isn't going to be all sunshine and roses. If we're surprised to read that God punished people for sin, we don't have an appropriate understanding of

God's holiness, the reality and seriousness of our sin, and the corresponding necessity of God's just response. *It's only when we naively read the Bible using childlike categories of "nice" and "mean" that verses like those in the introduction to this chapter are unexpected.* That said, it's helpful to understand some of the details of how God's justness translated into specific actions in the Bible. The next chapter is devoted to looking at several of those examples.

Second, God's justness didn't apply only to people who lived in biblical times—it applies to us. That sounds obvious, but sometimes we forget the seriousness of our own sin. So here's a reminder: God, in his authority as lawgiver, has set the penalty for sin as death (Rom. 6:23). The good news is that we know a perfectly good and holy God won't sentence anyone to death unjustly. We can trust in his perfect judgment. The bad news is that all of us have sinned and deserve the penalty of death (Rom. 3:23). That leaves us in a grave spot (pun intended), but God has offered a way out. He paid the penalty for us by sending Jesus to die in our place. In this way, he *justly* forgave us. He didn't ignore our sin—that would be inconsistent with his just character. Payment was made as required, but out of love, he made that payment himself. If we accept that payment, we are reconciled to God and will spend eternity with him. If we don't, we will pay the penalty ourselves and spend eternity without him.[1]

While the most common misunderstanding of justness is that God's just actions are cruel and arbitrarily vengeful, we should look at one other important misunderstanding as well: the idea that God is *fair*.

God Is Just but Not Necessarily Fair

In some contexts, the words *just* and *fair* can be used interchangeably. But we have to be careful in saying that God is fair, because there's at least one sense of the word *fair* that shouldn't be equated with the word *just*: the idea that everyone should be treated equally. This meaning of fairness does not apply to God's character.

That's right. God, in this sense, is not necessarily fair.

To understand the difference between treating people equally and treating them justly, let's look at the parable of the workers in the vineyard in Matthew 20. Jesus says the kingdom of heaven is like a landowner who went out early in the morning to hire workers for his vineyard. The landowner agreed to pay them a denarius for the day and sent them out to work. Throughout that day, he came across several others who also needed work and sent them out to the fields as well, promising to pay what was "right." By the evening, people in the vineyard had labored anywhere from one hour to a whole day. To the workers' surprise, the landowner paid everyone a full day's wage. When those who had worked all day complained, the landowner replied, "Don't I have the right to do what I want with my own money? Or are you envious because I am generous?" (Matt. 20:15).

In this parable, the landowner justly gave the first workers what he promised—a day's wage. The other workers were the beneficiaries of the landowner's generosity.

Similarly, God is just to everyone, but to some he is additionally gracious.

God expresses this prerogative directly in Exodus 33:19: "I will have mercy upon whom I will have mercy, and I will have compassion on whom I will have compassion."

God's gifts are his to give as he sees fit. His generosity is never required. If we don't understand this and inappropriately expect God to be fair—in the sense of treating everyone the same—we can become disappointed or even angry with him in our circumstances. This is why it's important for Christians to recognize the distinction between justness and fairness.

KEY POINTS

- God's justness means he can, should, and will judge perfectly between right and wrong and dispense justice accordingly.
- God must do something about sin—the breaking of his laws—because he is holy and good. A God who didn't care about the difference between right and wrong wouldn't *be* holy and good.
- All of us have sinned and deserve God's stated penalty of death, but God has offered a way out. He paid the penalty for us by sending Jesus to die in our place. In this way, he *justly* forgave us—not ignoring our sin but lovingly making the payment himself. It is our responsibility to accept his gift.
- God is just but not necessarily fair—when fair means treating everyone equally. God's gifts are his to give as he sees fit. His generosity is never required.

CONVERSATION GUIDE

Open the Conversation

- Think about the last time you received a consequence for breaking a rule. Do you think the adult who gave you that consequence was mean for doing so? Why or why not? *(Discuss how parents set rules and give consequences out of love.)*

Advance the Conversation

- Read Deuteronomy 32:4; Psalm 9:7–8; Isaiah 61:8. These verses describe God's just nature. Based on what they say, how would you describe what it means for God to be just? *(Discuss your child's definition, then offer the description given in this chapter. Emphasize the necessary relationship between God's* holiness, goodness, lovingness, and justness—and how justness is therefore not being "mean.")

- Read Isaiah 26:21; Nahum 1:2–3; Romans 2:5. Would you describe God as mean or just in these verses? Why? *(All these verses speak to God's actions specifically as a response to sin, indicating that they are the outworking of his just nature.)*

- If God is just, what do you think that means for us, given that we sin throughout our lives? *(God will judge us too. Discuss the points from this chapter on the good news of how God has chosen to justly forgive us if we accept his gift.)*

- Read Matthew 20:1–16. Did the landowner treat all the workers the same? *(Explain that they were treated differently—some were paid based on hours worked, while others were paid based on the landowner's generosity.)* Do you think the landowner was unjust in how he treated them? *(Explain the difference between justness and fairness. Discuss how God is like the landowner, just to everyone but to some additionally gracious.)*

Apply the Conversation

- A fourteen-year-old posted the following question online: "Why does God sound so mean in the Bible? I don't understand! All my life I have gone to Catholic school . . . and they always say how God is so loving and that's all they talk about in church. But in the Bible he doesn't sound nice, he sounds almost mean to me. Why is he so mean in it? I'm confused."[2] How would you respond to her?

16. Why Does God Seem So Harsh in Parts of the Old Testament?

The Old Testament contains a lot of death and killing: God wipes out humanity, the ground swallows people, God commands the Israelites to destroy nations. Some of the Bible's accounts can sound pretty ruthless.

In the New Testament, we don't see this. It's not that the New Testament subject matter is any less serious—Jesus speaks in no uncertain terms about the gravity of sin and its eternal consequences—but we don't see God taking immediate action in the same way.

While this striking difference can be a curiosity for Christians, it's a spiritual deal breaker for many skeptics. They often claim that the God of the Old Testament is downright evil and can't possibly be reconciled with the more "loving" God portrayed in the New Testament. A morally good God, they say, would never act in the ways the Old Testament says, so the Bible must be fiction.

How can we help our kids navigate such claims? While much could be said, we'll focus on one particularly important subject: how what we learned about God's justness can help us make sense of his supposed *harshness* in the Old Testament.

Context for Understanding God in the Old Testament

The most important starting point for this discussion is the fact that God's *character* is presented in a consistent way throughout Scripture. If we look back at chapters 13, 14, and 15, we'll see verses in both the Old and the New Testament that speak to every one of God's attributes. If we think God seems different in the Old and New Testaments, it's not because God actually changed. This, of course, doesn't say anything about whether the God of the Bible is evil, but it does focus our discussion on his actions rather than on his supposed character change.

Once we know God is just (see chap. 15) and that his justness has never changed, the question becomes whether his actions in the Old Testament can reasonably be seen as an outworking of that justness or if they're something else altogether. To answer that question, we can look at passages to see if the Bible specifies that God's actions were, indeed, a response to sin.

That said, we have to be realistic about how much we can understand. We can reasonably establish whether God's actions were a judgment, but we can't necessarily establish God's reasons for the timing, method, or extent of his judgment. We may sometimes think God's judgment seems extreme, but we can't possibly have his full perspective. If we know that (1) he's perfectly just and (2) he was acting in response to sin, it follows that he must have acted rightly. With this in mind, let's look at five commonly questioned passages.

Five Old Testament Passages Often Questioned

1. Noah's Great Flood

In Genesis 1:31, God looked upon his creation and said it was "very good." By Genesis 6, however, we read that the Earth had become terrible: the human race was wicked (v. 5); the thoughts of the human heart were all evil, all the time (v. 5); the Earth was filled with violence (v. 11); and all the people on Earth had "corrupted their ways" (v. 12).

The Bible identifies just one righteous man among all: Noah. In response to humanity's wickedness, God sent a great flood, but first he provided a way for Noah to be saved. He told him to build an ark, onto which Noah could take his family and all the animals that God commanded. God eventually flooded the Earth, destroying "every living thing" (Gen. 7:21) except those on Noah's ark.[1]

In this first passage, we can clearly see that the flood was God's response to sin—a case of God's judgment on his wicked creation.

2. The Destruction of Sodom and Gomorrah

In Genesis 18:20–33, the Lord told Abraham that the cities of Sodom and Gomorrah had sinned exceedingly. Judgment was near. Abraham pleaded with God for mercy on Sodom and Gomorrah, however, because that's where his nephew Lot and Lot's family lived. He asked God, "Will you sweep away the righteous with the wicked? What if there are fifty righteous people in the city? . . . Will not the Judge of all the earth do right?" (vv. 23–25). The Lord replied that he would spare the entire area if there were fifty righteous people. Abraham then asked what would happen if there were only forty-five righteous people. Again, the Lord said he would spare the area. Abraham proceeded to ask what would happen if only forty, thirty, twenty, or ten righteous people were found. Each time, the Lord said he would spare Sodom and Gomorrah. Ultimately, God saved Lot and his family, then "overthrew those cities and the entire plain, destroying all those living in the cities" (Gen. 19:25).

There's no doubt from this account that God's destruction of Sodom and Gomorrah was a response to sin—a case of God's judgment.

3. The Egyptian Plagues

After Joseph's family moved to Egypt to escape famine, their descendants became "so numerous that the land was filled with them" (Exod. 1:7). Their increasing numbers concerned the Egyptian king, so he forced them into harsh slavery to prevent them from gaining power. The Egyptians made their lives "bitter" and worked them "ruthlessly" (Exod. 1:14). Pharaoh even ordered all Israelite male infants to be thrown into the Nile River (Exod. 1:22).

God responded to this sinful oppression of his people by commanding Moses and Aaron to confront Pharaoh and to tell him to let the Israelites go. Pharaoh repeatedly refused to release them, so God sent ten plagues upon Egypt. The plagues culminated in the killing of every firstborn Egyptian child (Exod. 11:4–6). In response, Pharaoh finally let the Israelites go.

Once again, it's clear that God sent the plagues as a judgment on the nation of Egypt in response to sin.

4. The Destruction of the Canaanites

In Genesis 12:1–3, God promised Abraham that he would bless all the families of the Earth through his descendants. As a result, Abraham was to become the ancestral father of God's chosen people, the Israelites, and ultimately of Jesus himself. Part of this blessing included the Israelites' eventual inheritance of the land of Canaan (Gen. 15:18–21).

When the time came for the Israelites to inherit the land, it was occupied by the Canaanite people, who were extremely depraved—guilty of multiple abominations, including child sacrifice, bestiality, idolatry, witchcraft, and sorcery (Lev. 18:20–30; Deut. 18:9–14). God didn't want the Israelites to settle among a wicked people. He wanted the Israelites to be physically, morally, and theologically set apart so they would be in a position to carry his message forward hundreds of years—to the time of the Savior. Otherwise, Israel could be permanently led astray.

The time for fulfillment of God's land promise to Abraham ultimately converged with the time when God was ready to execute judgment upon that land's inhabitants. He commanded the Israelites to "completely destroy them" (Deut. 20:17).

When we understand God's command in view of history, we see he wasn't ordering an indiscriminate massacre. He was executing a judgment on the Canaanites' sinfulness.[2]

5. The Destruction of the Amalekites

The Amalekites repeatedly fought the Israelites. They first attacked them at Rephidim (Exod. 17:8), an attack recounted in Deuteronomy 25:17–19:

> Remember what the Amalekites did to you along the way when you came out of Egypt. When you were weary and worn out, they met you on your journey and attacked all who were lagging behind; they had no fear of God. When the LORD your God gives you rest from all the enemies around you in the land he is giving you to possess as an inheritance, you shall blot out the name of Amalek from under heaven.

The Amalekites later battled the Israelites on multiple occasions by joining forces with the Canaanites (Num. 14:45), the Moabites (Judg. 3:13), and the Midianites (Judg. 6:3). Eventually, God commanded King Saul to "attack the Amalekites and totally destroy all that belongs to them. . . . Put to death men and women, children and infants, cattle and sheep, camels and donkeys" (1 Sam. 15:3). The Amalekites who escaped King Saul's attacks harassed the Israelites for hundreds of years.

Yet again, God's command to destroy a people group did not pop up out of nowhere. The context was the Amalekites' hatred for the Israelites and their attacks over hundreds of years. Their sinfulness eventually brought God's judgment upon them.

What we've seen from this quick overview is that God's judgment was the background for each of these biblical passages that skeptics find so questionable. Again, we can't necessarily explain the timing, method, or extent of his judgment, but we don't have the full perspective of God.

As a final note, while we can morally justify God's actions in the Old Testament, that alone doesn't tell us why we don't continue to see such actions in the New Testament. The answer for the change largely lies in John 3:17: "God did not send his Son into the world to condemn the world, but to save the world through him." Jesus ushered in a new period of salvation and forgiveness of sins for those who accept it. We now await God's *final* act of judgment, which will occur at the end of time.

KEY POINTS

- God's character never changes, even if he sometimes seems different in the Old and New Testaments.

- Once we know God is just and that his justness never changes, the question becomes whether his actions in the Old Testament can reasonably be seen as an outworking of that justness . . . or something else altogether.

- To evaluate this question, we can look at biblical accounts to see if the Bible specifies that God's actions were, indeed, a response to sin.

- Five Old Testament passages have especially made people question God's goodness: the flood, Sodom and Gomorrah, the Egyptian plagues, the destruction of the Canaanites, and the destruction of the Amalekites. In each of these cases, the

Bible clearly demonstrates that God's actions were a *just* response to sin.

CONVERSATION GUIDE

Open the Conversation

- When you hear the Old Testament accounts of how God destroyed creation through Noah's flood or how God wiped out the cities of Sodom and Gomorrah or how God sent ten plagues on Egypt, do you think he seems different than he does in the New Testament? Why or why not?

Advance the Conversation

- Some people think God sounds harsher in the Old Testament because he did things like send plagues on Egypt. Do you think God's character may have changed from the Old Testament to the New? Why or why not? *(Go back to chapters 13, 14, and 15 to show your child that verses speak to every one of God's attributes in both testaments. Also read Malachi 3:6.)*

- In the previous chapter, we learned what it means for God to be just—and that the penalty for sin is death. If we wanted to know whether one of the "harsh" events in the Bible happened because God was acting out of his justness, what would we look for in the passage? *(Something that says the event happened because of sin.)*

- *(Walk through the five accounts in this chapter to show how the Bible says each one happened as an outworking of God's just nature. Clarify that we can't, however, always understand the timing, method, or extent of God's judgment.)*

Apply the Conversation

- A man left a comment on a blog post about Noah's flood, saying, "The big question is why Christians conveniently sweep [difficult] passages of the Bible under the rug. . . . It's right there in black and white and they shrug it off as though God became a changed man after the birth of his son Jesus. I think it's good that we all begin to ask why Christians consider the Bible their rock, their symbol for morality."[3] If you could talk to this man, what would you say?

17. How Can God Be Three Persons in One?

The belief that God is a Trinity is foundational to Christianity. The doctrine of the Trinity states:

1. There is one God.
2. God is three distinct persons.
3. Each person is fully God.

Of all Christian beliefs, the Trinity is often the most difficult to teach kids. It's a belief most *adults* struggle to comprehend, so we can fail miserably trying to make sense of it for our children. I know I have. When my kids were younger, I peeled a hard-boiled egg in front of them to demonstrate how the Trinity is like an egg—the shell, the white part, and the yolk all make up one egg, just as the Father, the Son, and the Holy Spirit make up one God. But that analogy makes a serious error by suggesting that God is made up of three parts combining to make one whole. (I'll explain more about why this isn't a good analogy later in the chapter.)

There are, of course, many other analogies Christians commonly use to explain the Trinity. The problem is that none of them are accurate. Nothing in the world manifests itself in a way comparable to the Trinity. The Trinity is a *mystery*, something we can never fully understand.

Note that saying the Trinity is mysterious is not the same as saying it's illogical—a claim commonly made by skeptics. In particular, skeptics often say the Trinity defies the rules of logic because it's a contradiction. A contradiction is when two different statements cannot both be true at the same time and in the same sense. It would be a contradiction, for example, to say that three gods are one God or to say that three persons are one person. But the doctrine of the Trinity says neither of these things. It says that one God exists as three persons. This statement, when properly understood, doesn't defy the rules of logic.

Although the Trinity is a mystery, there's much we can understand about it. In this chapter, we'll study what the Bible says about each of the three key points of the doctrine and why popular analogies fail to accurately teach each point.[1]

One God

Scripture states explicitly that there is only one God. For example:

- "Hear, O Israel: The LORD our God, the LORD is one" (Deut. 6:4).
- "Before me no god was formed, nor will there be one after me" (Isa. 43:10).
- "'The most important [commandment],' answered Jesus, 'is this: Hear, O Israel: The Lord our God, the Lord is one. Love the Lord your God with all your heart'" (Mark 12:29–30).
- See also 2 Kings 5:15; Isaiah 46:9; John 17:3; Galatians 3:20; 1 Timothy 2:5.

The belief in one God is called monotheism. Judaism, Christianity, and Islam are all monotheistic religions, but the belief that one God exists in three persons sets Christianity apart from Judaism and Islam. Jews and Muslims often interpret the belief that one God exists in three persons to mean that Christians believe in three Gods (tritheism). Christians, however, recognize tritheistic belief as heresy.

Mormonism is an example of a nonmonotheistic religion. Mormons believe many gods exist and that the Father, the Son, and the Holy Spirit are three Gods who function as one in purpose.[2] The belief that there is only one God sets Christianity apart from Mormonism.

The following trinitarian analogies inadvertently teach something other than monotheism and should be avoided:

- "The Trinity is like an egg, which is made of a yolk, the white, and the shell." This analogy denies the unity of God. An egg is composed of three distinct and unalike parts. Unlike the Father, the Son, and the Holy Spirit, they are not the same substance.
- "The Trinity is like a three-leaf clover." Again, this analogy denies the unity of God. Each leaf is distinct and does not share the same nature. In the Trinity, each member shares the same (divine) nature.

Three Distinct Persons

While the Bible explicitly tells us there is only one God, it does not explicitly state that God exists in three persons. To confirm that the Bible teaches this part of trinitarian doctrine, we need to establish two additional facts: (1) the Bible speaks of the Father, the Son, and the Holy Spirit as three distinct persons, and (2) each one of these distinct persons is fully God.

First, let's look at whether the Bible speaks of the Father, the Son, and the Holy Spirit as three distinct persons. If the Father, the Son, and the Holy Spirit are three distinct persons, we should see all three listed together or acting simultaneously. That's exactly what we find.

- "As soon as Jesus was baptized, he went up out of the water. At that moment heaven was opened, and he saw the Spirit of God descending like a dove and alighting on him. And a voice from heaven said, 'This is my Son, whom I love; with him I am well pleased'" (Matt. 3:16–17).

- "But the Advocate, the Holy Spirit, whom the Father will send in my name, will teach you all things and will remind you of everything I have said to you" (John 14:26).

- "You know . . . how God anointed Jesus of Nazareth with the Holy Spirit and power, and how he went around doing good and healing all who were under the power of the devil, because God was with him" (Acts 10:37–38).

- See also Matthew 12:28; 28:19; Luke 3:22; John 15:26; 2 Corinthians 13:14; 1 Peter 1:2.

These verses counter the idea that God is one person who acts in three different forms or modes (a heresy called modalism). If, for example, the Father, the Son, and the Holy Spirit are just three modes that God shifts between, all three couldn't simultaneously participate in Jesus's baptism (Matt. 3:16–17).

The following trinitarian analogies inadvertently teach modalism and should be avoided:

- "The Trinity is like water—it exists in the three forms of solid, liquid, and gas." Water can exist in the forms of solid, liquid, and gas, but the same molecule of water cannot exist in all three forms at the same time. This analogy implies God is not three distinct, coexisting persons.

- "The Trinity is like a man who is simultaneously a father, a husband, and a son." A man cannot simultaneously be a father, a husband, and a son to the same person. His role simply changes depending on the person he's interacting with. This analogy implies God too is one person who changes roles.

We've established thus far that the Bible says there is one God and that the Father, the Son, and the Holy Spirit are three distinct persons. The final piece of the puzzle is to establish that each of these persons is fully God.

Each Person Fully God

Below are key verses that equate each member of the Trinity with God himself.

The Father Is Fully God

- "For on [Jesus] God the Father has placed his seal of approval" (John 6:27).
- "Grace and peace to you from God our Father and from the Lord Jesus Christ" (Rom. 1:7).
- See also Isaiah 64:8; 1 Corinthians 8:6; Ephesians 1:3; 1 Peter 1:2.

The Son (Jesus) Is Fully God[3]

- "In the beginning was the Word, and the Word was with God, and the Word was God. . . . The Word became flesh and made his dwelling among us" (John 1:1, 14).
- "Theirs are the patriarchs, and from them is traced the human ancestry of the Messiah, who is God over all, forever praised!" (Rom. 9:5).

173

- See also John 20:28; Colossians 1:16; 2:9; Hebrews 1:8; 1 John 5:20.

The Holy Spirit Is Fully God

- "You, however, are not in the realm of the flesh but are in the realm of the Spirit, if indeed the Spirit of God lives in you" (Rom. 8:9).
- "Don't you know that you yourselves are God's temple and that God's Spirit dwells in your midst?" (1 Cor. 3:16).
- See also Matthew 10:20; John 14:17; Acts 5:3–4; 1 Corinthians 2:11; 1 John 5:6.

Arius, who lived from about AD 250 to 336, famously denied the deity of Jesus by claiming Jesus was *created* by God. This belief, called Arianism, was condemned by the church at the First Council of Nicaea in AD 325. As you might have guessed, there's an analogy that inadvertently teaches Arianism: "The Trinity is like the sun." In this analogy, the Father is like the sun, while the Son and the Holy Spirit are like the heat and the light created by the sun. This teaches Arianism because it implies that the Son and the Holy Spirit originated from the Father instead of having existed with the Father from the beginning. This is another analogy to avoid.

While we don't have an easy way to explain the Trinity to our kids, it's important that we teach with accuracy. Use the analogies discussed in this chapter to explain what the Trinity is *not*!

KEY POINTS

- The doctrine of the Trinity refers to the belief that (1) there is one God, (2) God is three distinct persons, and (3) each person is fully God.

- Scripture states explicitly that there is only one God.
- Verses in which the Father, the Son, and the Holy Spirit are acting together or are listed together demonstrate they are distinct persons—not just one God working in various forms throughout history.
- Many other verses indicate that the Father, the Son, and the Holy Spirit are each fully God.
- Popular analogies for the Trinity all teach heresies. Use them to explain what the Trinity is *not*.

CONVERSATION GUIDE

Open the Conversation

- As Christians, we believe there is one God, that God is three distinct persons (the Father, the Son, and the Holy Spirit), and that each of these persons is fully God. This is what we call the Trinity. Do you think the Trinity is easy or hard to understand? Why?

Advance the Conversation

- Read the verses from this chapter that show there is only one God. Do you think the idea that God is three persons *contradicts* these verses? Why or why not? *(Explain what a contradiction is and discuss the reasons given in this chapter for why the Trinity isn't a contradiction.)*
- Read Matthew 3:16–17. This passage is often used to show that the Father, the Son, and the Holy Spirit are three distinct persons—and that God the Father doesn't just change into Jesus or the Holy Spirit at different times. How do these verses show this? *(Three persons are simultaneously active in Jesus's baptism. Contrast this with the idea of modalism.)*

- Read the verses in this chapter that show each person in the Trinity is fully God. How does each verse show this? *(This is not necessarily obvious, so discuss how each one equates the Father, the Son, or the Holy Spirit with God.)*
- *(For additional discussion, offer analogies from this chapter and ask your kids to identify where they go wrong in describing the Trinity.)*

Apply the Conversation

- Consider the following quote: "The trinity is not exactly logical. . . . [Those who defend Christianity] have what they believe to be a clear, concise, and rational answer for this conundrum. I've heard it and don't buy it. I much prefer to ponder the idea of there being one, mysterious, and largely unknowable deity out there . . . somewhere."[4] How would you respond to this person's statement that the Trinity isn't logical and that he prefers to believe in something else?

18. Why Didn't God Reveal More of Himself in the Bible?

As we've seen, we can learn about God from nature and from studying what he has revealed about himself in the Bible. If we put these pieces together, we can gain a considerable understanding of who God is and who we are in relationship to him.

But let's face it: there's a lot more we'd like to know.

Why does God allow Satan to have as much influence as he does?

Why does God heal some people and not others?

Why doesn't God let everyone live to at least adulthood?

Why is God allowing so much time before Jesus returns?

These are just a few of the questions I'd personally like answers to. I've often wished the Bible were written more like a "Frequently Asked Questions" (FAQ) section on a website—a resource where we could ask any and all questions and receive answers that satisfy our every curiosity. In my humble opinion, a comprehensive life FAQ would have been an excellent choice for structuring God's

Word. Apparently, however, there must be a good reason why God didn't give us such a thing, because if that would have been best for us, he would have done so. Still, on a day-to-day basis, it can be frustrating that so many answers are out of our reach. We can't help but wonder why God didn't reveal more.

We'll close part 3 by looking at why—despite all God chose to reveal about himself in nature and in the Bible—there's still so much we just don't know.

The Bible Tells Us What We *Need* to Know

When a book has a blank page, we conclude one of two things: (1) there was a printing error, or (2) the author intended to leave the page blank. Because seeing a blank page can lead to reader confusion, publishers sometimes print the words "This page intentionally left blank." The answers God hasn't given us are, in a sense, like blank pages in the Bible. But God is perfect, so we don't have to wonder if our incomplete knowledge is a "printing error" on God's part. When we're faced with uncertain or missing answers, we can be confident that those pages were *intentionally* left blank.

While this may seem obvious (of course a perfect God didn't mess up!), we often don't consider the implication: God must have given us all the written revelation we *need*. If we truly needed more, that would imply God erred in some way. A perfect God cannot err. We may *want* more, but we do not *need* more.

But what exactly is the need that the Bible meets? The answer lies in 2 Timothy 3:15–17:

> From infancy you have known the Holy Scriptures, which are able to make you wise for salvation through faith in Christ Jesus. All Scripture is God-breathed and is useful for teaching, rebuking, correcting and training in righteousness, so that the servant of God may be thoroughly equipped for every good work.

In other words, the Bible teaches us what we need to know for salvation ("make you wise for salvation") and for how to live godly lives ("equipped for every good work"). This doesn't mean our spiritual lives can't benefit from other resources but rather that we don't need any additional written revelation from God himself.

Many of us would still reply, "Great! We have what we need! But why can't we have more of what we *want*?" I'm sure God has many reasons for not satisfying more of our intellectual curiosity, but two are especially important: (1) we're not capable of knowing all we want to know, and (2) it wouldn't be good for us to know all we want to know.

Let's explore these two points.

We're Not Capable of Knowing All We Want to Know

Time for a reality check. We all know that God is God and we are not. But we can't even *begin* to understand the great chasm of perspective that exists between God and humankind.

Take my question about why God heals some and not others. In my own little mind, I think God could have provided some kind of evaluation matrix in the Bible to explain how he decides whom to heal. In reality, of course, it's just not that simple. There's no way God *could* explain his thoughts to us. To know why God didn't heal any given individual, we would have to have God's full perspective—a comprehensive knowledge of the past, the present, and the future, as well as a complete understanding of how all possible life spans for a person would impact all other people's lives and ultimately the course of history.

Those are too many wheels for our wheelhouse.

Without the actual mind of God, there are many things we can't possibly begin to understand. But beyond that, it wouldn't be *good* for us to know all we want to know.

It Wouldn't Be Good for Us to Know All We Want to Know

I'm going to be honest with you. I do not like this point. On a prideful level, it annoys me. *Can't I decide for myself whether something's important for me to know? Don't lump me in with everyone else! Just put all the detail in the Bible and let individuals sort out what they care about!* In other words, I accept this point as well as children accept the point that they can't eat candy all day because parents know what's best, and parents know candy isn't good for them.

I still want my candy.

That said, I'll try to be a bit more spiritually mature for the moment and flush out this important point: not having all the answers we'd like teaches us to depend on and grow in our relationship with God.

For one thing, our lack of answers allows us to depend humbly on God rather than depend pridefully on ourselves. We were created in God's image, but we weren't created to *be* God. Not knowing everything—and knowing that God does—should remind us that we must "trust in the LORD with all [our] heart and lean not on [our] own understanding" (Prov. 3:5).

In addition, our lack of answers requires us to seek God through prayer. If we knew everything (or even just a lot more than we do), we would have little need to talk to God. But it's through prayer that we experience a living, breathing relationship with our Creator, the very relationship for which we were made.

Finally, when we internalize that God has given us all we need to know, we thirst for his Word. Instead of focusing on what God *hasn't* said, we focus on understanding everything he *has* said. *These are the words the Creator of the universe chose for us to have!* That makes them so very special, so very precious, and so very important to understand. If we fully appreciate this idea, it will forever change our view of the Bible and what it means that it's God's Word.

KEY POINTS

- When we learn about what God has revealed about himself in nature and in the Bible, we gain a considerable understanding of who he is and who we are in relationship to him. But there's still a lot we don't know.
- We have all we need to know from written revelation. More specifically, 2 Timothy 3:15–17 tells us that the Bible teaches us what we need to know about salvation and Christian living.
- There's no way God *could* explain much of what we'd like to know because our human perspective is too limited.
- Even if God could have explained more, it wouldn't be *good* for us to know all we want to know. Not having all the answers teaches us to depend on and grow in our relationship with him.

CONVERSATION GUIDE

Open the Conversation

- If you could ask God three questions, what would they be? *(Take time to talk about your child's questions, then share some of your own. Your honesty will show that everyone has questions and that this is okay.)*

Advance the Conversation

- All of us have questions we wish God would have answered. There's more we want to know. But do you think we have at least all we *need* to know? Why or why not? *(Explain that if we truly needed more written revelation, that fact would imply God erred in some way. A perfect God cannot err.)*
- Read 2 Timothy 3:15–17. What do these verses say the Bible teaches us? *(What we need to know for salvation and how to live*

godly lives. Explain that this doesn't mean other resources can't benefit us but that we have all the written revelation we need for these two things.)

- Even if we understand that the Bible tells us all we need to know for salvation and Christian living, many might still reply, "Great! We have what we need! But why can't we have more of what we *want*?" What are some possible reasons why God gave us all the information we *need* to know rather than all the information we *want* to know? *(Explore your child's reasons and offer the two discussed in this chapter: we aren't capable of understanding everything, and it wouldn't be good for us to know everything.)*

Apply the Conversation

- In an online discussion between theists and atheists, an atheist asked, "[If the Bible is God's inerrant Word,] why didn't God reveal more useful information to us through the Bible? Couldn't hundreds of years of famine have been averted if he'd simply told people about crop rotation in there? Does God want us to suffer?"[1] How would you respond? Be sure to address what this commenter means by "useful."

PART 4

Believing
in
God

Overview

A wonderful thing happened just before Thanksgiving last year: our bathroom scale broke. The display stopped working, so I happily didn't have access that weekend to the truth of what all the turkey, noodles, mashed potatoes, bread, and pie did to my body.

I'm fairly petite, but I still watch what I eat and weigh myself regularly. After experiencing the liberation of a scale-free Thanksgiving, however, I was in no rush to buy a replacement. Weeks came and went. No new scale. Christmas came and went. Definitely no new scale. On New Year's Day, however, I knew I had been detached from reality for too long: it was time to buy a replacement.

As it turns out, I was pleasantly surprised when I stepped onto our new scale for the first time. I hadn't gained as much weight after the holidays as I had thought. But then my husband stepped onto the scale. He shook his head in confusion and said, "This isn't right. It's underweighing by several pounds." He had just been to the doctor's office for a physical that morning, so he had a trustworthy point of reference. The scale was wrong.

Did we take it back?

No way.

I strangely liked the lower weight number, even though I knew it was incorrect. It was close enough to reality that I started looking forward to weighing myself each morning and wondering if the scale was somehow adjusting over time. Maybe it was now showing my real weight . . . maybe it wasn't. It was like a little inside joke I had with myself (perhaps I need some new hobbies).

In reality, of course, only one number reflects my true weight. I can choose how I *respond* to that reality—by ignoring it, by accepting a false alternative, or by embracing it—but the truth doesn't depend on what I do with it. That said, if I choose to ignore the truth or to accept a false alternative, there can eventually be serious implications.

We've just finished eighteen chapters laying out the truth of what God has revealed about himself in nature and in the Bible. This is a critical foundation for our kids to have. But it's not enough to acknowledge that God's truth exists, just as it's not enough for me to acknowledge that my true weight exists while living in blissful ignorance. How we *respond* to truth matters—there are real implications for our lives. And humans have responded to God's truth in many ways.

In part 4, we'll look at some key questions about *believing* in God, questions raised by skeptics and Christians alike. The first three chapters address topics concerning the variety of religious beliefs in the world: Why do people believe so many different things about God? Do all religions worship the same God? and Is what you believe about God simply a matter of where you grew up? The next three chapters deal with questions Christians have about the nature of belief: Why do Christians sometimes doubt their belief in God? How do we know God hears and answers prayers? and How can we develop a relationship with a God we can't see or hear? Kids often struggle with these questions in particular.

Knowing that these questions can be challenging for Christians, skeptics often use them as a tool for shame. For example, they say that people who believe in God will always have doubt because, deep down, they know God doesn't exist.[1] Other times they mock the idea that God answers prayers, as does the author behind the popular website Why Won't God Heal Amputees (whywontgodhealamputees.com). Still others make fun of Christians for believing they have a relationship with an invisible Being, calling God an "imaginary friend." In all these cases, the uncertainties Christians sometimes feel in their own faith can be used against them with devastating consequences. It's important that we (1) acknowledge the challenges that can exist in the life of a believer and (2) equip our kids with an understanding of what to do with these challenges.

The conversations in part 4 will help your kids consider the importance of how they—and others—respond to the weightiness of God's truth. Through these conversations, they'll see that faith isn't a matter of choosing the scale we like the most but rather shaping our lives around reality.

Three Keys to Impactful Conversations about Believing in God

1. *Explain the transition in the nature of topics.* In the first three parts of this book, we discussed what God has revealed about himself in nature and in the Bible. Now we're looking at how humans *respond* to God's revelation. Help your kids connect the dots so they understand the progression of conversations.

2. *Emphasize the need to speak the truth in love.* The first three chapters of part 4 talk about what non-Christians believe. When we have these conversations, it's important we don't speak poorly or condescendingly about those who believe differently than we do. As Christians, we must show our love to everyone, as every human is made in the image of God.

At the same time, our kids need to know that speaking the truth about what God has revealed is not hateful or intolerant in and of itself, as our culture likes to claim. Tolerance simply means bearing with ideas other than our own—not accepting them as true. We must be willing to speak the truth while doing so with gentleness and respect (1 Pet. 3:15).

3. *Be prepared to take conversations to a more personal level.* Throughout this book, the questions have asked kids for their opinions but, for the most part, haven't focused on their own relationship with God. In the last three chapters of part 4, this will change. Some kids will be comfortable sharing, and others won't. For those who are reluctant to open up, sharing your own experiences and letting your kids know you genuinely value what they have to say can be especially helpful.

19. Why Do People Believe So Many Different Things about God?

One evening when I was cooking dinner, our doorbell rang. I opened the door, assuming it was a package delivery, but instead found a woman and a young girl. They introduced themselves, and the woman asked, "Can my daughter show you a short video about God?"

I quickly realized they were Jehovah's Witnesses.

If my son hadn't been right next to me, I would have said, "No, thanks," and headed back to save my soon-to-be-burnt dinner. But I knew this would be a great opportunity to at least briefly demonstrate how to talk with people who have different beliefs than we do, so I left a small opening for conversation.

"I'm in the middle of cooking dinner right now, so I don't have time to watch a video or talk long, but I'm a Christian—"

She interjected, "We're Christians too! It's so nice to talk to someone who believes in God. Most of the people we talk to don't believe in God at all."

"I know what you mean—our world is becoming so secular, and it's important to help people understand the evidence for God's existence. You and I share that belief. But where we *differ* is still very important. For example, your church has its own translation of the Bible, which it uses to deny that Jesus is God. [I elaborated on the significance of this point.] I'm curious, have you ever had the opportunity to study why almost all Bible scholars reject that translation?"

She hesitantly replied, "Well, kind of, I mean, not a lot . . ."

"I have to get back to cooking, but one of the ways I'm working to prepare my kids' faith for this tough world is by reading about and discussing opposing viewpoints with them. I encourage you to do the same with your daughter. Whether Jesus is God makes a big difference for all else we believe." (Jehovah's Witnesses are taught that reading opposing literature is dangerous, but I hoped to get her thinking, in light of her own child's faith.[1])

I thanked them for coming, and, with that, they left.

As soon as the door closed, my son pondered out loud, "So the reason they believe different things is because they have their own translation of the Bible . . ."

I found it interesting that he had picked this key point out of our conversation and had phrased it in this way. We had talked informally about other religions before, but we had never done so in a way that would have helped my son systematically categorize what divides people's beliefs—something important for putting the Bible in context.

When it comes to religious beliefs about God that differ from what the Bible teaches, people can generally be divided into five groups:

1. Those who don't believe God exists and reject the truth of all holy books.
2. Those who believe God exists but reject the truth of all holy books.

3. Those who reject the Bible but accept another holy book.

4. Those who accept the Bible but interpret it in an unorthodox way.

5. Those who accept the Bible but don't believe all it teaches (intentionally or not).

These categories don't exhaustively capture the world's beliefs, but they do account for the majority of them. Let's look at each group to see how its beliefs compare with what the Bible teaches.

Group 1: Not Believing God Exists *and* Rejecting All Holy Books

Atheism

Atheism, as most commonly understood, is the belief that there's no God (which also implies a rejection of the world's holy books as divinely inspired revelation). Many atheists, however, prefer to say that atheism is simply the *lack* of a belief in God. The reason they care to make the distinction is that if they lack belief in something, they have no burden of proof. They're not technically making any claims, so they don't have to prove their case. If, however, atheists make the claim that God does not exist, doing so requires them to make a case for what they believe. There's a fine distinction between these definitions, but the distinction has many implications for the nature of conversations between theists and atheists.

Agnosticism

Agnosticism is the belief that nothing can be known about the existence and/or nature of God. Note that this is not the same as saying, "I *don't know* if there's a God" (a statement describing a person's knowledge status). Agnostics are saying, "Humans *can't* know if there's a God" (a statement claiming such knowledge isn't possible). Agnostics don't technically reject God, but I've included them in this category because, like atheists, they don't have a positive belief in God. As with atheism, agnosticism implies a rejection of all holy books. People who accept a written source as divine revelation believe something can be known about God's existence, and they therefore are not agnostic.[2]

Group 2: Believing God Exists but Rejecting All Holy Books

Deism

Deism is the belief that a supreme being created the universe but remains aloof and doesn't actively intervene in human affairs. As with atheists and agnostics, deists reject any books claiming to be the revealed Word of God. Because deists do not accept a written source of revelation, their beliefs about God are limited to what can be observed in nature and determined through reason. They therefore can't (or at least shouldn't) claim to know anything about how God relates to humans, such as why we're here, what we're supposed to do while we're here, or what happens after we die. Such beliefs would be only personal speculation, since deists don't believe God has revealed these things.

"Spiritual, Not Religious"

A growing number of people in the United States—nearly 1 in 5—label themselves "spiritual, not religious."[3] This typically means they believe in God or some kind of higher power but reject the truth of any organized religion.

Some of these people are technically deists—they feel some connection to a Creator God but don't believe he's active in creation. The group as a whole, however, warrants a separate acknowledgment because many of them *do* believe God interacts with creation.

They just don't think he's revealed himself in any particular holy book. They tend to believe they can reach God however they want, and they pray or meditate accordingly.

Group 3: Rejecting the Bible but Accepting Another Holy Book

When it comes to religious beliefs, arguably the most significant dividing factor is the existence of a wide variety of holy books. Here are some of the most important ones used by the world's major religions:

Christianity: Bible

Islam: Quran

Hinduism: Vedas

Buddhism: Tipitaka

Sikhism: Guru Granth Sahib

Judaism: Tanakh (includes the Torah, Nevi'im, and Ketuvim)

Mormonism: Book of Mormon

Baha'ism: Kitáb-i-Aqdas

Jainism: Agam Sutras

Shintoism: Kojiki

These sacred writings teach vastly different answers to questions about the existence and nature of God as well as the nature, purpose, and direction of humanity. While holy books may have some teachings in common, they contradict one another in many important ways. *They are not simply different versions of one truth.* Religious pluralism—the popular idea that multiple religions can be true—is illogical. It fails to acknowledge the fact that holy books make irreconcilable truth claims about the nature of reality. The appropriate question regarding the truth of world religions is not "How do all these religions point us to God?" but rather "Which, if any, of their holy books is true?"

Group 4: Accepting the Bible but Interpreting It in an Unorthodox Way

Trust in different holy books will inevitably lead people to a wide variety of beliefs about God. But sometimes, even when people say they believe in the Bible, their beliefs about God can vary greatly. This is because some "Bible-based" religions *interpret* the Bible in an unorthodox way—a way that differs from the historic Christian faith. As a result, they end up denying central tenets of Christianity.

Jehovah's Witnesses are one example of this. They believe the church corrupted the Bible over the centuries, so it was necessary to retranslate it into what they call the New World Translation. Based on their translation, Jehovah's Witnesses deny the deity of Christ, the bodily resurrection of Christ, and the personhood of the Holy Spirit. Another religion in this category is Oneness Pentecostalism. Oneness theology teaches that God is a single person who has manifested himself in three different ways (as the Father in creation, as the Son for our redemption, and as the Holy Spirit in our regeneration). This is similar to the heresy of modalism, which we discussed in chapter 17.

From these examples, we can see that Christians must be discerning when considering a church to attend. Even when a church claims to be "Bible-based," we need to ask what, exactly, it teaches.

Group 5: Accepting the Bible but Not Believing All It Teaches

Many people say they believe the Bible but hold beliefs contrary to what the Bible says. For some, this is unintentional. They simply aren't familiar enough with the Bible. Oftentimes, this manifests itself in an oversimplified view of God in which one attribute (for example, God's love) is focused on to the exclusion or the minimization of other attributes (for example, God's justness).

Other people make a more conscious decision to pick and choose beliefs from the Bible. They willfully reject parts they don't like. Second Timothy 3:16 makes clear, however, that "*all* Scripture is God-breathed" (emphasis mine). We are not in a position to cherry-pick. It's our responsibility as Christians to study God's Word so we have an accurate and comprehensive understanding of what it says.

Understanding these categories can give our kids significantly more insight into what divides people's beliefs about God and can enable them to share their faith more effectively.

KEY POINTS

- Atheists and agnostics don't have a positive belief in God and reject all holy books as divinely inspired revelation. Deists and people who say they are "spiritual, not religious" reject all holy books but believe God exists.
- When it comes to religious beliefs, arguably the most significant dividing factor is the existence of a wide variety of holy books. These holy books contradict one another in many important ways. They are not simply different versions of one truth.
- Sometimes even when people say they believe the Bible, their beliefs about God vary greatly. This is because some "Bible-based" religions interpret the Bible in an unorthodox way.
- Many people say they believe the Bible but hold beliefs contrary to what it teaches because they haven't studied it enough or they intentionally cherry-pick what they want to believe.

CONVERSATION GUIDE

Open the Conversation

- We've been studying how God has revealed himself in nature and in the Bible. But people around the world believe all kinds of different things about God. Why do you think that is?

Advance the Conversation

- *(Walk through each of the five groups described in this chapter. Explain in your own words how their beliefs differ from what the Bible teaches, or read from the chapter directly.)*
- How can an increased understanding of what someone else believes help you share your faith more effectively?
- If you were sharing your faith with someone who's a Muslim, would you focus more on the evidence for God's existence or why we have good reason to believe the Bible is true? Why? *(Muslims already believe in God, so discussion should center on the reliability of the Bible versus that of the Quran.)*
- How would your approach to sharing your faith with a Muslim differ from your approach to sharing your faith with an atheist? *(Unlike Muslims, atheists do not already have a positive belief in the existence of God, so conversations with atheists about the evidence for God's existence are often an important starting point.)* How about with a Jehovah's Witness? *(Jehovah's Witnesses already believe in God and their translation of the Bible, so discussion may best center around the validity of their translation.)* And how about with someone who's "spiritual, not religious"? *(People who say they are "spiritual, not religious" may have any number of beliefs about the existence, nature, and revelation of God, so it would be important to start by asking questions to better understand what, exactly, they believe.)*

Apply the Conversation

- How would you respond to this statement: "We could argue until the cows come home about which religion is the best or truest, and it would be a monumental waste of breath. God is not concerned about which religion is better than other religions. God is concerned with how well each religion brings its people closer to God, and how well each religion moves its believers to love and serve their fellow human beings."[4]

20. Do All Religions Worship the Same God?

In 2015, Wheaton College professor Larycia Hawkins became the center of a global controversy when the school suspended her for saying on Facebook that Muslims and Christians worship the same God. Administrators at Wheaton, a Christian institution in Illinois, said there were significant questions regarding the theological implications of her remarks and that it was essential for faculty and staff to "engage in and speak about public issues in ways that faithfully represent the College's evangelical Statement of Faith."[1] Hawkins's suspension was followed by a firestorm of articles and TV news pieces debating whether Muslims and Christians do, indeed, worship the same God.

If this had been a one-off story, it wouldn't have ended up in this book. But the broader question of whether all (or most) religions worship the same God frequently comes up in popular culture. For example, people make statements like these:

- "I think all religions worship the same god, whether it is Allah, God, or Yahweh. In Hinduism they divide the god from one of the other religions in fractions and let each represent a small part of the world and its problems."[2]
- "The God of Abraham, Mohammed, and Jesus is the same as the God worshiped by Sikhs. We simply are seeing different aspects of it and approach it from a differ[ent] understanding."[3]
- "All theists are worshipping the same God but have chosen a way to worship him that fits their specific histories, traditions and cultures. Though the creation myths differ and the actions of His prophets differ, God himself, the deity, is basically the same in most religions."[4]

What's the potential problem with these kinds of comments? That's what we'll look at in this chapter.

Are We All Worshiping the Same God?

My son has a treasured stuffed turtle that we affectionately call Old Tortue. After years of calling him that, however, we discovered one day that the turtle came with a name printed on his store tag: Shelley. After the discovery, my son continued to call him Old Tortue, but my daughter thought it would be fun to annoy her brother and has called the turtle Shelley ever since (of course).

We all know that Old Tortue and Shelley are just two names that refer to one thing (just as Morning Star and Evening Star can both refer to the planet Venus). No one would think my son sleeps with two turtles just because his single turtle is referred to by two names. We intuitively know that whatever is true of Old Tortue is true of Shelley because they are, in reality, the same thing.

So is this the case with various religions' concepts of God? For example, are Allah and God truly just different names for the same Being—a Being that's exactly the same? At first glance, it seems that's definitely *not* the case, as the Muslim and Christian concepts of God are very different. Muslims believe God is one person, while Christians believe God is three persons. This is not a trivial difference, and it's just one of many ways Muslims and Christians disagree on who God is. As another example, recall from chapter 17 that Mormons believe many gods exist and that the Father, the Son, and the Holy Ghost are three of them. Again, this is not a trivial difference, and it's just one of many theological differences between Mormons and Christians.

When compared, the Christian, Muslim, and Mormon concepts of God differ significantly. We're not all describing the stuffed turtle in the same way. Does this mean, then, that we're worshiping different gods? Not necessarily. Stay with me here. Two people can describe the same object in different ways without the object actually being different. For example, my son may correctly describe Old Tortue as being green with a plain brown shell, while I may incorrectly describe him as being green with a spotted brown shell. We're still talking about the same turtle, but one of us is describing him incorrectly. Some philosophers and theologians believe this is the case with God. They say we're all referring to the same Being, but concepts of him differ across religions because some people simply have an incorrect *understanding* of him.

Other philosophers and theologians disagree and push the debate a step further. Imagine that you asked me and my son to describe the stuffed turtle he has in his room. He says it's green with a brown shell, and I say it's blue with a pink shell. You want to find out who's right, so you go to his room. As it turns out, there are two different turtles there. When you asked us to describe the stuffed turtle, we each thought of a different one and gave a description accordingly. In this case, you couldn't legitimately say that we were simply describing one turtle differently—we had two different turtles in mind. Similarly, some philosophers and theologians say the concepts religions have about God are so fundamentally different that they can't possibly be referring to the same Being.

So where does this leave us? Well, it all depends on which concepts of God we're comparing and what our criteria are for saying, "These are so different that we *must* be talking about two different Beings." For these reasons, there's no black-and-white, catchall answer that even philosophers and theologians agree on.

You may be thinking, *We just had to talk a whole lot about turtles to get to the bottom line that there's no simple answer.* Yes, we did. But it's important to understand why the answer to this chapter's question isn't so simple. Unfortunately, many Christians and nonbelievers have fought vigorously over this question without ever stopping to acknowledge the important nuances we just discussed.

Four Underlying Claims to Understand

Oftentimes when people say all religions worship the same God, they're actually making a different, more specific claim. We should be careful to identify exactly what their claim is before getting into philosophical "turtle talk" that might not answer their underlying point at all. In particular, people often mean one of the following four things.

1. There's Only One True God

As Christians, we affirm there's only one true God (see chap. 17). If this is the only point being made when a person says everyone worships the same God, then we can agree once the point is clarified. However, the fact that only one true God exists doesn't imply many of the other things people commonly assume. For example, acknowledging that there's only one true God doesn't mean that all religions are basically the same, that people believe the same things about God, or that all worship is acceptable to God.

2. All (or Most) Religions Are Basically the Same

The claim that all (or most) religions are basically the same is simply not true. The core beliefs of major religions contradict one another in logically irreconcilable ways. For example, Hinduism affirms a cycle of rebirths called reincarnation, while Christianity teaches that a person has one life, after which they will be judged. Christian Science denies the reality of sin, while Christianity affirms the reality of sin and teaches that it's an eternally significant problem. Religions differ in all kinds of important ways like these, making vastly different claims about where we came from, why we're here, the nature of reality, and where we're eventually headed. Religions can have *some* beliefs in common, but it's meaningless to say that religions in their totality are basically the same.

3. All (or Most) Religions Have the Same Concept of God

Similarly, the claim that all (or most) religions have the same *concept* of God is not true. Not only do religions make vastly different claims about reality in general (see the previous point), but they also make vastly different claims about the nature of God specifically. For example, Mormonism teaches the existence of many gods, while Christianity teaches the existence of one God (in three persons). Islam denies the deity of Jesus, while Christianity affirms the deity of Jesus. Jainism teaches that the universe is eternal and that there's no Creator God, while Christianity teaches that the universe is finite and required a Creator God to bring it into existence. When we consider the specific teachings about God across religions, we see that religions have very different concepts of who God is.

4. All Worship Is Acceptable to God

The claim that all worship is acceptable to God, just as a matter of logic, doesn't work. Even if we all agreed that people are worshiping the same God, this wouldn't mean that all beliefs about God are true or that God would approve of how every person worships him. To give an extreme example, I could say I'm worshiping God by throwing rocks through the windows of homes where atheists live. Most people would agree such worship would not be acceptable. A God who would approve of *any* kind of worship would not be a morally good Being. So where do we draw the line? As humans, we can't. The only One who can draw the line on the acceptability of worship is God himself. The pertinent questions, therefore, are whether God has revealed himself and his desires in a holy book, and, if so, which holy book is true? Saying or implying that all worship is acceptable to God ignores these logically important considerations.

As we can see, how we talk about God matters. While it might not initially sound like a big deal if people want to say that all religions worship the same God, the spiritual significance of these underlying claims makes this chapter's topic an important one to understand.

KEY POINTS

- A long history of debate exists among philosophers and theologians over whether different religions worship the same God. There's no easy answer—it depends on which concepts of God we're comparing and what our criteria are for saying, "These are so different that we *must* be talking about two different Beings."

- When people say all religions worship the same God, they're often making one of four more specific claims: (1) there's only one true God, (2) all (or most) religions are basically the same, (3) all (or most) religions have the same concept of God, or (4) all worship is acceptable to God.
- The spiritual significance of these underlying claims makes this chapter's topic important to understand.

CONVERSATION GUIDE

Open the Conversation

- Do you think all religions worship the same God? Why or why not? *(This is an opportunity to simply get your kids thinking about the subject.)*

Advance the Conversation

- People get into some big debates over this question and feel strongly about the answer. Why do you think those who say all religions worship the same God feel this is important to believe? *(With this and the next question, try to get your kids to think from someone else's perspective and to consider why someone would care to make the statements at all.)*
- Why do you think those who say religions worship very different Gods feel this is important to believe?
- Many times when people say all religions worship the same God, they're actually making a different, more specific point. I'm going to read four things people often mean when they say this, and I want you to tell me if you agree or disagree with each one—and why. *(Read the four points, one at a time, and allow your child to explain why he or she agrees or disagrees. Discuss the key points raised in this chapter for each. Conclude*

by explaining that it's more helpful to ask clarifying questions to understand what a person means by "all religions worship the same God" than to debate the statement itself.)

Apply the Conversation

- A member of the Sikh religion stated, "The God of Abraham, Mohammed, and Jesus is the same as the God worshiped by Sikhs. We simply are seeing different aspects of it and approach it from a differ[ent] understanding."[5] How would you respond?

21. Is What You Believe about God Simply a Matter of Where You Grew Up?

We all want to be the best parents we can be and spend a lot of time doing things we think will ensure that. But deep down, we also know our kids will grow up believing some weird things because they grew up in our particular home. For example, my kids will believe:

- The definition of freezing is when the thermostat dips below 70.
- Coffee is a necessary start to every day, but if you're a mom, it's not enjoyable unless it's served in a mug that reflects the season (fall = mug with falling leaves, winter = mug with snowman).
- An exciting date night for adults is a nice dinner followed by side-by-side reading.
- You can never pick a movie to watch before evaluating multiple possibilities. You must spend at least thirty minutes watching trailers, checking out the new-release list, and

debating with the rest of the family what to choose (possibly concluding it's not worth watching anything at all).

I'm sure you could come up with a list for your home too.

Undoubtedly, there's a relationship between how we see the world and how our parents see the world. On a broader scale, there's also a relationship between how the culture in which we grew up views the world and how we view the world. Skeptics have noted, in particular, that a strong relationship exists between religion and geography—if you grew up in Saudi Arabia, for example, you'd almost certainly be a Muslim. What's the significance of this point? Skeptics say this relationship demonstrates that belief in God isn't a response to the truth of any divine revelation but rather a function of where you happen to have been born.

In this chapter, we'll evaluate this popular claim. We'll begin by looking at the facts themselves: Is it true there's a relationship between religion and geography? Then we'll dig more deeply into the underlying reasons why skeptics raise the issue of the relationship between religion and geography in the first place. Understanding these reasons can help kids think more critically about this subject and respond to challenges more effectively.

Is It True There Is a Relationship between Religion and Geography?

Consider these facts about the distribution of religion around the world:

- Twenty-eight countries have a population that is 95 percent or more Muslim.[1]
- More than 80 percent of the Hispanic countries in South America are Roman Catholic.[2]

207

- About 80 percent of India's and Nepal's population is Hindu.[3]
- More than 75 percent of people in the Czech Republic, Estonia, Sweden, and Norway are atheist.[4]
- More than 70 percent of people in Cambodia, Thailand, Myanmar, Bhutan, and Sri Lanka are Buddhist.[5]
- More than 70 percent of people in the United States identify as Christian.[6]

Based on this data, it would be fair to say that if you grew up in India, there's a good chance you'd be a Hindu. If you grew up in the Czech Republic, there's a good chance you'd be an atheist. If you grew up in Thailand, there's a good chance you'd be a Buddhist.

But this is not the whole picture. In other countries, there's much more religious diversity. For example, in Singapore, 34 percent of people are Buddhist, 18 percent are Christian, 16 percent are unaffiliated with a religion, and 14 percent are Muslim, with the remainder belonging to other religions.[7] And *within* many countries, there's a significant amount of religious "switching." In the United States, for example, 34 percent of people currently have a religious identity different from the one in which they were raised.[8]

What does this tell us? In many parts of the world, there's a strong relationship between religion and geography—in certain parts, an extremely strong relationship. That said, there's at least some religious diversity in almost every country, so statements like, "If you were born in [country], you would be a [member of specific religious group]" are untrue, as that's not always the case. Multiple factors will always affect religious belief, and the weight of their influence will vary. The fact that geography is a particularly strong influencer in many areas is undeniable, but it's just a descriptive fact about the world, and it's something we can all agree on.

Why Skeptics Raise This Issue

Affirming that there's a relationship between religion and geography doesn't get us far. We need to understand *why* skeptics believe the relationship is relevant to the question of truth. Typically, they say it demonstrates one of three things: (1) religions are nothing more than a cultural fluke, (2) evidence for the truth of any given religion is lacking, or (3) if God is just, no religion can be an exclusive path to God. Each point requires a different response, so we'll consider them individually.

Religions Are Nothing More than a Cultural Fluke

For some skeptics, the relationship between religion and geography matters because they believe it shows that religion must be nothing more than a cultural fluke—not something that could reflect the real existence of a deity. One blogger put it this way:

> Most children inculcated into Catholicism remain Catholics, most children indoctrinated into Islam remain Muslims, most children raised as Hindus remain so, etc. . . . Perhaps religion finally shall go extinct once more people realize that one's piety, at least with regard to a particular superstition, is a mere accident of geography. A fundamentalist Christian, in other words, in an alternate reality, would be just another [Muslim warrior].[9]

When skeptics such as this person suggest that all religions are untrue because people's beliefs are inherently influenced by culture, they're committing a logical error called the genetic fallacy. People commit a genetic fallacy when they judge a claim to be true or false on the basis of its origin rather than its merits. In this case, some skeptics assume that all religions are untrue because they in some way originate from culture. But even when the origin of a certain belief is primarily cultural in nature, that has nothing to do with whether the belief itself is true. The truth of any claim about reality must be evaluated on its own merits—not on the geographical distribution of those who believe it.[10]

Evidence for the Truth of Any Given Religion Is Lacking

Other skeptics acknowledge that religious distribution across geography, in and of itself, doesn't suggest that all religions are untrue, but they raise the issue because they believe it shows that evidence is lacking for the truth of any *one* religion. For example, one writer says:

> Religion is a cultural trait like customs, fashion, or traditional foods. If there really were a god, we would expect people to be drawn to the true religion over all the others because its claims were supported by far better evidence, not that people would mirror their environment and religions would fill their ranks by indoctrinating children before their critical thinking skills are developed.[11]

An important thing to understand about this claim is that there are *many* things people do not typically form beliefs about by studying all available evidence and then making a decision—and religion is one of them. The worldwide distribution of beliefs is not the outcome of each person's thorough evaluation of evidence, so the distribution itself *says* nothing about the evidence. And even *if* every single human did thoughtfully evaluate evidence for the truth of various religions, we know from chapter 1 that they would inevitably interpret the evidence in different ways. For these reasons, it's not possible to look at the global distribution of religious beliefs and determine which religion, if any, is best supported by evidence.

If God Is Just, No Religion Can Be an Exclusive Path to God

A third reason people sometimes raise the issue of the relationship between religion and geography is that they believe it shows the absurdity of any religion claiming an exclusive path to God, especially if there are supposedly eternal consequences for what people believe. Consider the words of one skeptic with this view:

> I shall venture a guess as to what [a Christian] would propose would have caused a child born in India to Hindu parents to become a Christian. It works like this: Jesus would have recognized him as a person MEANT to be Christian, and thus would have implanted in his mind a "Christian Gene," or some such predisposition toward Christianity. . . . This then sets him above the one billion-plus Hindus Jesus doesn't deem worthy of hypnotizing, enticing, or otherwise receiving His "revealed" singular truth. All those others would be ignored and condemned to hell for not abandoning their historic Hindu faith and coming to the Lord independently, without His divine intervention.[12]

If religions didn't claim that what we believe about God actually matters, many skeptics probably wouldn't raise the issue of religion and geography at all. But for those like this commenter, the Christian belief that people go to heaven or hell based on their relationship with Jesus—when many people worldwide have never heard about Jesus—is irreconcilable with the existence of a loving God. They believe that if God is just, there must be multiple religious paths to reach him.

A chapter in *Keeping Your Kids on God's Side* is dedicated to the question of what happens to those who have never heard about Jesus. For our current purpose, we'll just note the key takeaway: the Bible does not explicitly state what happens to those who have never heard about Jesus, but because we know God is perfectly just, we can be confident he'll do what is right on judgment day. There's no reason to assume that God's verdicts will be unjust simply because we don't know how he'll make those decisions.

The most effective response to the claim that geography determines a person's religion is to say, "I agree there's a relationship between religion and geography. What do you believe this says about the truth of various religions?" Once you identify why a person is raising the issue, a more productive discussion can follow.

KEY POINTS

- In many (though not all) parts of the world, there's a strong relationship between religion and geography. Skeptics use this fact to suggest that belief in God isn't a response to the truth of any divine revelation but rather a function of where you happen to have been born.
- People typically raise the issue of the relationship between religion and geography because they believe it demonstrates one of three things: (1) religions are nothing more than a cultural fluke, (2) evidence for the truth of any given religion is lacking, or (3) if God is just, no religion can be an exclusive path to God.
- The first two points don't logically follow. Even when the origin of a certain belief is primarily cultural in nature, that has nothing to do with whether the belief itself is true or whether the belief is based on good evidence.
- The third point ignores the biblical context that God is perfectly just. The Bible never explicitly states what happens to those who have never heard about Jesus, but because we know God is just, we can be confident he will judge rightly.

CONVERSATION GUIDE

Open the Conversation

- Ninety-nine percent of people in Afghanistan are Muslim. Do you think that if you had been born in Afghanistan, you would be a Muslim too? Why or why not?

Advance the Conversation

- *(Read the bullet-pointed statistics under the section "Is It True There Is a Relationship between Religion and Geography?")* Skeptics sometimes think facts like these suggest that all religions must be untrue. Why do you think they say this? *(At first glance, it seems that beliefs are merely an "accident" of geography. Explain the genetic fallacy and discuss why geographical relationships can say nothing about the truth of religious claims.)*

- Do you think that if the evidence for the truth of any one religion was especially strong, the majority of people in all countries would adhere to that religion? Why or why not? *(Discuss the fact that people form beliefs for all kinds of reasons not necessarily related to evidence and that even when people look at the same evidence, there will be multiple interpretations.)*

- Some people think there can't be only one path of salvation if religious beliefs are highly influenced by the country in which a person grows up. Otherwise, they say, God would be unjust. Why do you think they say this? *(Explain that this question boils down to what happens to people who have never heard about Jesus, and discuss the response from this chapter.)*

Apply the Conversation

- How would you respond to this question posted online: "Given that a person's religion is most often a simple accident of geography, how can religious people be so convinced that their particular one just happens to be the only one that is right?"[13]

22. Why Do Christians Sometimes Doubt Their Belief in God?

The most-read article on my blog to date is one from 2014 called "5 Things to Do When You're Struggling with Faith Doubts."[1] Several thousand people land on it every month after searching online for help with their doubt about God. The comment section after the post has turned into a virtual support group for Christians struggling with unresolved spiritual questions.

One commenter shared:

> For 35 years I have always lived in the fact I KNEW God was there, and I KNEW Christ died for me. Most who struggle with faith are living in hard times and it causes them to doubt. That's not me. I have a wonderful family, am blessed with all I need and so much more . . . yet in the last week I suddenly and abruptly started to question everything I knew. Before getting online tonight I found myself on the floor crying, asking God to speak to me, just one

word, and when I laid there for 30 minutes with no answer and no signal, I let it drive me even more toward the feeling.

Dozens of heart-wrenching comments like this one follow my blog post. In the midst of them, one person attempted to offer encouragement by saying, "Let go and let God. You'll be just fine."

I'm pretty sure no one found that advice helpful.

Unfortunately, this is often the feedback Christians get when they admit to struggling with doubt. Well-meaning people trivialize the severity of the problem and chalk up the solution to just having *more* faith—the exact thing people are struggling to have in the first place. On the other hand, skeptics often retort that the commonality of doubt betrays the fact that *no one* wholeheartedly believes in God.

Both reactions are extreme. We can more reasonably address doubt by (1) acknowledging that some amount of doubt is normal, (2) discussing why doubt arises, and (3) evaluating what to do with doubt.

Doubt Is Normal

One of the most difficult aspects of having doubt about our faith is feeling that we're somehow abnormal—that if we experience doubt, we're not a "real" Christian. But doubt is actually a normal part of faith. When we don't have certainty about something, there is always room for doubt. For example, we can be confident that an airplane will safely deliver us to our destination, but we can't be certain of that, so some doubt should necessarily exist. Skeptics who claim that the commonality of spiritual doubt somehow demonstrates that people don't really believe in God are ignoring this everyday reality. Skeptics should doubt their skepticism as well.

The Bible itself reveals the normality of doubt. One of my favorite examples is from Luke 7. John the Baptist had been passionately preaching in the wilderness of Judea about the need for people to repent. He survived on a diet of locusts and honey, baptized scores of people, and preached the coming of Jesus. This was a man convicted of his beliefs. But when he was eventually imprisoned for condemning the immoral actions of Herod Antipas, he began to have doubt. He sent two of his disciples to ask Jesus, "Are you the one who is to come, or should we expect someone else?" (v. 20). Jesus replied, "Go back and report to John what you have seen and heard: The blind receive sight, the lame walk, those who have leprosy are cleansed, the deaf hear, the dead are raised, and the good news is proclaimed to the poor" (v. 22). Jesus didn't criticize John for having doubt. Instead, he confirmed that he was, indeed, the Messiah.

Jesus's disciple Thomas also had doubt. After spending years learning from Jesus and witnessing his miracles, Thomas still doubted the initial reports of Jesus's resurrection. He said, "Unless I see the nail marks in his hands and put my finger where the nails were, and put my hand into his side, I will not believe" (John 20:25). A week later, Jesus appeared to Thomas and said, "Put your finger here; see my hands. Reach out your hand and put it into my side. Stop doubting and believe" (v. 27). Again, Jesus didn't criticize Thomas for his doubt—he provided the evidence Thomas needed to believe.

Still, the fact that doubt is normal doesn't necessarily mean it's a good thing. In some cases, it *can* be a good thing, such as when dealing with the questions that led to doubt results in a more convicted faith. But doubt isn't something we should celebrate. Jesus spoke on several occasions about how doubt can hinder our spiritual lives (Matt. 14:31; 21:21; Mark 11:23; Luke 24:38). When we experience doubt, we must recognize it as something that requires our attention and not let it passively snowball to a point where our faith is destroyed by an avalanche of uncertainty.

So how do we give doubt our attention? It depends on the *kind* of doubt we experience.

Three Kinds of Doubt

New Testament scholar Gary Habermas, in his book *Dealing with Doubt*, identifies three types of spiritual doubt people experience: factual, emotional, and volitional.[2] These distinctions can help us understand why doubt arises in the first place and what to do about it.

1. Factual Doubt

Factual doubt is doubt about the evidence for God's existence and/or the truth of Christianity. I know a young Christian who was an undergraduate student taking a humanities class. He shared online that, so far in the semester, he'd "learned" that Jesus never claimed to be God, Christianity borrowed ideas from earlier pagan myths, and the church arbitrarily picked which books to include in the Bible. He noted that the other students reacted in shock and disbelief. When a professor asked one student how these facts made her feel, she said she was going to give her parents and pastor a piece of her mind.

As we've discussed, kids today are being presented with volumes of conflicting information online, in the media, and in classrooms. Factual doubt will inevitably arise when a person, like this student, faces an abundance of information without the preparation needed to accurately evaluate it.

How, then, should we respond when factual doubt arises?

- *Make sure the doubt is truly factual in nature.* Oftentimes, people claim they doubt God because of facts, but in reality, they have a bigger emotional or volitional objection to God. As we'll see, those kinds of doubt require a different response.
- *Identify root question(s).* Factual doubt usually manifests itself in many questions at one time. For example, many people have a long list of "why would God . . ." questions.

But often at the root of them all is a single nagging feeling that if we don't understand God, he must not really exist. In such a case, it's often best to study the evidence for God's existence rather than dive into answers for every individual question. Once we're fully convicted of God's existence, we can come back to individual questions with a fresh look.

- *Seek answers from trustworthy sources.* Googling "Does God exist?" results in over seven million webpage results. But reading the thoughts of some guy in the corner of the internet is hardly going to convince us that our "research" was trustworthy and our doubt should go away. There are millions of pages of *mis*information that will exacerbate our doubt without good reason. We need to be intentional in selecting resources written by experts in the area of interest (for both Christian and opposing views).

2. Emotional Doubt

Emotional doubt is doubt that arises because our feelings about God can fluctuate due to life circumstances. The comment at the beginning of this chapter is an example of such doubt. This person had a strong faith, and then suddenly and without warning he started questioning everything and wanted a sign from God. He wasn't presented with information that shook him—he just started *feeling* differently. As he himself acknowledged, this kind of doubt most commonly arises when we encounter hard times and are tempted to ask, "How can God exist when all this bad stuff is happening?" Emotional doubt is an unwanted feeling that can come upon us suddenly in both good times and bad.

What can we do when emotional doubt arises?

- *Pray and read the Bible.* With any kind of doubt, it's important to read God's Word and pray for his help in our struggles.

But this is especially the case with emotional doubt because the feeling of distance from God is often the result of not reading the Bible and praying in the first place—two of the spiritual activities most central to the life of a believer.

- *Revisit the objective evidence for God's existence . . . or learn about it for the first time.* Most people come to believe in God based on experiences rather than any kind of study of the evidence for his existence. When emotional doubt sets in, they have no objective evidence to counter their subjective feelings so that they can say, "Well, I don't *feel* like God is there, but I *know* he's there because [the kinds of evidence we discussed in part 1]." During difficult times, the objective evidence for God's existence can serve as an intellectual anchor in an emotional storm.

3. Volitional Doubt

Volitional doubt arises when our will conflicts with God's will—we, effectively, are choosing to doubt. When this is the case, there's often sin in our lives that we don't want to acknowledge as sin, and we begin to question God because of it. A teenager, for example, may reject God because they're engaging in sexual sin and don't want to believe it's wrong. For this reason, most people won't admit that their doubt about God is volitional in nature—they usually claim their doubt is factual. How can we tell the difference? People who sincerely have questions about the facts tend to have their doubt satisfied after exploring answers. People with volitional doubt tend to raise a new question for every question answered, as if they don't *want* to resolve their doubt.

How should we handle volitional doubt?

- *Recognize that doubt is rarely neutral.* We typically doubt *toward* God (wanting to believe) or *away* from God (not wanting to believe).[3] If we're doubting away from God, it's important to consider why. Understanding the underlying reason why we don't want to believe in God—regardless of any evidence—should make us really think about whether our doubt is well-founded.

- *Study why there's good reason to believe the Bible is really God's Word.* Because volitional doubt is typically rooted in a desire to live in a way that conflicts with what the Bible says, the core issue is whether the Bible is actually God's Word. If it's not, there's no objective reason why we shouldn't carry on however we want. But if it is, we're confronted with the fact that what the Bible says has bearing on our lives—there's a moral authority to whom we have a moral obligation, whether *we* feel something should be considered sinful or not.[4]

Few people are happy when doubt creeps in, and for some, the situation can feel devastating. But when we stop to identify the nature of our doubt, we can address it in a God-honoring way that actually deepens our faith for the future.

KEY POINTS

- Doubt is normal—even John the Baptist and the disciple Thomas doubted.
- Doubt can be good if we deal with it appropriately and allow it to lead us into a deeper faith. But left unattended, doubt can snowball into a spiritually dangerous outcome.
- *How* we should give doubt our attention depends on the type of doubt we have: factual, emotional, or volitional.
- Factual doubt is doubt about the evidence for God's existence and/or the truth of Christianity.

- Emotional doubt is doubt that arises because our feelings about God can fluctuate with life circumstances.
- Volitional doubt is doubt that arises when our will is in conflict with God's will—we are choosing to doubt.

CONVERSATION GUIDE

Open the Conversation

- Do you think it's common or unusual for Christians to go through periods of time when they doubt that God exists? Why? *(Use this as an opportunity to acknowledge that some amount of doubt is normal anytime we lack absolute certainty about something—skeptics should doubt too. Share the stories of John the Baptist and Thomas.)*
- Have you ever doubted that God exists? Why or why not?

Advance the Conversation

- Do you think having doubt about your faith is a good thing, bad thing, or both? Why? *(Discuss your child's answer, then talk about the good and bad aspects from this chapter.)*
- What do you think are some reasons why people sometimes have doubt about their faith? *(Write down your child's reasons for use with the next question.)*
- There are three kinds of doubt people sometimes have: factual, emotional, and volitional. *(Explain what each is using the information from this chapter.)* Think back to the reasons you just gave for why people have doubt. Are those reasons factual, emotional, or volitional? Why?
- If you were having factual doubt, what do you think would be good ways and bad ways to handle it? *(Talk about the*

points from this chapter. For extended conversation, have a similar discussion about emotional and volitional doubt.)

Apply the Conversation

- A Christian commented online, "I feel that I've lost all ground and have spiraled out of control with fear, doubt, and confusion. Why is someone believing in Islam (or any other religion) wrong, and why am I right? I have always felt that Christianity was right because it confirmed my sense of compassion and goodness, but what if my sense of 'goodness' is just from my personal morality I've built thus far? How do I really know it's right?"[5] What kind of doubt is this person having? What would you recommend she do?

23. How Do We Know God Hears and Answers Prayers?

When my kids were toddlers, we had a treadmill in our garage. Despite our many warnings never to touch it, curiosity got the best of my son one day. He snuck into the garage, stepped onto the treadmill, and hit the start button. The treadmill immediately ramped up to running speed and threw my son against the wall. His legs got stuck in the small space between the wall and the treadmill, and he couldn't escape. The treadmill kept running, creating so much friction against my son's legs that he ended up with second-degree burns before we were able to rescue him.

After a long day at the hospital, we were ready to tuck the kids into bed for the night. We all got together and prayed that God would heal my son's wounds and relieve his suffering. The next night the family gathered to pray for him again. But before we could, my daughter asked, "Why didn't God answer our prayer yesterday? The wounds are still there."

I'll never forget that question. As adults, when we pray something like, "Please heal these burn wounds," we don't expect the wounds to disappear the next day. But why not? Why don't we have the expectation that God will answer prayers in such a clear, immediate way? Do we as adults simply temper our prayer expectations based on experience in a way that kids haven't yet learned to? And if so, what does this say about the legitimacy of believing there's a God who truly hears and answers prayers?

These questions haven't been lost on skeptics. For example, a popular atheist website called Why Won't God Heal Amputees? focuses on this challenge (whywontgodhealamputees.com). It attacks the idea that God exists based on the alleged lack of examples in which God answers prayers in a clear, undeniable way—like making an amputated limb grow back.

An important starting point for a discussion about how we know God hears and answers prayers is what we learned in part 1: there's compelling evidence that a universe-creating, life-designing, and moral-lawgiving God exists, and this evidence doesn't depend on whether God hears and answers prayers. If God doesn't respond to prayers in certain ways, or in any way at all, it doesn't follow that God must not exist. At most, a skeptic of *Christianity* can question whether our human experience with prayer is consistent with what the *Bible* says about prayer. If the Bible makes claims about prayer that we don't see fulfilled, skeptics can rightly question the legitimacy of those claims.

With that in mind, let's look at what, exactly, the Bible says about prayer.

How Do We Know God *Hears* Prayers?

There's no way to look at the world around us and conclude that the God who created it hears our prayers. Those who believe God has revealed himself in the Bible, however, can turn to Scripture for that information, and the Bible clearly says God is listening when we pray:

- "The LORD is far from the wicked, but he hears the prayer of the righteous" (Prov. 15:29).
- "If my people, who are called by my name, will humble themselves and pray and seek my face and turn from their wicked ways, then I will hear from heaven, and I will forgive their sin and will heal their land" (2 Chron. 7:14).
- "We know that God does not listen to sinners. He listens to the godly person who does his will" (John 9:31).
- "For the eyes of the Lord are on the righteous and his ears are attentive to their prayer, but the face of the Lord is against those who do evil" (1 Pet. 3:12).

Note that these verses connect God's hearing of prayers with the righteousness of the person praying. This doesn't mean God isn't *aware* of the prayers of the unrighteous but that the presence of unrepentant sin in our lives can be a barrier to God *considering* our prayers. This leads us to the next question.

How Do We Know God *Answers* Prayers?

Once again, let's look at what the Bible says:

- "If you, then, though you are evil, know how to give good gifts to your children, how much more will your Father in heaven give good gifts to those who ask him!" (Matt. 7:11).
- "Therefore I tell you, whatever you ask for in prayer, believe that you have received it, and it will be yours" (Mark 11:24).
- "So I say to you: Ask and it will be given to you; seek and you will find; knock and the door will be opened to you" (Luke 11:9).

- "Until now you have not asked for anything in my name. Ask and you will receive, and your joy will be complete" (John 16:24).

No one who trusts that the Bible is God's Word should wonder if God truly answers prayers. These and many other verses explicitly state he does. But we also know from personal experience that God doesn't answer all prayers in the way we hope. And when we experience the disappointment of unanswered prayers, it can lead us to question the Bible's promises. To avoid this uncertainty, we need a foundational understanding of why some prayers are not answered.

In Mark 11:24, Jesus said that *whatever* we ask for will be ours, but it doesn't take much to show that he didn't *literally* mean "whatever." There must be at least some qualification to "whatever" in order for God to be consistent with his nature. The Bible lists several reasons why God sometimes says no:

- We *have unrepentant sin in our lives* (see the verses listed previously under "How Do We Know God Hears Prayers?").
- We're *asking for something not good for us*: "Which of you, if your son asks for bread, will give him a stone? Or if he asks for a fish, will give him a snake?" (Matt. 7:9–10).
- We *have selfish motives*: "When you ask, you do not receive, because you ask with wrong motives, that you may spend what you get on your pleasures" (James 4:3).
- We're *asking for something not in line with God's will*: "This is the confidence we have in approaching God: that if we ask anything *according to his will*, he hears us" (1 John 5:14, emphasis mine).

Most of us have no trouble accepting the first three points and can identify when, perhaps, these are the problems with our prayers. But the last one can be challenging. At times we pray for something and can't imagine how it would *not* be God's will to respond in the way we hope. For example, anyone who has prayed desperately for God to heal a loved one, only to see that person die, knows how difficult it can be to find comfort in the cold, intellectual fact that healing "just wasn't God's will" in that case. When we're hurting, we want to know *why* something was or wasn't his will. But the difficult reality is that we can't know, given our limited perspective.

Nowhere is this clearer than in Luke 22:42, when Jesus himself faced the gruesome prospect of death on the cross. He prayed, "Father, if you are willing, take this cup from me; yet not my will, but yours be done." His prayer request was not granted. It was the Father's will, instead, that humanity be saved through Jesus's sacrifice on the cross. What seemed like the ultimate prayer denial turned out to be for the ultimate good of humankind.

Similarly, we can be confident that God will respond to *our* prayer requests by answering in the way that is best in view of eternity, but that doesn't mean the answers will always look like what's best in the present.

But What about Amputees?

Let's conclude by returning to the question of why God doesn't heal amputees. Recall that the core question identified earlier was whether our human experience with prayer is consistent with what the Bible says. So what have we learned the Bible says? God answers prayers, but there are many reasons why he doesn't answer all prayers in the way we'd like. The question of why God doesn't heal amputees is no different from numerous other questions we could ask: Why doesn't God answer a prayer for a million dollars to instantly appear in a person's front yard? Why doesn't God answer a child's prayer to fly like a bird? Why doesn't God answer a prayer for a child's burn wounds to heal immediately rather than gradually? If we know from the Bible that God doesn't answer *all* prayers, we logically can't look at the outcome of any *particular* prayer to determine whether God *ever* answers prayers. What we're looking at may be one of many examples of requests that God, in his wisdom, does not grant.

A lack of certain prayer outcomes is not inconsistent with the Bible. *What would be inconsistent with the Bible is if God never answered prayers.*

But millions of people throughout history have claimed they've received answers to prayers. Today, according to Pew Research, almost one-third of Americans say their prayers result in "definite and specific answers from God" *at least once a month*, with almost one in five adults saying they receive direct answers to specific requests at least once a week.[1] While a skeptic might claim every single one of these millions of people is mistaken every single time, *that's* a belief worth being skeptical about.

There's no way for Christians to prove God answers prayers, just as there's no way for a skeptic to prove God *doesn't* answer prayers. But if (1) there's good reason to believe God exists (as we saw in part 1), (2) the Bible claims God answers some but not all prayers, and (3) it's the overwhelming experience of Christians that God does, indeed, answer prayers on a regular basis, then the (possible) fact that God doesn't heal amputees has no logical bearing on the truth status of Christianity. It's a theologically shallow question rooted in a misguided understanding of what the Bible actually says.

KEY POINTS

- The Bible explicitly states in many places that God both hears and answers prayers.

- The Bible doesn't say God will answer all prayers in the way we hope. We can't always know *why* it isn't God's will to grant a given prayer request, but we can be confident that God will answer in the way that is best in view of eternity.
- If we know from the Bible that God doesn't answer *all* prayers, we logically can't look at the outcome of any *particular* prayer request to determine whether God *ever* answers prayers. What we're looking at may be one of many examples of requests that God, in his wisdom, does not grant.
- What would be inconsistent with the Bible is if God never answered prayers, but this would be contrary to the experience of millions of people throughout history.
- In light of these points, questions like "Why won't God heal amputees?" are inconsequential.

CONVERSATION GUIDE

Open the Conversation

- All Christians have some prayers answered in the way they hope and others that are not. What are some examples of answered prayers in your life? What are some examples of unanswered prayers?

Advance the Conversation

- Read Mark 11:24. Jesus said *whatever* we ask for we'll receive. Yet we know there are certain prayer requests God would never grant. What are some examples you can think of? *(Discuss your child's examples, and explain that Jesus's use of the word whatever must be understood in the context of God's character and other Bible verses. Read the verses about unrepentant sin, asking for things that aren't good for us, having selfish motives, and praying in line with God's will as additional examples.)*

- Think again about the unanswered prayers you've experienced. Do any of the reasons we just discussed explain why your prayers were unanswered? Why or why not? *(Discuss the fact that we can't always understand why answering a specific prayer is or isn't God's will, so we have to trust in his eternal perspective. Give the example of Jesus's unanswered prayer request.)*

- If you knew that people throughout history have prayed to grow wings and be able to fly and that this prayer has never been answered, would you question whether God exists? Why or why not? *(Explain that God's existence is independent of how he interacts with prayers. Discuss how we can't look at the outcome of any particular prayer request to determine whether God ever answers prayers. Share the statistics of people who say they experience answered prayers every week/month. For older kids, tie the discussion to the question of amputees in particular.)*

Apply the Conversation

- In response to a survey asking people to explain in their own words why they left Christianity, one respondent said it was in part because "prayer never worked for me."[2] If you could talk to this person about their comment, what questions would you ask to better understand what they mean? What are some key points from this chapter you might share?

24. How Can We Develop a Relationship with a God We Can't See or Hear?

A few years ago, we attended a church with a large and vibrant children's program. The Sunday school classes often put on performances for the congregation. One song the kids sang regularly was called "I Am a Friend of God." They would enthusiastically jump up and down during the chorus, gesturing to symbolize their close friendship with Jesus.

One Sunday after such a performance, I ran into a friend who was perturbed by the whole thing.

"Are we really *friends* with God? I don't know what to make of that," he said.

"What do you mean? Kids shouldn't think they're friends with God?" I asked.

"It's just kind of weird. I mean, God is God and we are creatures. We aren't really *friends*. I think it's kind of misleading."

"Well, we *are* supposed to have a relationship with God. I think that's what they're trying to teach them. Stop being a theological curmudgeon."

Despite my attempt to dismiss my friend's concerns, I looked into the subject when we got home. I quickly realized that all commentary on this topic leads back to Jesus's words in John 15:13–15:

> Greater love has no one than this: to lay down one's life for one's friends. You are my friends if you do what I command. I no longer call you servants, because a servant does not know his master's business. Instead, I have called you friends, for everything that I learned from my Father I have made known to you.

Here we can see that Jesus does, indeed, say we are friends. Yet something about this "friendship" signals that it's different from what we experience with our earthly friends. Jesus says, "You are my friends *if you do what I command*." That's quite different from the nature of human friendships. Can you imagine how your friends would respond if you laid down this criterion for friendship?

And let's not ignore the other obvious difference: Jesus is a friend we can't physically see or hear.

Yet millions of kids are told each week that they need to have a relationship with God, as if that's the most natural thing in the world. If we want our kids to have a relationship with God—as we should—they're going to need more guidance than simply hearing that Jesus is their friend. Let's take a look at how we can help our children understand (1) how God speaks to us and (2) how we can respond.

Hearing from God

Today, God's primary way of communicating with us is through the Bible.[1] If we want a close relationship with him, we start by reading and listening to what he has said. Unfortunately, many Christians don't take this to heart. Research shows that only 45 percent of those who regularly attend church read the Bible more than once a week. Over 40 percent say they read the Bible occasionally—once or twice a month. And almost one in five say they never read the Bible.[2] These are tragic statistics, considering the importance of Bible reading in developing a relationship with God.

Many Christians, however, don't think of reading the Bible as something relational in nature. They see the Bible as static information rather than God's living Word. But Hebrews 4:12 tells us, "The word of God is alive and active. Sharper than any double-edged sword, it penetrates even to dividing soul and spirit, joints and marrow; it judges the thoughts and attitudes of the heart." In addition, Romans 10:17 says, "Faith comes from hearing the message, and the message is heard through the word about Christ." Note that it doesn't say, "Faith comes from having a Bible on your nightstand." In order to have a relationship with God, we have to live in a way that allows us to continually hear God's message—we have to read the Bible. And as Hebrews 4:12 makes clear, this is not a onetime event. God's Word continually works through us.

More specifically, reading the Bible facilitates a relationship with God in four important ways:

1. *We learn about who God is.* Just as we develop relationships with other humans by getting to know who they are, we develop a relationship with God by getting to know who he is. Throughout the Bible, we learn about God's attributes (see chap. 13), which leads us to the necessary knowledge of his identity. We need this biblically accurate understanding of who God is in order to have an authentic relationship with him.

2. *We learn about what God has done.* The God of the Bible is not a remote God who created the universe and stepped

away. He's been active throughout the history of the world. In the Old Testament, we see how he worked through his chosen people to reveal himself to the world and ultimately bring forth our Savior, Jesus. In the New Testament, we see how he offered us salvation through Jesus's sacrifice on the cross and how he guided the growth of the early church. Understanding what God has done is another important part of getting to know who he is and what his purposes are for humankind.

3. *We learn about who we are in relation to God.* There's an inherent hierarchy in our relationship with God. We aren't buddies on equal ground, and this necessarily colors how we relate to each other. An obvious example of a relational hierarchy is that between parents and kids. As much as our kids may like to say they can do whatever they want and assert their independence, the reality is that they depend on us while they are young. When they don't respect the relationship and live in rebellion, they can bring great harm to themselves. Similarly, when we don't have a proper respect for who we are in relation to God and try to live outside his boundaries, we put ourselves in spiritual danger. By reading the Bible regularly, we remain mindful that God is God and we are not.

4. *We learn about God's deep love for us.* A close relationship with our children requires that they know how much we love them. A relationship without love is only a cold association. Just as our kids long to know we love them, we long to know God loves us. God tells us he loves us in Scripture. And not just in a couple of verses. The Bible is a love story from beginning to end—God created us, pursued us, saved us, and made a way for us to be with him forever. If we want to be assured that we're in a loving relationship with our heavenly Father, we have to read the Bible.

Now that we've seen how God speaks to us, let's look at how we should respond.

Responding to God

When we respond to God, we do so in two primary ways: through our words (prayer) and through our actions (living out our faith).

Words: Prayer

In the previous chapter, we talked about petitionary prayers—prayers in which we make requests. But petition is not the only or even the primary purpose of prayer. Prayer is ultimately about nurturing our relationship with God. We won't have much of a relationship with someone if all we ever do is ask that person for what we want from him or her, and it's no different with God.

Perhaps this is why Jesus modeled for us how we should pray:

> Our Father in heaven, hallowed be your name, your kingdom come, your will be done, on earth as it is in heaven. Give us today our daily bread. And forgive us our debts, as we also have forgiven our debtors. And lead us not into temptation, but deliver us from the evil one. (Matt. 6:9–13)

In the Lord's Prayer, we see the necessity of adoration ("hallowed be your name"), confession ("forgive us our debts"), and petition ("deliver us from the evil one"). Many other Bible verses speak to the additional importance of thanking God in prayer (Col. 4:2; 1 Thess. 5:16–18; Heb. 13:15). The ACTS acronym is a helpful way to remember these core prayer elements: Adoration, Confession, Thanksgiving, and Supplication (supplication is another word for petition). When we pray, we should speak with God in all these ways. If we only make requests, we miss the awestruck humility that comes from expressing adoration, the freedom that comes from confession, and the joy that comes from thanksgiving.

Actions: Living Out Our Faith

When we have a healthy relationship with God, we live out our faith—our actions reflect our love for our Creator. Volumes could be written on this topic, but in the interest of space, we'll highlight three key ways in which we should live out our faith:

1. *We should strive to live a Christlike life.* In Ephesians 5:1, the apostle Paul tells us to be "imitators of God" (ESV). This, of course, is no easy thing. But when we are in Christ, we become a new creation (2 Cor. 5:17) and the Holy Spirit lives within us (Rom. 8:9). The Spirit then bears fruit in our lives—love, joy, peace, patience, kindness, goodness, faithfulness, gentleness, and self-control. Because we still have a sin nature during our earthly existence, we'll never perfectly manifest these fruits. We remain in a struggle against sin, but as Christians, we have God's help to fight it.

2. *We should be part of a church—a body of believers.* Unfortunately, it's become "fashionable" for people today to say they're Christians but don't want to be part of a church. This idea, however, is unbiblical. When we put our faith in Jesus, we become a member of the body of Christ (1 Cor. 12:27). A church body needs all its "parts" to be present and working together in order to function as designed (1 Cor. 12:14–20). When we're part of a body of believers, we're able to teach one another (Rom. 15:14), serve others (both inside and outside the church [Gal. 5:13]), love one another (1 John 4:12), and encourage one another (Heb. 3:13). Given the importance of these things, it should be no surprise that the author of Hebrews explicitly urged early Christians to

"not [give] up meeting together, as some are in the habit of doing" (Heb. 10:25). Part of being in a relationship with God is being in a relationship with other believers—our spiritual brothers and sisters.

3. *We should tell others about Jesus.* When we love someone dearly, we want others to know that person. It's no different with God. Part of the outworking of our relationship with Jesus is that we want others to know him and experience the joy that comes from that relationship. As if that's not reason enough, the Bible calls us to do so as well: "Go and make disciples of all nations, baptizing them in the name of the Father and of the Son and of the Holy Spirit" (Matt. 28:19).

It's easy to lose sight of the fact that our relationship with God is different from all other relationships we experience. But when we acknowledge the differences and teach our kids how to have a healthy relationship with God, we give them a practical faith foundation they'll use for the rest of their lives.

KEY POINTS

- A relationship with God is a key part of a Christian's life, but we should never take it for granted that others (including our kids) understand what that means.
- Our primary way of hearing from God is by reading the Bible. In doing so, we develop a relationship with him by learning (1) who God is, (2) what God has done, (3) who we are in relation to God, and (4) how deeply God loves us.
- We respond to God through our words (prayer) and through our actions (living out our faith).

- A healthy prayer life should include Adoration, Confession, Thanksgiving, and Supplication (ACTS).
- When we have a healthy relationship with God, we live out our faith—our actions reflect our love for our Creator. Among other things, such actions include living a Christlike life, being part of a church, and telling others about Jesus.

CONVERSATION GUIDE

Open the Conversation

- What do you think it means to have a relationship with Jesus? *(Acknowledge that a relationship with Jesus is quite different from a relationship with another human being.)*
- Do you feel like you have a relationship with Jesus? Why or why not?

Advance the Conversation

- The most important way God speaks to us is through the Bible. How do you think reading the Bible develops your relationship with God? *(Discuss the four things highlighted in this chapter and why each is important for relationship building.)*
- One way we respond to God is through prayer. In the previous chapter, we talked about petitionary prayers, in which we ask God for things. But prayer should be more than making requests. What are some other important parts of prayer? *(Read the Lord's Prayer, then introduce the ACTS acronym.)*
- Another key way we respond to God is by living out our faith—our actions should reflect our love for our Creator. What are some ways Christians can do that? *(Discuss living a Christlike life, being part of a church, and telling others about Jesus.)*

Apply the Conversation

- An atheist group put up a billboard that says, "God is an imaginary friend. Choose reality, it will be better for all of us."[3] If someone said this to you and asked how you can have a relationship with someone you can't see or hear, what would you say?

PART 5

The Difference God MAKES

Overview

During vacation Bible school one summer, our church collected an offering to help an orphanage in Mexico. The kids were encouraged to bring what they could to contribute to the cause.

The morning after the collection was announced, my daughter came running down the stairs with a ziplock bag of piggy bank money. I smiled with appreciation for her giving heart and told her, "I'm so proud of you. You always want to share what you have with others. That's wonderful, sweetheart."

She looked at me, gave a slight shrug, and replied, "It's just money I had in my piggy bank. It doesn't really matter."

My blood immediately went to a rolling boil. I have worked really hard to teach my kids the value of money and to emphasize how grateful we need to be for every small thing we have. I couldn't believe her attitude.

"You have got to be kidding me. I seriously can't believe you just said that when we have talked so much about gratitude and generosity. That's several dollars you have in that bag! How can you say it doesn't matter?"

She looked down at the bag, which held two dollar bills and many coins. Then she looked at me in confusion and said, "Mommy, this is not several dollars. This is two dollars and some change that doesn't matter."

I took the bag and dumped everything out on the floor, then made piles of four quarters each. I counted it all up and told her she had $8.36.

She was shocked.

She scooped up the bills and coins, promptly put them back in the bag, and announced there was no way she was giving away $8.36. Before I could launch into a sermon on generosity, she was halfway up the stairs, on her way to deposit her newly found riches.

I've reflected several times since then on what it means to accurately value something. There was $8.36 in that bag before and after our conversation. But something happened that drastically changed the value my daughter assigned to it—to the point that I couldn't pry the money out of her hands just a few minutes later.

When kids grow up in a Christian home, they can take their beliefs for granted, believing that Christianity is true but not fully understanding its *value* for everyday life. This was certainly the case for me as a kid. I spent hundreds of hours in church, but when I left home, I didn't know what to do with my faith, other than continue to wear the Christian label and bide my time as a good person until I was beamed up to heaven someday. Those hundreds of hours hadn't taught me what it meant to see *all* of life differently than someone who wasn't a Christian; I had no idea what it meant to have a Christian worldview—a biblically coherent understanding of life.

That fact eventually affected me spiritually. Not long after I left home, I discovered the bestselling novel *The Celestine Prophecy*. This book promotes non-Christian ideas rooted in New Age spirituality, but I quickly became enamored with it, telling all my friends they just *had* to read it. I started paying attention to how the book's insights applied to my everyday life . . . and suddenly felt life was more meaningful.

My faith was so shallow that the first exciting philosophy I encountered after high school swept me off my feet. It never occurred to me that my Christian beliefs should have immediately rendered these New Age ideas false. Sadly, I felt I understood more about the meaning of life from *The Celestine Prophecy* than I did from my time in church.

In this final section, we'll look at six critically important questions that affect our everyday lives—What is the meaning of life? Do we really have free will? What should we do with our lives? What is our responsibility to other people? How should we make sense of evil? Why does biblical hope matter?—and see how the answers differ between the perspectives of an atheistic worldview and a theistic worldview.

These conversations will show kids why it doesn't work to mix and match worldviews—the meaning of life, for example, isn't up for grabs between God and the author of *The Celestine Prophecy*. When they have the opportunity to consider the profound differences a worldview makes for everyday life, kids learn to value their faith in a new way. Like my daughter clutching her newly treasured $8.36, they'll understand why they need to hold on to their faith—and never let go.

Three Keys to Impactful Conversations about the Difference God Makes

1. *Introduce this section by explaining the shift to questions about how we live our daily lives.* Many kids have never considered just how much a belief in God should impact their lives. They think of Christianity more in terms of what happens after they die than in terms of how to live on Earth. As you prepare your kids for these conversations, acknowledge that many people—both children and adults—think this

way but that our faith has numerous implications for our earthly lives. Explain that in this final section we're moving from conversations on *knowing* truth to conversations on *applying* truth.

2. *Emphasize the importance of living consistently within a worldview and explain that many people do not.* Even though a worldview should affect a person's answers to the above six questions, people often don't live consistently within their beliefs. Atheists, for instance, often acknowledge that evil exists in the world and live accordingly, but they don't have an objective basis for calling anything evil (see chap. 29). The chapters draw out this point, but make sure not to miss it in your conversations.

3. *Talk to your kids about what they want to learn next.* We've covered a lot of ground in this book—but don't stop here! When you get to the end, talk with your kids to decide what to learn next. Ask them (1) Which subjects did you find most interesting? (2) Which subjects did you find least interesting? and (3) Which subjects would you like to know more about? Use their answers to make a game plan for your continued conversations. If you've made it this far, you've got momentum. Don't stop now.

25. What Is the Meaning of Life?

When I was in high school, I was one of four girls taking an advanced physics class with about thirty boys. We girls were spread throughout the room, so each of us sat surrounded by our male classmates. This, of course, is a high school recipe for teasing.

In my case, the teasing was religion-based. The boys who sat around me all happened to be atheists. Anytime I would mention church, youth group, or God in general, they would all snicker and reply, "No! The meaning of life is forty-two!"

I had no idea what that meant, but they thought it was just *so* clever. They would laugh hysterically at their inside joke.

Eventually, someone let me in on the joke. In Douglas Adams's science fiction classic *The Hitchhiker's Guide to the Galaxy*, the number forty-two is the "Answer to the Ultimate Question of Life, the Universe, and Everything."[1] This number was calculated by a supercomputer over a period of 7.5 million years. The computer, however, points out that the answer is meaningless because the beings that programmed it never knew what the question was.

My classmates had been referring to the atheist's "answer to the universe": our existence is as objectively meaningless as the number forty-two. Though I doubt they understood why at the time, they were right about the implications of atheism. If God doesn't exist, there can be no objective meaning to life. People can create their *own* meaning, but there's no meaning that applies to all people. A belief that the meaning of life is to love others can be no more legitimate than a belief that the meaning of life is to watch television and eat bonbons all day.

In a theistic worldview, however, things look much different. If there's a God who created the universe and life with a purpose and imbued his creation with value, then there's an objective meaning to life that exists independently of our choosing—meaning that is to be discovered, not created.

In this chapter, we'll dig deeper into the contrast between an atheistic worldview and a theistic worldview to see how a person's view of God fundamentally drives his or her view of the meaning of life—and how we, as Christians, should live in light of this fact.

The Meaning of Life—without God

In an atheistic worldview, the universe and everything in it developed by strictly natural forces; there's no creative or sustaining intelligence behind the universe and no ultimate reason for its existence. It just *is*. And it follows that life within such a world has no special value. To understand why, let's recount how atheists say life unfolded.

Atheists believe the universe sprang into existence about 13.7 billion years ago with no intelligent cause behind it. Eventually, about 4.5 billion years ago, the Earth formed, and 0.5 billion years later, the first life developed by chance from nonliving matter. As life continued to reproduce, random changes (called mutations) occurred in DNA. Some of these mutations offered an advantage to their organisms, leading to improved survival and reproduction. When the organisms with the beneficial mutations no longer reproduced with the original population, a new species came into existence. Over billions of years, this process created every species on Earth. All of this happened with no guiding intelligence. Humans just happened to be one of many evolutionary products.

Without assessing the truth of this account, we can note two important implications of it.

First, what we call life is nothing more than a bunch of molecules in motion. Nothing exists apart from the basic matter of which we—and everything else in the universe—are comprised. Famed astronomer Carl Sagan, who believed the cosmos is "all that is or ever was or ever will be,"[2] acknowledged this implication while downplaying its significance:

> I am a collection of water, calcium and organic molecules called Carl Sagan. You are a collection of almost identical molecules with a different collective label. But is that all? Is there nothing in here but molecules? Some people find this idea somehow demeaning to human dignity. For myself, I find it elevating that our universe permits the evolution of molecular machines as intricate and subtle as we.[3]

While an atheist may marvel at the beauty of our identity as "molecular machines," it's hard to ignore the fact that in a world without God, we're . . . "machines." Marvel all you want, but that's a difficult pill for most people to swallow. We certainly feel like much more than machines. This idea counters our deepest human intuition.

Second, there's no objective meaning to life. If there's no author of life, then there's no one with the authority to say, "This is what life is all about." Many people are enamored with this thought; they don't *want* someone telling them what to make of their lives. They want to create their own meaning and often vigorously defend the idea that self-defined meaning is a beautiful—even preferable—thing. For example, one of the highest grossing publishing projects ever on the funding website Kickstarter was a book called *A Better Life: 100 Atheists Speak Out on Joy & Meaning in a World without God*. Christians often think that atheists can't claim there's *any* meaning to their lives, but that's not accurate, as the contributors to this book are eager to point out. Remember what we noted earlier: in a world without God, there can be no *objective* meaning that applies to all people, but people can create *subjective* meaning for themselves. The question is, however, how meaningful can subjective meaning be? This is an important question we'll return to after looking at the meaning of life *with* God.

The Meaning of Life—with God

In a theistic worldview, life is the product of purposeful intelligence. All living things were meant to be here—no cosmic accidents involved. And the author of life who purposefully created us has the authority to tell us the objective meaning behind our existence. For Christians, this meaning is revealed in the Bible, and a biblical worldview has two key implications for this discussion.

First, life is precious. One of the first things the Bible tells us is that God created humankind—and only humankind—in his image (Gen. 1:26). We're spiritual beings capable of knowing God and having a relationship with him that lasts forever. We're not just molecules labeled in a special way. We're the product of God's handiwork and the pinnacle of creation. This means there's a significant difference between humans and animals, and between life and nonliving matter.

Second, our existence has objective meaning. In a Christian worldview, because there's a Creator of life, he—and only he—can say what the meaning is behind his creation. While no verse in the Bible explicitly says, "The meaning of life is . . . ," a good summary of Scripture would be, "The meaning of life is to know God and make him known." In John 17:3, Jesus prayed, "Now this is eternal life: that they know you, the only true God, and Jesus Christ, whom you have sent." This is a powerful statement about the meaning of our existence—we are to know God, which ultimately leads to eternal life. But that's not all. We also have a responsibility to share this knowledge with others so that they too can have eternal life. In Matthew 28:19–20, Jesus says, "Therefore go and make disciples of all nations, baptizing them in the name of the Father and of the Son and of the Holy Spirit, and teaching them to obey everything I have commanded you." In a Christian worldview, the meaning of our existence is knowing God and making him known, whether individuals choose to acknowledge it or not.

The Difference God Makes

So what difference does a belief in God, and more specifically, the Christian God, make in how a person sees the meaning of his or her life? All the difference in the world. From a Christian perspective, human lives are meant to be shaped around knowing God and making him known, and when we don't live in this way, it leads to a feeling of emptiness. God has set eternity in our hearts (Eccles. 3:11), so when we're not living in light of our true meaning, we *know* we're missing something, even if we haven't yet figured out what it is. When we live to know God and to make him known, however, we're fulfilled and can find true and lasting joy.

Recall that in a world without God, there's no objective meaning to life; individuals can only craft their own meaning. While on the surface that may sound like an exciting prospect, we should stop to ask how meaningful such meaning can ever be. Without God, we're just chemical specks in a vast, indifferent universe. We can choose to find meaning in saving the endangered hawksbill turtle, but, ultimately, the hawksbill turtle is just molecules in motion like every other living thing. So why bother? We can choose to find meaning in art, but scientists say the sun will eventually explode and swallow the Earth. If that's the case, do paint patterns on canvas really matter? We can choose to find meaning in ending human suffering, but if humans have no more inherent value than rocks, why not just *end* those lives instead?

That's not being overly dramatic. We're merely taking a world without God to its natural conclusions. Christian apologist and author Gregory Koukl, in *The Story of Reality: How the World Began, How It Ends, and Everything Important that Happens in Between*, draws this out further:

> We should not be surprised, then, when those who take [the athe-istic] view seriously—if they were brutally honest—are eventually overcome with a gnawing sense of futility. For to take it to its logical and proper conclusion, in the final analysis life is ultimately empty, meaningless, purposeless, cold, and void. Philosophers call this "nihilism," which means "nothing-ism." And when someone starts really believing nothing-ism about themselves and other human beings, bad things begin to happen.[4]

Of course, just because life is devoid of any lasting meaning in a world without God doesn't mean God exists. But there's little reason to *celebrate* the ability to live according to our small, self-defined meanings when, ultimately, such an existence leads to nothingness.

KEY POINTS

- In a world without God, there can be no objective meaning to life. People can create their *own* meaning, but there's no meaning that applies to all people.

- In a Christian worldview, God purposefully created the universe and life and imbued his creation with value. This means there's an objective meaning to life that exists independently of our choosing—meaning that is to be *discovered*, not created.

- According to the Bible, we were made to know God and to make God known. God has set eternity in our hearts, so when we're not living in view of this true meaning, we know we're missing something.

- Without God, we're just chemical specks in a vast, indifferent universe. We might be able to create our own meaning, but such meaning has no lasting value.

CONVERSATION GUIDE

Open the Conversation

- Do you think there's a meaning of life that applies to all people? Why or why not?

Advance the Conversation

- No verse in the Bible says the exact words, "The meaning of life is . . ." But based on what you know about the Bible, what do you think the meaning of life is? *(Discuss how life is precious and has an objective meaning that applies to all people whether they accept it or not—to know God and to make him known.)*

- If God didn't exist, how do you think that would change the meaning of life? *(If there were no God who created life and gave it value and meaning, then there would be no meaning that applied to everyone. Meaning would be whatever each person decided. For older kids, read the account of how atheists say life unfolded for deeper understanding.)*

- How do you think a person's view of the meaning of life affects how they live?

Apply the Conversation

- In an article in which several atheists commented on how they find meaning in life, one said, "I find the fact that there is no external force in charge of us all makes the life we do have much more interesting. We get to derive our meaning, and create our own purpose, and that makes it a much richer experience than playing out pre-written scripts for the amusement of an omniscient almighty. That we all just get one life to live means we don't have the safety net of a do-over, and it makes the time that we do have more meaningful to me."[5] How would you respond?

26. Do We Really Have Free Will?

My husband is the chief operating officer of one of the largest Gospel Rescue Missions in the United States. Since the late 1800s, rescue missions have served people dealing with hunger, homelessness, abuse, and addiction. At the rescue mission where my husband works, those who need help getting off the streets can enter a program for one to two years in which they live at the facility, receive all their meals, get counseling, participate in Bible studies, and receive job and life-skills training. By the time "students" graduate, they're ready to be self-sufficient—and for some, it's the first time in their lives. Countless people have been impacted by rescue missions, as they've changed their ways of thinking, broken strongholds, and decided to give their lives to Jesus.

Underlying the work of rescue missions (and many other charitable organizations) is the assumption that, with the right support, people have the ability to choose a different life direction. But the ability to freely make such a choice shouldn't be taken for granted.

The reality and the meaning of what we commonly call free will depend on whether God exists.

The definition of free will and the extent to which humans have it have been debated by philosophers and scientists for ages. We cannot possibly plumb the depths of the debate here. What we will do, however, is look at free will from the big-picture perspective of what it means to make choices in the context of both an atheistic and a theistic worldview. For our purposes, we'll define free will as the ability to choose a specific course of action from a variety of alternatives.

Free Will—without God

In the previous chapter, we learned that, according to an atheistic worldview, life is the product of purely natural forces. We saw that if we're nothing more than molecules in motion, it follows that (1) life has no special value and (2) life has no objective meaning. It also follows that there's little reason to believe we would have the ability to freely make choices in such a world. If all we are is our biology, then a logical implication is that our decisions are driven by strictly physical impulses—we're bound by the shackles of physical law.

To be sure, few people feel as though this is the reality of their lives. No one sits around waiting to see what their molecules will do next. But atheists who grant there can be no free will in a world without God say this is the reality nonetheless. Consider the following quotes from several well-known atheist scientists:

- Evolutionary biologist Jerry Coyne: "To assert that we can freely choose among alternatives is to claim, then, that we can somehow step outside the physical structure of our brain and change its workings. That is impossible. Like the output of a programmed computer, only one choice is ever physically possible: the one you made."[1]

- Plant biologist Anthony Cashmore: "The reality is, not only do we have no more free will than a fly or a bacterium, in actuality we have no more free will than a bowl of sugar. The laws of nature are uniform throughout, and these laws do not accommodate the concept of free will."[2]
- Molecular biologist Francis Crick: "'You,' your joys and your sorrows, your memories and your ambitions, your sense of personal identity and free will, are in fact no more than the behavior of a vast assembly of nerve cells and their associated molecules."[3]
- Cornell historian of biology William Provine: "It starts by giving up an active deity, then it gives up the hope that there is any life after death. When you give those two up, the rest of it follows fairly easily. You give up the hope that there is an imminent morality. And finally, there's no human free will. If you believe in evolution, you can't hope for there being any free will. There's no hope whatsoever in there being any deep meaning in life."[4]

Although most of us live each day assuming we're freely making choices, these scientists say it's only an illusion. In a purely material world, we cannot escape our biology to make choices other than the ones we made (a view called naturalistic determinism). If that's the case, we can never assign moral responsibility to our actions because those actions were entirely determined by past events. *Blame and praise become meaningless concepts because a person could not have done anything other than what they did.* Just as we wouldn't blame a robot for running over a mouse, we wouldn't blame a human for committing murder—it's just how that person was "programmed" by biology.

It should be noted that some atheists do believe free will is compatible with a purely material world (a view called compatibilism). While we don't have space to discuss the various hypotheses concerning how this could work, these ideas typically involve defining free will in ways other than how we usually think of it. Regardless of the definition, however, if we're only material beings with no souls, there's no objective moral significance to how free or determined our choices are. In a world with no moral authority and no ultimate accountability, our choices are simply a descriptive fact of our existence.

Free Will—with God

In a theistic worldview, we reach very different conclusions about the reality and the extent of free will. More specifically, from a Christian perspective, the Bible teaches that humans have the ability to make choices and are accountable to God for the choices they make.

The following verses, for example, take it as a given that humans have the ability to choose from among various actions:

- "Anyone who chooses to do the will of God will find out whether my teaching comes from God or whether I speak on my own" (John 7:17).
- "No temptation has overtaken you except what is common to mankind. And God is faithful; he will not let you be tempted beyond what you can bear. But when you are tempted, he will also provide a way out so that you can endure it" (1 Cor. 10:13).
- "If anyone, then, knows the good they ought to do and doesn't do it, it is sin for them" (James 4:17).

Furthermore, the Bible is filled with verses that indicate we will be held morally accountable to God for the choices we do make. For example:

- "I tell you that everyone will have to give account on the day of judgment for every empty word they have spoken" (Matt. 12:36).

- "There is a judge for the one who rejects me and does not accept my words; the very words I have spoken will condemn them at the last day" (John 12:48).
- "We will all stand before God's judgment seat.... Then, each of us will give an account of ourselves to God" (Rom. 14:10, 12).
- "We must all appear before the judgment seat of Christ, so that each of us may receive what is due us for the things done while in the body, whether good or bad" (2 Cor. 5:10).

While these and other verses suggest that humans have the ability to make choices and will be held accountable for their actions, Christians have varying views on *how* the human will works within the context of God's sovereignty. The basic question is this: If all things are under God's control (see chap. 13), how can people make free choices? This isn't a purely philosophical question. We see difficult cases in the Bible in which it appears that God *overrides* the human will (for example, Exod. 7:3–4; John 6:44; Rom. 8:29–30; Eph. 1:5, 11). The relationship between God's sovereignty and the human will is the topic of several important theological debates, but, ultimately, God didn't explain the mechanics of that relationship. The Bible clearly teaches both God's sovereignty and humanity's moral responsibility, however, so Christians hold these truths in balance, trusting that the mystery exists because humans lack God's infinite perspective.

The Difference God Makes

While it's difficult (if not impossible) for atheists to reconcile our common intuition concerning free will with a purely material universe, few people live as though they have no control over their choices. Whether they believe in God or not, people normally give significant consideration to their daily behaviors, feeling that they're genuinely deciding what to do in their lives.

For Christians, these choices have great moral significance. Belief in the reality of some degree of free will fundamentally shapes how we live. Questions such as those in the chapters that follow—What should we do with our lives? What is our responsibility to other people? and How should we make sense of evil?—have meaning *because* we presume humans have the ability to make choices that matter. Christians believe programs like those offered through rescue missions are important because people can choose to follow Jesus and turn their lives around, no matter the circumstances that led them to seek help. They're not molecular robots at the mercy of their machinery but invaluable people made in the image of God who can choose to enter into a relationship with their Creator. In a Christian worldview, the most important decision anyone will ever make is how to respond to God. That's a choice that not only matters but also matters for eternity.

KEY POINTS

- In a world without God, there's little reason to believe we would have the ability to freely make choices. If all we are is our biology, then a logical implication is that our decisions are driven by strictly physical impulses over which we have no control.

- In a Christian worldview, humans have the ability to make choices and are morally accountable to God for the choices they make.

- The Bible teaches both God's sovereignty and humanity's moral responsibility, so Christians hold these truths in balance. How they work together is beyond our understanding.

- In a Christian worldview, the most important decision anyone will ever make is how to respond to God.

CONVERSATION GUIDE

Open the Conversation

- Do you think robots and humans make choices in the same way? Why or why not?

Advance the Conversation

- If God didn't exist, people could be made only of physical "stuff"—we'd be like biological robots with no souls. If that were true, what would it suggest about our ability to freely make choices? *(Our choices would all be physical in nature too. Like robots, we would be driven to act by how we were made, not by our own free will. Discuss how this means it wouldn't make sense to ever blame or praise someone. Read the quotes from atheist scientists in this chapter.)*

- Read John 7:17; 1 Corinthians 10:13; James 4:17. What do these verses tell us about the biblical view of human choices? *(These verses take it as a given that humans have the ability to choose from among various actions.)*

- Read Matthew 12:36; John 12:48; Romans 14:10, 12; 2 Corinthians 5:10. What do these verses tell us about the *importance* of our choices? *(They matter greatly—we'll be held morally accountable for them.)*

- From a Christian perspective, what do you think is the most important choice a person will ever make in life? *(How to respond to God.)*

Apply the Conversation

- Read the quote from Francis Crick in this chapter. If that's what you believed to be true, how do you think it would affect how you live your life?

27. What Should We Do with Our Lives?

Gretta Vosper is a United Church of Canada minister. She's also an atheist.

In 2015, a review committee from her denomination found that she was "not suitable" to continue in her role because . . . wait for it . . . she doesn't believe in God. If Vosper had been let go by her church and denomination at that point, she likely never would have made the news. But when her two-hundred-member congregation insisted on standing by her, despite the fact that she no longer preached about Christianity, it created more than a few headlines.

One loyal church member's comment may sum up the feelings of the many others who stayed: "It's not about coming to hear that I'm a sinner. That is so yuck. This fulfills my need to feel upbeat. The services are more happy and joyful, more interested in community and justice."[1]

Vosper has authored several books, including one called *With or Without God: Why the Way We Live Is More Important Than What We Believe*. On her website, she emphasizes, "We're not going to stop trying to make the world a better place. We hope you don't either."[2]

Vosper and her church community are obviously committed to living lives that benefit the Earth and those who live on it. They're presumably doing many great things for society, and that's commendable. But is it true that how we live is more important than what we believe? That's the conclusion many today have reached: we should all just be good people, do good things, and forget about religion.

The underlying question of what we should do with our lives is fundamental to our human existence. In this chapter, we'll see how the answer, once again, depends on whether God exists. Along the way, we'll also see that saying how we live is more important than what we believe is nonsensical from *both* an atheistic and a theistic perspective.

What We Should Do with Our Lives—without God

Anytime we hear the word *should* in the context of an atheistic worldview, our "inconsistency alarm" should go off.

If God doesn't exist, there's no objective reason why anyone should live in any particular way. *Should* implies a moral obligation. But if we're all just molecules in motion, to whom would we be morally obliged? To other molecules in motion? Clearly not. In an atheistic world, no one can prescribe a way of living for anyone else because there's no moral authority and therefore no objective basis for doing so. How a person "should" live his or her life can be only a matter of opinion. One way cannot be morally better than another way.

With this in mind, let's return to Vosper's statement (and the common sentiment) that how we live is more important than what we believe. In the context of an atheistic worldview, this claim has three significant problems:

1. *Vosper can't prescribe how all people should live if she's assuming God doesn't exist.* And surely she wouldn't say that all ways of living are good. As someone committed to social justice, she almost certainly doesn't believe it's fine to kill someone. But saying that how we live is more important than what we believe presumes there is some way all people *should* live. No one has an objective basis for claiming this, however, if God doesn't exist.

2. *Saying how we live is more important than what we believe is a belief itself.* Ironically, it's Vosper's belief that how we live is more important than what we believe that *determines* how she lives. (Think about that for a minute.) We cannot separate what we believe from how we live.

3. *This discussion assumes people have the free will to choose what to do with their lives.* But as we saw in the previous chapter, this is highly questionable in a world without God. If we're nothing more than our biology, and free will isn't a reality, it's a nonstarter to talk about how we should live our lives. We don't have the freedom to decide.

What should we do with our lives if God doesn't exist? No one has the authority to say. It's simply a matter of opinion. And we likely don't even have the freedom to form that opinion if we're nothing more than molecules in motion.

What We Should Do with Our Lives—with God

My husband and I recently drove by a local church that was promoting a Wednesday night class called "Submitting to Authority." My husband looked at me and said, "I'm sure *that* title is really going to pack the room!" It makes me laugh every time I think of it.

Most people feel at least some innate resistance to authority. The idea that we can live our lives however we want sounds appealing.

But if God exists and has created human beings with a purpose (see chap. 25), the reality is that he's the authority over our lives and how we respond to that authority matters. The good news, of course, is that the Christian God is all-knowing and all-good, so we can trust that he *knows* what's best for us and will *do* what's best for us—any negative views we have of earthly authority figures don't apply to him. While we might initially bristle at the idea of attending a "Submitting to Authority" class, there's no reason to do so if we're talking about *God* as the authority.

So what does the Bible say God wants us to do with our lives? As we learned in chapter 24, we should strive to live in a Christlike way. When we put our faith in Jesus, we are a new creation and the Holy Spirit works through us to bear godly fruit in our lives (Gal. 5:22–23). In other words, according to the Bible, there is a direct connection between what we believe and what we do—good works flow out of our belief in, knowledge of, and relationship with God. The apostle Paul writes of this connection in Colossians 1:9–10:

> We continually ask God to fill you with the knowledge of his will through all the wisdom and understanding that the Spirit gives, so that you may live a life worthy of the Lord and please him in every way: bearing fruit in every good work, growing in the knowledge of God.

This tells us that Spirit-led discernment is what helps us determine what we should do with our lives. The Bible doesn't dictate specifics on things like what career to choose or where to live but rather says that people have been given different gifts with which to glorify God (1 Pet. 4:10–11). When Christians want guidance on how best to utilize these gifts and how to make specific life choices, they can seek God's will through prayer.

With this discussion in mind, let's return once more to Vosper's claim that how we live is more important than what we believe.

From a Christian perspective, what we believe about Jesus has eternal significance. John 3:16 says, "For God so loved the world that he gave his one and only Son, that whoever believes in him shall not perish but have eternal life." Romans 10:9 says, "If you declare with your mouth, 'Jesus is Lord,' and believe in your heart that God raised him from the dead, you will be saved." These verses make the importance of belief very clear: belief in Jesus leads to eternal life. Furthermore, John 14:6 says that Jesus is the *only* way to God: "I am the way and the truth and the life. No one comes to the Father except through me."

If the Bible is true, how we live *cannot* be more important than what we believe—what we believe determines where we will spend eternity. But this doesn't mean that the way in which a Christian lives his or her life doesn't matter. To the contrary, the Bible says that "faith by itself, if it is not accompanied by action, is dead" (James 2:17). A genuine love for God results in a life of good works for God's glory. In a Christian worldview, therefore, belief and action go hand in hand. Without belief in Jesus, people remain in their sins; without action, faith is dead.

As we've seen, the statement that how we live is more important than what we believe is an objective truth claim that isn't consistent with atheism *or* theism.

The Difference God Makes

People, regardless of what they believe about God, can do good things with their lives. Christians, atheists, and people with all kinds of other beliefs help the homeless, give money to charities, participate in environmental causes, fight child abuse, advocate for crime victims, and much more. For atheists, doing such things, which Christians and other theists would call "good," is a matter of preference. While some atheists might say all people *should* live to make the world a better place, we saw in this chapter that such a claim is inconsistent with an atheistic worldview. An atheist who chooses a life of crime because they don't believe there's any moral significance to our existence is living more consistently within an atheistic worldview than one who claims all people *should* do good things.

Living consistently within a Christian worldview, however, means living a life of good works as the fruit of a love for God. Because Christians believe there's an objective moral standard and that God's moral law has been revealed in the Bible, they have an objective basis for *determining* what it means to live a good life. This doesn't mean Christians always live as they should, however. Christians still sometimes sin (Rom. 3:10; 1 John 1:8). But 1 John 1:9 tells us, "If we confess our sins, he is faithful and just and will forgive us our sins and purify us from all unrighteousness." As the overly used bumper sticker says, Christians aren't perfect, just forgiven. This doesn't mean we should sin because we know God will forgive us but that we acknowledge when we do sin and repent accordingly.

The lives of atheists and Christians can look similar in the good works they do, but the similarities don't make believing in Jesus any less important. The Bible is clear: belief matters in an eternally significant way.

KEY POINTS

- If God doesn't exist, no one has the authority to say how anyone else should live. It's simply a matter of opinion.
- If God exists and has created human beings with a purpose, he's the authority over our lives and it matters how we respond to that authority.
- In a Christian worldview, there is a direct connection between what we believe and what we do—good works flow out of our belief in, knowledge of, and relationship with God.

- If the Bible is true, how we live *cannot* be more important than what we believe—what we believe determines where we will spend eternity. A genuine love for God, however, results in a life of good works for God's glory.

CONVERSATION GUIDE

Open the Conversation

- Who are some people in your life who have the authority to tell you what to do?
- Do you think their authority is a good or bad thing? Why?

Advance the Conversation

- If God created us, that means he has authority over our lives and how we respond to him matters. How is God a different kind of authority than the people you just thought of? *(God is a perfect authority. Because God is all-knowing and all-good, we can trust that he knows what's best for us and will do what's best for us. No human can be a perfect authority.)*
- If someone asked you what God wants us to do with our lives, what would you say? *(Recall what it means to live a Christlike life. Read James 2:17, then discuss the importance of the connection between belief in God and a life of good works for God's glory.)*
- If God didn't exist, how would that change what people should do with their lives? *(What they should do would be only a matter of opinion. Discuss how no one could say anyone else should live in a certain way if there were no moral authority.)*
- Do you think atheists can do as many good things in their lives as people who believe in God? Why or why not? *(People*

can do good things whether they believe in God or not, but only in a world with God can something be called good.)

Apply the Conversation

- An atheist author wrote that parents should "teach kids that it's what they do in life that matters, not what they believe."[3] Do you agree with her advice? Why or why not?

28. What Is Our Responsibility to Other People?

When our twins were four and our youngest was two, my husband and I took them to serve the homeless in a nearby downtown area. We brought apples, bananas, and tangerines and put them in a small wagon that the kids could pull. We walked around, and the kids took turns offering fruit to the people lining the streets in tents and sleeping bags.

We ended up giving out 150 pieces of fruit that day. Some of the homeless beamed when they saw the kids. Some didn't respond because they were high on drugs. Some said they didn't like fruit. Some explained they couldn't eat apples because they had no teeth. But nothing deterred the kids. Their young hearts truly embraced the opportunity to serve.

When we got into the car to leave, I told them how happy they had made the people they helped and how happy they had made God by spending time loving others. My daughter, however, started crying.

In a soft, quivering voice, she said, "We didn't make them happy. What they need is comfortable beds."

My son, who rarely gets serious, offered a solution in a hushed voice filled with heaviness. "Mommy, I know where there's a bed store. We can buy beds to put on the sidewalks."

Oh, the tears that came.

It hit me at that moment how complex a Christian's responsibility to others is. On the one hand, we want serving to be an investment in tangible outcomes, like providing beds for the homeless. On the other hand, tangible outcomes aren't always possible, and we need to be willing to simply love people however we can—one piece of fruit at a time. And, ultimately, we aren't meeting people's greatest need of all if we're not sharing Jesus with them.

In the previous chapter, we looked at the broad question of what we should do with our lives. Here we're focusing on one particular part of that question: What is our responsibility to others? For Christians, we'll see that responsibility is weighty and multifaceted, just as I came to appreciate after my experience serving the homeless with our kids. For atheists, however, the answer is very different—and quite bleak.

Responsibility to Others—without God

Given what we've learned about the implications of an atheistic world, you should see this one coming a mile away: in a world without God, no one has any responsibility to anyone else. If life has no special value because it's the product of purely natural forces, and there's no moral authority to establish relational obligations, then the idea of responsibility to one another is senseless. As we've seen, molecules can't owe other molecules anything.

Despite this implication of a world without God, many atheists consider themselves "humanists" and stress the importance of believing in human dignity and equal rights. For example, *The Humanist* magazine says:

> Humanism is a rational philosophy informed by science, inspired by art, and motivated by compassion. Affirming the dignity of each human being, it supports the maximization of individual liberty and opportunity consonant with social and planetary responsibility. It advocates the extension of participatory democracy and the expansion of the open society, standing for human rights and social justice.[1]

It sounds good, but there's a logical problem with the humanist position. If God doesn't exist, natural rights that are equally held by all people also don't exist. A "right" is something to which a person is entitled, and we can't be entitled to something unless someone entitles us to it. Who has the authority to give rights to humankind if God doesn't exist? At most, a government can pass laws to create rights for its citizens, but that doesn't mean those rights are universal in nature—anyone can see they vary by country. Humanists fight for the idea of fundamental equality but have no way to objectively justify the idea given their worldview.

From an evolutionary perspective, in which organisms fight for survival and the fittest win, a more consistent view is that people are very *unequal* in a world without God because they can be compared only on a physical basis. Some people are strong, others are weak, and there's no Creator who has given everyone a more fundamental value. Several years ago, Princeton University philosopher Peter Singer shocked America by making statements consistent with such a worldview. Singer suggested that no newborn should be considered a person until thirty days after birth and that doctors should kill some disabled babies immediately. Singer explained:

> When the death of a disabled infant will lead to the birth of another infant with better prospects of a happy life, the total amount of

happiness will be greater if the disabled infant is killed. The loss of the happy life for the first infant is outweighed by the gain of a happier life for the second.[2]

Singer's position led to moral outrage, but it's actually just taking an atheistic worldview to its natural conclusions: life has no inherent value, so there's no moral problem if the strong win and the weak lose. They never had equal rights to begin with.

Responsibility to Others—with God

In a world with God, the picture is far less bleak. The foundation for a Christian's view of people's responsibility to one another is what we learned in chapter 25: all human lives are precious and equal in value because every human is created in the image of God. A disabled newborn is as precious as a nondisabled adult. Value doesn't depend on physical or intellectual capabilities. It comes from our identity as image bearers of God.

In a Christian worldview, not only is there an objective basis for believing all humans are equal in value, but there's also a moral authority who has directed us to actively care for one another. In Matthew 22:37–40, Jesus tells us, "'Love the Lord your God with all your heart and with all your soul and with all your mind.' This is the first and greatest commandment. And the second is like it: 'Love your neighbor as yourself.' All the Law and the Prophets hang on these two commandments." Loving our neighbors (other humans) as ourselves means caring for people's physical *and* spiritual needs. Let's look more closely at what this requires.

The physical needs of humanity today are great. According to World Vision International, 870 million people don't have enough to eat, one out of every four children under age five is stunted (prevented from growing or developing properly), and two billion people lack access to vitamins and minerals that are essential for good health.[3]

While we know that people's eternal destination is of utmost importance, Christians cannot ignore the physical needs of millions of suffering people like these. As Christian apologist Norman Geisler put it, "Man is more than a soul destined for another world."[4]

Jesus says in Matthew 25:31–46 that when we serve others by feeding the hungry, giving a drink to the thirsty, clothing those without clothes, caring for the sick, and visiting those in prison, we serve him. And 1 John 3:17 says, "If anyone has material possessions and sees a brother or sister in need but has no pity on them, how can the love of God be in that person?" According to the Bible, when we love God, we love others, and that love necessarily manifests itself in caring for others' physical needs.

That said, a biblical love for others cannot stop with physical concerns. In a Christian worldview, people are more than molecules with physical needs for continued existence—they're spiritual beings with the need for a relationship with their Creator. They'll either spend eternity in the presence and glory of God or face eternal separation in hell. If that's reality, it's the most unloving thing imaginable for Christians *not* to care for people's spiritual needs by telling them about Jesus.

Atheist Penn Jillette, of the magician duo Penn & Teller, puts this in perspective:

> I've always said that I don't respect people who don't proselytize. I don't respect that at all. If you believe that there's a heaven and a hell, and people could be going to hell or not getting eternal life, and you think that it's not really worth telling them this because it would make it socially awkward . . . how much do you have to hate somebody to not proselytize? How much do you have to hate somebody to believe that everlasting life is possible and not tell them that? I mean, if I believed, beyond the shadow of a doubt, that a truck was coming at you, and you didn't believe that truck was bearing down on you, there is a certain point where I tackle you. And this is more important than that.[5]

To care for the physical needs of others while ignoring their spiritual needs is like giving a hamburger to a hungry man sitting on train tracks and not telling him a train is coming. The Bible calls Christians to care for both physical and spiritual needs, and ignoring either puts people in serious danger.

The Difference God Makes

Atheists can passionately fight for equal rights and the dignity of all persons as much and as well as Christians and other theists. But again, they have no objective basis for claiming those beliefs are anything more than personal opinion.

Christians, however, have a weighty responsibility to others. Unfortunately, many nonbelievers misunderstand the nature of that responsibility. They cite Jesus's words to "love your neighbor as yourself" (Matt. 22:39) and boil Christianity down to a simple moral directive to care for people's physical needs. But doing so ignores the critically important words right before those: "'Love the Lord your God with all your heart and with all your soul and with all your mind.' *This is the first and greatest commandment*" (Matt. 22:37–38, emphasis mine). The commandments to love God and to love others are given in that order for a reason. Our love for God informs *how* we love others. Without God, there's no objective moral basis for determining what love even looks like. It could mean never telling someone that what they believe is wrong, and this is exactly what many people today think love is. But when we follow God's commands in the proper order, by loving him first, we understand that this is not what it means to love others at all. Loving others requires us to graciously share God's truth, even when it's not the popular thing to do. As Jillette recognized as an atheist, *not* doing so because it's sometimes socially awkward is a pitiful excuse when we believe a person's eternity hangs in the

275

balance. Whether we're dealing with food or the gospel, Christians must treat our responsibility to others with the utmost seriousness.

KEY POINTS

- In a world without God, no one has a responsibility to anyone else. If life has no special value because it's the product of purely natural forces, and there's no moral authority to establish relational obligations, then the idea of responsibility to one another is senseless.
- If God doesn't exist, there's no objective basis for equal human rights. The secular humanist view is inconsistent.
- In a Christian worldview, all human lives are precious and equal in value because every human is created in the image of God. As Christians, we have an objective basis for believing in equal human rights and a moral authority who has directed us to actively care for one another.
- The Bible calls Christians to care for the physical *and* spiritual needs of others, and ignoring either puts people in danger.

CONVERSATION GUIDE

Open the Conversation

- Do you think humans have responsibilities to one another? If so, what kinds of responsibilities? If not, why not?

Apply the Conversation

- Read Matthew 22:37–40. What do you think Jesus meant when he said we should love our neighbors? *(Discuss how loving others involves caring for two kinds of needs: physical and spiritual. Give examples of each. Read Penn Jillette's quote and discuss the importance of caring for spiritual needs even when it's hard.)*

- In Matthew 22:37–40, Jesus's first command is to love God and his second command is to love others. Why do you think he gave the commands in that order? *(Our love for God informs how we love others. Without God, there's no objective moral basis for determining what love even looks like.)*

- If God didn't exist, what do you think our responsibility would be to one another? *(No one would have any responsibility to anyone else. Review why from the discussion in this chapter. With older kids, explain the idea of humanism and why it's an inconsistent view.)*

Advance the Conversation

- A person made the following comment about an online article about the truth of Christianity: "Unlike Christians, my spiritual path is highly personal and subjective. I will never say that you'd better believe what I believe or you will suffer eternal consequences. Christians like to intimidate me with this 'Jesus is the high way' tactic. I believe that God is like an ocean, and different spiritual paths are like rivers. I am not the one who decides which river is the best to reach the ocean."[6] How would you respond to this person's frustration with Christians for saying he'd "better believe" in Jesus or he'll suffer eternal consequences?

29. How Should We Make Sense of Evil?

I sometimes marvel at how different my twins are. Although I know they're unique people with unique sets of DNA, it seems like people who enter the world on the same day and grow up in the same family would somehow converge in personality. Not so. My son and daughter could not be more different in how they approach life.

Nowhere is this more obvious than in how they undertake their piano lessons. My daughter learns a new song by carefully figuring out each note and ensuring accuracy as she plays. My son, however, tackles new songs with brute force and is happy to get them *mostly* right.

Last week at lessons, my son started to play his latest piece but was quickly stopped by his teacher. "Whoa! Wrong notes! Wrong notes!"

Frustrated that he had to fix something, my son replied, "How can any note even be wrong? They're just keys on the piano!"

His teacher responded, "All notes are wrong except the one you were supposed to play."

If my son had just been messing around and hitting keys on the piano without trying to play a song, he would have been correct—those notes couldn't have been wrong because there were no "right" notes to play. But as soon as he was playing notes in the context of a song, there was an objective standard each of his notes could be compared to. His notes either matched the song's notes, making them *right*, or didn't match them, making them *wrong*.

I was immediately struck by how analogous this is to the problem of evil that atheists face. Like piano notes, human behavior can be right or wrong only if there's an objective standard to compare it to, but in a world without God, there *is no* objective standard; evil can't actually exist. Let's look at this atheistic problem of evil more closely, then we'll turn to the better known *theistic* problem of evil.

The Problem of Evil—without God

In the last few chapters, we've seen that many things can't exist in a world without God. There can be no objective meaning, no free will (at least in the sense we commonly assume), no objective way people should live their lives, and no innate human responsibility to one another. Now we can add one more to the list: there can be no evil.

On any given day, we can scroll through news headlines and read about people being murdered, children being abused, women being raped, and much more. It's part of our most basic human intuition to categorize such things as "evil." But in a world without God, there's no objective standard for *calling* anything evil. Just as people can't hit wrong piano notes unless there's an objective standard to which the notes can be compared, people can't do *anything* wrong unless there's an objective moral standard to which their behavior can be compared. When it comes to evil, the challenge for atheists is this: no human action can be evil in a world without God, despite the fact that our deepest human intuition tells us certain things are horribly wrong. A person's view of murder, child abuse, and rape can be only a matter of opinion. That's a tough thing for most people to say they believe.

As counterintuitive as it is, however, many atheists bite the bullet for consistency and admit this is the implication of their worldview. For example, in an online debate on this subject, one atheist said:

> There is no innate good or evil. Good and evil are just two words and feelings that humans use to categorize things. Love, family, kindness—good. Murder, rape, drug abuse—evil. The extreme majority of the population would agree with those six categorizations, but in reality that's only because we've been taught that certain things are good and evil. Nothing, by itself, is either way, but only becomes so in a human's eye.[1]

This view, of course, is consistent with the idea of unguided evolution. If all life originated from a single cell via blind evolutionary forces, then humans are just another animal. And as we discussed in chapter 4, we don't assign moral categories to animal behavior—a dog doesn't do something morally wrong by biting someone. Similarly, if there's no God, then there's no reason to assign moral categories to *human* behavior. We're just animals, and what we do is simply a fact of our existence. Good and evil are meaningless.

The Problem of Evil—with God

The problem of evil for Christians and other theists is often more obvious than the one for atheists: How can so much evil exist in a world created by a good God? It seems that such a God would never permit the many terrible things we see. Christians have an objective basis for calling things evil but face the challenge of explaining how evil exists given what they believe about God.

This difficulty is not easily resolved. Thoughtful philosophers and theologians have grappled with the problem of evil for centuries. There's nothing you'll find here or anywhere else that will make you say, "Oh! I get it now. The extent of evil in the world is actually quite easy to understand!" What we can do, however, is look at two important points that can help us *begin* to understand the problem of evil from a Christian perspective.

First, the coexistence of God and evil is logically possible. This is an important starting point for discussion because some philosophers have suggested that there's no logical way to resolve the problem of evil without removing one of God's biblical attributes. The argument basically goes like this:

- If God is all-good, he *would* eliminate evil.
- If God is all-powerful, he *could* eliminate evil.
- Evil exists.
- Therefore, (1) God doesn't exist, (2) he exists but is not all-good, or (3) he exists but is not all-powerful.

In order to demonstrate that this conclusion doesn't follow and that the coexistence of God and evil is at least logically possible, we need to show that one of the first two statements isn't necessarily true. Christian philosopher Alvin Plantinga did exactly that in his classic work *God, Freedom, and Evil*. Plantinga demonstrated that an all-good God wouldn't necessarily eliminate evil if the existence of human free will is a greater good. This is known as the free will defense. Plantinga explains:

> A world containing creatures who are significantly free (and freely perform more good than evil actions) is more valuable, all else

being equal, than a world containing no free creatures at all. Now God can create free creatures, but He can't cause or determine them to do only what is right. For if He does so, then they aren't significantly free after all; and they do not do what is right freely. To create creatures capable of moral good, therefore, He must create creatures capable of moral evil; and He can't give these creatures the freedom to perform evil and at the same time prevent them from doing so. As it turned out, sadly enough, some of the free creatures God created went wrong in the exercise of their freedom; this is the source of moral evil. The fact that free creatures sometimes go wrong, however, counts neither against God's omnipotence nor against His goodness; for He could have forestalled the occurrence of moral evil only by removing the possibility of moral good.[2]

Plantinga's free will defense shows that the existence of evil doesn't disprove the existence of God—there's at least one possible way to reconcile them, and most philosophers today acknowledge as much. But even if the existence of evil doesn't disprove the existence of God, many people go on to say that the existence of evil at least counts as significant evidence *against* the existence of God.

This brings us to our second point. *Evil must be considered in the context of all the evidence* for *God's existence.* If we look only at evil, the picture indeed looks bleak. It certainly seems this world is inconsistent with the idea of a perfectly good and loving God. But we must remember that evil is only one of many pieces of evidence we have to consider. Recall what we learned in part 1: the origin of the universe, the origin and the development of life, and our innate moral understanding are all pieces of evidence that point *to* God's existence. In addition, there are other important pieces of evidence we didn't have space to discuss, such as the historical evidence for the resurrection of Jesus.[3] All this compelling evidence remains, even when evil exists alongside it. So the question is, What's the best explanation for *all* that we observe? Perhaps surprisingly, Christians believe the existence of God is the best explanation for all that we see, *including* evil—if we acknowledge that evil is an objective reality that can be accounted for only by the existence of a moral authority.

As it turns out, evil can actually be evidence *for* God.

The Difference God Makes

Atheists can feel as much moral outrage at the evil in the world as anyone who believes in God. But they have no objective basis for appealing to others to feel the same way. The most they can do, based on their own opinion of what's evil, is work toward corresponding laws and justice on Earth. But remember: no one can be morally blamed for their actions in a world without God. Putting a person in jail for murder is the moral equivalent of putting an elephant in jail for stepping on a toad.

For Christians, however, evil isn't an illusion that ends with the earthly imprisonment of various molecules in motion. We understand evil to be the result of humans using their free will to rebel against God's perfect laws. We mourn human bondage to such sin. And we recognize that the solution to evil is not to deny its existence but to turn to Jesus, who conquered evil on the cross. Revelation 21:1–5 tells us of the glorious day when that victory will be realized in full through the creation of a new heaven and a new earth:

> Then I saw "a new heaven and a new earth," for the first heaven and the first earth had passed away, and there was no longer any sea. I saw the Holy City, the new Jerusalem, coming down out of heaven from God, prepared as a bride beautifully dressed for her husband. And I heard a loud voice from the throne saying, "Look!

God's dwelling place is now among the people, and he will dwell with them. They will be his people, and God himself will be with them and be their God. 'He will wipe every tear from their eyes. There will be no more death' or mourning or crying or pain, for the old order of things has passed away." He who was seated on the throne said, "I am making everything new!" Then he said, "Write this down, for these words are trustworthy and true."

Not only does a Christian worldview make sense of evil in a way that atheism cannot, but it also offers the hope that evil will be forever eliminated. In our final chapter, we'll look at why hope matters so greatly for humankind.

KEY POINTS

- A problem of evil exists for both atheists *and* theists.
- The problem of evil for atheists is that there's no objective standard for calling anything evil, despite the fact that our deepest human intuition tells us certain things are horribly wrong. A person's view of murder, child abuse, and rape, for example, can be only a matter of opinion.
- Christians and other theists have an objective basis for calling things evil but face the challenge of explaining how evil exists given what they believe about God.
- The free will defense demonstrates that God and evil can logically coexist if human free will is a greater good than the elimination of evil.
- Christians believe the existence of God is the best explanation for all that we see, *including* evil—if we acknowledge that evil is an objective reality that can be accounted for only by the existence of a moral authority.

CONVERSATION GUIDE

Open the Conversation

- When you hear the word *evil*, what actions come to mind? Why do you consider these things evil?

Advance the Conversation

- People sometimes think God must not exist if we see evil in the world. Why do you think they say that? *(It seems that if God is all-good and all-powerful, he would and could stop evil from happening.)*

- Can you think of any reasons why a good God would allow evil to happen? *(Discuss your child's answer, then explain the free will defense—human free will may be a greater good than the elimination of evil.)*

- Think back to what we learned in part 1: the origin of the universe, the origin and the development of life, and our moral understanding are all pieces of evidence that convincingly point to God's existence. Do you think the existence of evil is stronger evidence that God *doesn't* exist? Why or why not? *(Discuss the importance of looking at all the evidence together and not looking at evil alone. Explain why evil is actually evidence for God if we believe it's an objective reality.)*

- If God didn't exist, do you think there could still be evil? Why or why not? *(Share the piano analogy and discuss how there would be no objective basis for labeling anything evil. Explain why that means atheists have their own problem of evil.)*

Apply the Conversation

- A person asked online, "How does an atheist justify experiencing moral outrage?" An atheist responded, "Moral outrage is based on a value system. Does being religious entitle you to a better value system because it comes from the Bible? What about all the other holy books? Or because it's not Christian, are their value systems worth less? Atheists derive their values as well. They just don't come from a holy book. They come from values instilled by our parents, community and our own personal goals. As far as I can tell, these values are not worth less or more than any other value based system."[4] Based on what you learned in this chapter, do you feel this person is justified in feeling moral outrage as an atheist? Why or why not?

30. Why Does Biblical Hope Matter?

Each month at my kids' Christian school, the teachers give out Christian character awards. Last month they recognized the character trait of hope. My son commented one morning, "That's so weird. Hope? Why is that even a Christian thing?"

As I told him, that's a great question—and one that's misunderstood by Christians and nonbelievers alike. Hope can have everything or nothing to do with Christianity. It depends on what is meant by *hope*.

To understand the various ways in which people use the word, it helps to think of it along two spectrums. First, hope runs along a spectrum of *significance*. The significance of a given hope is based on its importance to us and determines how vested we are in it. Second, hope runs along a spectrum of *justification*. The justification for a given hope is how well-founded it is and determines how confident we are that it will be realized.

If we combine the ends of these spectrums, four categories of hope emerge:

1. *Insignificant hope/low justification*: This is wishful thinking with little consequence, like crossing our fingers that we'll happen to find a good parking spot when we get to the store.

2. *Insignificant hope/high justification*: This applies to things we trust will happen but don't really care if they don't. For example, I hope it rains tomorrow based on a reliable weather forecast, but if it doesn't, that's fine too.

3. *Highly significant hope/low justification*: This is the sad state of believing something of great importance to one's life while having little reason to do so. At best, it's a recipe for extraordinary disappointment; at worst, it's delusion.

4. *Highly significant hope/high justification*: This is the kind of hope we want to build our lives around—hope of great importance that we have reason to be confident in. This is the hope of Christianity.

It's critically important to understand why Christian hope falls in this last category rather than the categories of parking spots, rain, or delusion. We'll soon look at that question in detail. But for perspective, let's first consider what kind of hope we can reasonably have in a world *without* God.

Hope—without God

In case you haven't noticed, the picture we've drawn of an atheistic worldview isn't exactly hope-filled:

- Life is an accident with no special value and no objective meaning.

- We're chemical specks in a vast, indifferent universe, here for a brief moment in time.
- There's little reason to believe we can freely make choices.
- No one should live in any particular way, because doing so makes no moral difference.
- No one has a responsibility to anyone else because we're just molecules in motion with no moral obligations.
- There's no such thing as objective moral evil, so we can't even condemn the worst actions of society as objectively wrong.

Like anyone else, atheists can have "hope" in life if we're talking about the hope of good parking spots or rain. Some hopes have greater significance for a while—the hope of getting married, finding a good job, beating cancer, or having a family—but all these hopes end in the same place after being realized: a grave.

Atheist philosopher Bertrand Russell famously described the ultimate hopelessness of a world without God:

> That Man is the product of causes which had no prevision of the end they were achieving; that his origin, his growth, his hopes and fears, his loves and his beliefs, are but the outcome of accidental collocations of atoms; that no fire, no heroism, no intensity of thought and feeling, can preserve an individual life beyond the grave; that all the labors of the ages, all the devotion, all the inspiration, all the noonday brightness of human genius, are destined to extinction in the vast death of the solar system, and that the whole temple of Man's achievement must inevitably be buried beneath the debris of a universe in ruins—all these things, if not quite beyond dispute, are yet so nearly certain, that no philosophy which rejects them can hope to stand. Only within the scaffolding of these truths, only on the firm foundation of unyielding despair, can the soul's habitation henceforth be safely built.[1]

Are you ready to build your life on "the firm foundation of unyielding despair"? I doubt most people crave such hopelessness. But is a godless world "so nearly certain" that we have no intellectually honest choice other than to accept this devastating fate?

Thank God, the answer is no.

Hope—with God

The picture we've been drawing of a world with God, from a biblical perspective, couldn't be more different:

- Life is precious and is the product of a purposeful Creator. All living things were meant to be here—no cosmic accidents involved.
- Every person's life has objective meaning: to know God and to make him known.
- We have the ability to make choices and moral accountability for the choices we make. What we do matters.
- Living a life of good works is the natural outcome of our belief in, knowledge of, and relationship with God.
- There's an objective basis for equal human rights because every human is created in the image of God and is therefore equally valuable.
- Evil is an objective reality worthy of condemnation and will eventually be eliminated.

In addition to what we've learned above, the Bible assures us that death is not the end of our existence—instead of a grave, those who have put their trust in Jesus enter the glorious presence of the Lord and live with him forever in a place free from pain and suffering (Rev. 21:4). This is a "new birth into a living hope through the resurrection of Jesus Christ from the dead, and into an inheritance that can never perish, spoil or fade" (1 Pet.1:3–4).

That's hope.

And not parking spot hope.

Deeply significant hope.

In 1 Corinthians 15:54–57, the apostle Paul looks forward to the day when such momentous hope is realized:

> When the perishable has been clothed with the imperishable, and the mortal with immortality, then the saying that is written will come true: "Death has been swallowed up in victory." "Where, O death, is your victory? Where, O death, is your sting?" The sting of death is sin, and the power of sin is the law. But thanks be to God! He gives us the victory through our Lord Jesus Christ.

No question about it, the hope of Christianity is a highly significant one. But we can't forget that highly significant hope without justification is delusional. If there's no good reason to believe Christianity is true, who cares if it offers so much hope? Even Paul acknowledged this, saying, "If only for this life we have hope in Christ, we are of all people most to be pitied" (1 Cor. 15:19). Paul knew that false hope is worthless hope. It would be pitiful to waste one's brief existence living for a gospel built on wishful thinking.

So that brings us to the all-important final question: How confident can we be that God exists and offers us the hope the Bible describes? We've now come full circle to what we studied in parts 1 and 2. As we've seen, the evidence in the universe compellingly points to the existence of God. Recall the following:

- The beginning of the universe requires a cause consistent with whom we call God.

- The universe appears to be purposely structured (finely tuned) for life to exist and flourish.

- The complexity of life is more consistent with a purposeful Creator than blind chance.

- There's good reason to believe objective moral laws exist, which implies a moral lawgiver.
- The universe is rationally intelligible, which is to be expected in theism but not in atheism.
- Humans trust in their ability to reason, but only in a theistic world would we expect to have the mental tools necessary for discovering truth.

These are just *some* of the pieces of evidence for God's existence and the truth of Christianity.[2]

This is no delusion.

Belief in the existence of God—the God of the Bible specifically—is extremely well-founded.

This is a hope worth having.

The Difference God Makes

Most atheists acknowledge that their worldview offers little hope, but they aren't willing to put their faith in Jesus because they think Christianity is only wishful thinking. Unfortunately, many never take the time to consider the evidence for the truth of Christianity and end up living a life of ultimate hopelessness, believing this is all there is. That's why it's so crucial that Christians "always be prepared to give an answer to everyone who asks you to give the reason for the hope that you have" (1 Pet. 3:15). When we're prepared to give people reasons—like the ones discussed in this book—for believing Christianity is true, we have the opportunity to give them the well-founded hope of a glorious eternity.

As Christians, we live in light of that well-founded hope, remaining confident that God is in control, God is good, and God will make all things right in the end. This doesn't mean we don't feel the many pains of this earthly experience, but we do view them with an eye toward eternal life. We know this isn't the end of the story.

It's a fitting end to this book to leave you with Paul's "hopeful" words in Romans 15:13:

> May the God of hope fill you with all joy and peace as you trust in him, so that you may overflow with hope by the power of the Holy Spirit.

KEY POINTS

- Hope can have everything or nothing to do with Christianity. It depends on what is meant by hope.
- Hope runs along spectrums of significance and justification.
- Atheists can have hope for things of temporary significance, but, ultimately, atheism is a hopeless worldview because all life ends in a grave.
- Christians have a highly significant hope that those who put their trust in Jesus will enter the glorious presence of the Lord and live with him forever in a place free from pain and suffering—"an inheritance that can never perish, spoil or fade" (1 Pet. 1:4).
- Highly significant hope without justification is delusional. But that's not the status of Christianity. There's very good reason to believe God exists and that he offers the hope the Bible describes.

CONVERSATION GUIDE

Open the Conversation

- What is something you hoped for recently?
- Was that hope very important or very unimportant for your life overall? Why?

- Did you have good reason for believing that what you hoped for would happen? Why or why not?

Advance the Conversation

- When Christians say they have "hope" in Jesus, what kind of hope do you think they're talking about? *(Read Rev. 21:4; 1 Pet. 1:3–4. Discuss the hope of entering the presence of the Lord and living with him forever in a place free from pain and suffering.)*
- Do you think Christian hope is the kind of hope that impacts a person's life in a big or small way? Why? *(Christian hope is the most important hope we can possibly have. For perspective, compare it to other kinds of hope—for example, doing well on a test, making friends with someone, or getting a good job someday.)*
- If there weren't good reasons to believe Christianity is true, would it be worth putting your hope in Jesus? Why or why not? *(Explain that even the Bible tells us that if Christianity is not true, hope in Jesus is to be pitied. Hope can be a wonderful thing, but only if it's justified. Discuss how this makes the evidence for God's existence and the truth of Christianity so important.)*
- Here's a review of what we've learned about an atheistic worldview in the last few chapters. *(Read the review points at the beginning of the "Hope—without God" section.)* What kind of hope do you think atheists can have, given what you've learned about their worldview? *(Atheists can have hope for the temporary things of life, but these things are ultimately insignificant if our existence ends at death.)*

Apply the Conversation

- An atheist made the following comment to show that atheists have hope too: "Atheists have less hope than Christians have in the same way that adults have less hope than young children on Christmas Eve. But this does not mean atheists are without hope. It just means we hope for more realistic goals. It also means we face reality square in the face, figure out how reality works, and use that knowledge to better mankind. I'm a dreamer. I dream of a better world, and I think we can make a better world if we decide to figure it out, together."[3] How hopeful do you find this person's view of life? Based on what you've learned in this book, what are some things you might share with him if you could have a discussion?

Notes

All websites last accessed 3/1/2017.

Introduction

1. J. Warner Wallace has compiled an excellent summary of the many studies on this subject: "Are Young People Really Leaving Christianity?," Cold-Case Christianity, updated January 8, 2017, coldcasechristianity.com/2016/are-young-people-really-leaving-christianity/.

2. Natasha Crain, *Keeping Your Kids on God's Side: 40 Conversations to Help Them Build a Lasting Faith* (Eugene, OR: Harvest House, 2016).

Part 1 The Existence of God Overview

1. Daniel Dennett, *Darwin's Dangerous Idea: Evolution and the Meanings of Life* (New York: Simon & Schuster, 1996), 18.

2. Atheists define atheism in varying ways. Some prefer to say that atheism is simply the lack of a belief in God, as opposed to the belief that there is no God. (The reason for their interest in the distinction is discussed in chap. 19.) Throughout this book, when I use the word *atheist*, I'm referring to those who believe there is no God. In my personal experience, I find that the majority of atheists truly believe there is no God and don't simply lack a belief in deities.

Chapter 1 What Can We Learn about God from Nature?

1. Dan Barker, *Losing Faith in Faith* (Madison, WI: FFRF, 1992), 87.

Chapter 2 Where Did the Universe Come From?

1. Alexander Vilenkin, *Many Worlds in One: The Search for Other Universes* (New York: Hill and Wang, 2007), 177.

2. See this article for more background on Einstein's "fudge factor": Karen Wright, "The Master's Mistakes," *Discover*, September 30, 2004, discovermagazine .com/2004/sep/the-masters-mistakes.

3. Christians who are young-Earth creationists do not believe cosmic background radiation is residual heat from the beginning of the universe (for an explanation of young-Earth creationism, see chap. 8). As such, they would not personally accept it as scientific evidence for the beginning of the universe (see Danny R. Faulkner, "Comments on the Cosmic Microwave Background," Answers in Genesis, March 19, 2014, answersingenesis.org/astronomy/cosmology/comments -on-the-cosmic-microwave-background/). I include cosmic background radiation here, despite the fact that not all Christians accept it, because the focus of this section is on explaining why *mainstream scientists* have come to accept that the universe began to exist.

4. Here's a brief article that explains the findings in more detail: "Mathematics of Eternity Prove the Universe Must Have Had a Beginning," *MIT Technology Review*, April 24, 2012, www.technologyreview.com/s/427722/mathematics -of-eternity-prove-the-universe-must-have-had-a-beginning.

5. William Lane Craig and Quentin Smith, *Theism, Atheism, and Big Bang Cosmology* (Oxford: Clarendon, 1993), 135.

6. "Humanist Manifesto," American Humanist Association, americanhuman ist.org/Humanism/Humanist_Manifesto_I.

7. Stephen Hawking and Leonard Mlodinow, *The Grand Design* (New York: Bantam, 2010), 180.

8. For further discussion of this fact, see John Lennox, *Gunning for God: Why the New Atheists Are Missing the Target* (Oxford: Lion Hudson, 2011), chap. 1.

9. Lawrence M. Krauss, *A Universe from Nothing: Why There Is Something Rather Than Nothing* (New York: Free Press, 2012).

10. "How Can Atheists Argue That the Universe Came from Nothing without Redefining Nothing?" Quora, www.quora.com/How-can-atheists-argue-that-the -universe-came-from-nothing-without-redefining-nothing.

Chapter 3 Where Did Life Come From?

1. Life "as we know it" utilizes molecules—two or more atoms chemically bonded together—built primarily out of carbon. Skeptics sometimes claim that the fine-tuning argument discussed in this chapter is meaningless because, if different laws existed, different (non-carbon-based) life forms could have existed. Life could have just taken on whatever chemical basis would have appropriately matched the given laws of the universe. This is speculative. However, it's important to realize that much of the fine-tuning we see would be required for *any* life to exist—not just carbon-based life.

2. For a more detailed exploration of fine-tuning in the constants of nature, see Hugh Ross, *Creator and the Cosmos: How the Latest Scientific Discoveries of the Century Reveal God* (Colorado Springs: NavPress, 2001), chap. 14.

3. Hugh Ross, "Fine-Tuning for Life on Earth," Reasons to Believe, June 8, 2004, www.reasons.org/articles/fine-tuning-for-life-on-earth-june-2004.

4. Hugh Ross, "Probability for Life on Earth," Reasons to Believe, April 1, 2004, www.reasons.org/articles/probability-for-life-on-earth.

5. See, for example, Brian Greene, *The Elegant Universe: Superstrings, Hidden Dimensions, and the Quest for the Ultimate Theory* (New York: W. W. Norton, 2010).

6. William A. Dembski and James M. Kushiner, eds., *Signs of Intelligence: Understanding Intelligent Design* (Grand Rapids: Brazos, 2001), 110.

7. For a detailed look at this research and its difficulties, see Stephen C. Meyer, *Signature in the Cell: DNA and the Evidence for Intelligent Design* (New York: HarperOne, 2010).

8. Stephen C. Meyer, "Word Games: DNA, Design, and Intelligence," chap. 8 in *Signs of Intelligence*, ed. Dembski and Kushiner.

9. Ibid., 110.

10. Daphne Sashin, "Godless Mom Strikes a Chord with Parents," *Belief Blog*, January 18, 2013, religion.blogs.cnn.com/2013/01/18/godless-mom-strikes -a-chord-with-parents/comment-page-69/.

Chapter 4 Where Did Our Moral Understanding Come From?

1. An excellent book that elaborates on this and related topics is Francis J. Beckwith and Gregory Koukl, *Relativism: Feet Firmly Planted in Mid-Air* (Grand Rapids: Baker, 1998).

2. Richard Taylor, *Ethics, Faith, and Reason* (Englewood Cliffs, NJ: Prentice-Hall, 1985), 83–84.

3. Sam Harris, *The Moral Landscape: How Science Can Determine Human Values* (New York: Free Press, 2011), 1.

4. For an excellent longer (but still brief!) critique of Harris's book, see William Lane Craig, "Navigating Sam Harris' *The Moral Landscape*," Reasonable Faith, www.reasonablefaith.org/navigating-sam-harris-the-moral-landscape.

5. See this article by an atheist physicist as one example: Sean Carroll, "The .Moral Landscape," *Discover*, January 18, 2011, blogs.discovermagazine.com /cosmicvariance/2011/01/18/the-moral-landscape/#.WQy-89wpCUI.

Chapter 5 What Is the Difference between God and a Flying Spaghetti Monster?

1. Bobby Henderson, "Open Letter to Kansas School Board," Church of the Flying Spaghetti Monster, www.venganza.org/about/open-letter. See chapter 40 in *Keeping Your Kids on God's Side* for more information on intelligent design theory.

2. It should be noted that Henderson's comparison of intelligent design to religion is a mischaracterization of intelligent design theory. Intelligent design is the scientific theory that says some features of the universe and living things are best explained by an intelligent cause. While intelligent design theory is *consistent* with theism, it doesn't make any claims about the *identity* of the intelligent cause.

3. William Lane Craig, "God and the Flying Spaghetti Monster," Reasonable Faith, December 3, 2007, www.reasonablefaith.org/god-and-the-flying-spaghetti -monster.

4. Richard Dawkins, *The God Delusion* (New York: Houghton Mifflin, 2008), 77.

Chapter 6 How Much Evidence Do We Need to Be Confident God Exists?

1. See ratiochristi.org.

2. Eric Chabot, "The Most Common Objection to God's Existence on a College Campus," ThinkApologetics.com, September 23, 2016, chab123.wordpress .com/2016/09/23/the-most-common-objection-to-gods-existence-on-a-college -campus.

3. Leo Rosten, "Bertrand Russell and God: A Memoir," *Saturday Review*, February 23, 1974, 25–26, emphasis mine.

4. Greta Christina, "6 (Unlikely) Developments that Could Convince This Atheist to Believe in God," Alternet, July 4, 2010, www.alternet.org/story/147424 /6_%28unlikely%29_developments_that_could_convince_this_atheist_to_believe _in_god.

5. Blaise Pascal, *Pensées* (New York: E. P. Dutton, 1958), 118.

6. J. Warner Wallace, *God's Crime Scene: A Cold-Case Detective Examines the Evidence for a Divinely Created Universe* (Colorado Springs: David C Cook, 2015), 201.

7. I highly recommend Wallace's *God's Crime Scene*, for further explanation of the evidence introduced in this book as well as an exploration of additional pieces of evidence not covered here.

Part 2 Science and God Overview

1. "Frequently Asked Questions," American Humanist Association, american humanist.org/about/faq/.

2. David Kinnaman, *You Lost Me: Why Young Christians Are Leaving Church . . . and Rethinking Faith* (Grand Rapids: Baker Books, 2011), chap. 7.

3. Ibid.

4. For more on these trends, see "'Nones' on the Rise," Pew Research Center, October 9, 2012, http://www.pewforum.org/2012/10/09/nones-on-the-rise/.

Chapter 7 Can Science Prove or Disprove God's Existence?

1. For more information on Camp Quest's mission, vision, goals, and values, see campquest.org.

2. Richard Dawkins, "The Great Unicorn Hunt," *Guardian*, July 29, 2009, www.theguardian.com/science/2009/jul/29/camp-quest-richard-dawkins.

3. Amir Aczel, *Why Science Does Not Disprove God* (New York: William Morrow, 2014), 242.

4. Jerry A. Coyne, *Faith versus Fact: Why Science and Religion Are Incompatible* (New York: Penguin, 2015), 29.

5. Richard Dawkins, "Why There Almost Certainly Is No God," *Huffpost* (blog), May 25, 2011, www.huffingtonpost.com/richard-dawkins/why-there-almost -certainl_b_32164.html.

6. Thomas D. Williams, "Fellow Scientists Reprimand Atheist Richard Dawkins for 'Misrepresenting Science,'" Breitbart, November 3, 2016, www .breitbart.com/big-government/2016/11/03/fellow-scientists-reprimand-atheist -richard-dawkins-misrepresenting-science/; and David R. Johnson, Elaine How-ard Ecklund, Di Di, and Kirstin R. W. Matthews, "Responding to Richard: Ce-lebrity and (Mis)representation of Science," Public Understanding of Science, October 10, 2016, pus.sagepub.com/content/early/2016/10/06/0963662516673501 .abstract.

7. Richard Dawkins, *The God Delusion* (New York: Houghton Mifflin, 2008), 72.

8. "Can Science Disprove God?," Debate.org, www.debate.org/opinions /can-science-disprove-god.

Chapter 8 Do Science and Religion Contradict Each Other?

1. One example of this is certain claims of Mormonism. An excellent sum-mary of the historical and archaeological challenges to Mormonism is J. War-ner Wallace, "Investigating the Evidence for Mormonism in Six Steps," Cold-Case Christianity, June 27, 2014, coldcasechristianity.com/2014/investigating -the-evidence-for-mormonism-in-six-steps/.

2. Most Christians sense this as well. When Pew Research surveyed Christians who say there is a conflict between science and their religious beliefs and asked them to name the three most significant issues, by far the most commonly cited one was evolution and the creation of the universe (mentioned by 36 percent). The second most popular answer, stated by 18 percent of respondents, was "don't know." For full study results, see Cary Funk and Becka A. Alper, "Religion and Sci-ence," Pew Research Center, October 22, 2015, www.pewinternet.org/files/2015/10 /PI_2015-10-22_religion-and-science_FINAL.pdf.

3. Research shows this is the most prevalent Christian view, held by 46 percent of Americans. See Frank Newport, "In U.S., 46% Hold Creationist View of Human Origins," Gallup, June 1, 2012, www.gallup.com/poll/155003/Hold-Creationist -View-Human-Origins.aspx for further data. http://www.huffingtonpost.com /2012/06/05/americans-believe-in-creationism_n_1571127.html

4. For an overview of verses used in this approach, see *Keeping Your Kids on God's Side*, 206–7.

5. See this exchange as an example of what is debated: William Lane Craig, "Who Speaks for Science?," Reasonable Faith, June 10, 2012, www.reasonablefaith .org/who-speaks-for-science.

6. BioLogos (biologos.org) is the leading organization that promotes the the-istic evolution view.

7. Reasons to Believe (reasons.org) is the leading organization that promotes the old-Earth creationism view.

8. For a brief overview of how theistic evolutionists respond, see this article from BioLogos (an organization that promotes theistic evolution): "Were Adam and

Eve Historical Figures?," www.biologos.org/common-questions/human-origins /were-adam-and-eve-historical-figures.

9. See, for example, Michael Behe, *Darwin's Black Box: The Biochemical Challenge to Evolution* (New York: Free Press, 2006); and Michael Behe, *The Edge of Evolution: The Search for the Limits of Darwinism* (New York: Free Press, 2008).

10. This chapter is an exceedingly short overview of a vast and highly complex subject. For a book-length treatment, I highly recommend Alvin Plantinga, *Where the Conflict Lies: Science, Religion, and Naturalism* (New York: Oxford University Press, 2011).

11. "Why Do Christians Hate Science?," Dangerous Talk, February 12, 2010, www.dangeroustalk.net/?p=846.

Chapter 9 Do Science and Religion Complement Each Other?

1. John C. Lennox, *God's Undertaker: Has Science Buried God?* (Oxford: Lion Hudson, 2009), 58.

2. Paul Davies, "Physics and the Mind of God," *First Things*, August 1995, www .firstthings.com/article/1995/08/003-physics-and-the-mind-of-god-the-templeton -prize-address-24.

3. Thomas Nagel, *Mind and Cosmos: Why the Materialist Neo-Darwinian Conception of Nature Is Almost Certainly False* (New York: Oxford University Press, 2012), 26.

4. Frank Turek, *Stealing from God: Why Atheists Need God to Make Their Case* (Colorado Springs: NavPress, 2015), 37.

5. See whisper.sh/whisper/050bc680a81e7f484927d1cc28e090f1c9d8ec/No-its -not--Science-doesnt-need-religion-to-answer-anything--We-don.

Chapter 10 Is God Just an Explanation for What Science Doesn't Yet Know?

1. See the transcript of the debate at www.stephenjaygould.org/ctrl/barker -howe.html.

2. "Can Science Disprove God?," Debate.org, www.debate.org/opinions/can -science-disprove-god?ysort=3&nsort=5.

Chapter 11 Can Science Explain Why People Believe in God?

1. David G. McAfee and Chuck Harrison, *The Belief Book* (London: Dangerous Little Books, 2015), 4.

2. Aku Visala, *Naturalism, Theism, and the Cognitive Study of Religion: Religion Explained* (New York: Routledge, 2016), 6.

3. Justin L. Barrett, "Are We Born Believing in God?," Big Questions Online, March 5, 2013, www.bigquestionsonline.com/2013/03/05/are-born-believing-god/.

4. Deborah Kelemen, "Are Children 'Intuitive Theists'?," *Psychological Science* 15, no. 5 (May 2003): 295–301, www.bu.edu/cdl/files/2013/08/2004_Kelemen _IntuitiveTheist.pdf.

5. Ibid.

6. Justin L. Barrett, "Cognitive Science of Religion and Christian Faith: How May They Be Brought Together?," *Perspectives on Science and Christian Faith*, November 16, 2015, www.csca.ca/wp-content/uploads/2015/11/Barrett2015.pdf.

7. Charles Taliaferro, Victoria S. Harrison, and Stewart Goetz, eds., *The Routledge Companion to Theism* (New York: Routledge, 2013), 229–31.

8. Justin L. Barrett, "Cognitive Science of Religion: What Is It and Why Is It?," *Religion Compass* 1, no. 6 (2007): 768–86.

9. Quoted in J. Wentzel Van Huyssteen, *Evolution, Religion, and Cognitive Science: Critical and Constructive Essays* (Oxford: Oxford University Press, 2014), 135.

Chapter 12 What Do Scientists Believe about God?

1. Sam Harris, "10 Myths—and 10 Truths—about Atheism," *LA Times*, December 24, 2006, www.latimes.com/news/la-op-harris24dec24-story.html.

2. James H. Leuba, *The Belief in God and Immortality: A Psychological, Anthropological, and Statistical Study* (Boston: Sherman, French & Co., 1916).

3. Belief in a personal God was determined by agreement with the statement "I believe in a God in intellectual and affective communication with humankind, i.e., a God to whom one may pray in expectation of receiving an answer. By 'answer' I mean more than the subjective, psychological effect of prayer." More recent researchers have pointed out that this definition is problematic. For example, the wording may have suggested to some respondents that such a God would answer all prayers affirmatively. Other people may believe in a personal God who doesn't answer prayers at all.

4. Edward J. Larson and Larry Witham, "Scientists Are Still Keeping the Faith," *Nature* 386 (April 3, 1997): 435–36.

5. Edward J. Larson and Larry Witham, "Leading Scientists Still Reject God," *Nature* 394 (July 23, 1998): 313.

6. Elaine Howard Ecklund and Christopher P. Sheitle, "Religion among Academic Scientists: Distinctions, Disciplines, and Demographics," *Social Problems* 54, no. 2 (2007): 289–307, www.owlnet.rice.edu/~ehe/doc/Ecklund_SocialProblems_54_2.pdf.

7. Ibid.

8. Ibid.

9. David Masci, "Scientists and Belief," Pew Research Center, November 5, 2009, www.pewforum.org/2009/11/05/scientists-and-belief/.

10. Elaine Howard Ecklund, "Religious Communities, Science, Scientists, and Perceptions: A Comprehensive Survey," February 16, 2014, www.aaas.org/sites/default/files/content_files/RU_AAASPresentationNotes_2014_0219%20(1).pdf.

11. "93% of Scientists Are Atheist or Agnostic?," Yahoo Answers, answers.yahoo.com/question/index?qid=20100115000850AA3zhcL.

Part 3 The Nature of God Overview

1. See whisper.sh/whisper/05187fb235642a3099947f945d8d3be780fa63/Im-a-Christian-conservative-but-I-think-that-God-wants-us-to-be-happy.

2. "Christians: Do You Admit Your God Is an Arrogant, Cruel and Violent God?," Yahoo Answers, answers.yahoo.com/question/index?qid=2010052322243 1AA2TnzK.

Chapter 13 What Can We Learn about God from the Bible?

1. A. W. Tozer, *The Knowledge of the Holy* (New York: HarperCollins, 1961), preface and 79.

2. For a good comparison of Christian views on this subject, I recommend Stanley N. Gundry and Dennis Jowers, eds., *Four Views on Divine Providence* (Grand Rapids: Zondervan, 2011).

3. C. S. Lewis, *Mere Christianity* (New York: HarperOne, 2015), 39.

4. "Why Is the God of Christians, Jews, and Muslims So Arrogant?," Yahoo Answers, answers.yahoo.com/question/index?qid=20111109224533AAb llXD.

Chapter 14 What Does It Mean That God Is Love?

1. D. A. Carson, *The Difficult Doctrine of the Love of God* (Wheaton: Crossway, 2000), 11–12.

2. Ibid., 39.

3. There is much theological debate over whether God's saving love (point 3) and God's love for the elect (point 4) are one and the same. That discussion is outside the scope of this chapter, so I've chosen to stay faithful to Carson's original five-point framework and simply note that some Christians would collapse points 3 and 4 into a single kind of love.

4. "The Doctrine of I Don't Care Ministries," I Don't Care Ministries, www .idcministries.org/what-we-believe-about-god/.

Chapter 15 What Does It Mean That God Is Just?

1. For help talking to your kids about hell, see chapter 4 in *Keeping Your Kids on God's Side*. For help talking about why Jesus had to die for our sins, see chapter 20 in *Keeping Your Kids on God's Side*.

2. "Why Does God Sound So Mean in the Bible?," Yahoo Answers, answers .yahoo.com/question/index?qid=20110515103519AAnLFIj.

Chapter 16 Why Does God Seem So Harsh in Parts of the Old Testament?

1. Christians have varying views on whether Noah's flood was global (literally covering the whole earth as we know it today) or local (covering some smaller area). For our purposes, the distinction doesn't matter. Whether God wiped out every living thing in a local area or a global area, the same question remains: Is such an action consistent with the character of a good God?

2. For a more detailed examination of the Canaanite question, see chapter 3 in *Keeping Your Kids on God's Side*.

3. Steve Wells, "The Flood of Noah: All Flesh Died that Moved upon the Earth," *Dwindling in Unbelief* (blog), January 24, 2009, dwindlinginunbelief.blogspot .com/2009/01/gods-killings-1-all-flesh-died-that.html.

Chapter 17 How Can God Be Three Persons in One?

1. Note that the word *Trinity* is never used in the Bible. The first person to use the term *Trinity* and explicitly define it as the Father, the Son, and the Holy Spirit was the early church father Tertullian, writing in the early third century. Importantly, however, this doesn't mean the idea of the Trinity was invented a couple hundred years after Jesus. The word *Trinity* was created to summarize what Scripture had already revealed about God's nature.

2. While Mormons acknowledge the existence of many gods, they emphasize that they *worship* only the Godhead—God, Jesus, and the Holy Ghost (their preferred term for the Holy Spirit).

3. An important additional aspect of this discussion is whether Jesus himself claimed to be God. The verses listed here demonstrate that *others* spoke of him as God. For a detailed look at the many ways Jesus personally claimed to be God, see chapter 18 in *Keeping Your Kids on God's Side*.

4. "Am I Crazy for Thinking the Trinity Is Illogical?," Quora, October 4, 2015, www.quora.com/Am-I-crazy-for-thinking-the-Trinity-is-illogical.

Chapter 18 Why Didn't God Reveal More of Himself in the Bible?

1. "The Bible as Truth," The Rational Response Squad, June 27, 2007, www .rationalresponders.com/forum/sapient/atheist_vs_theist/8388.

Part 4 Believing in God Overview

1. See this article as one example: Anonymous, "Introducing Cognitive Dissonance," *Debunking Christianity* (blog), November 25, 2007, debunkingchristianity .blogspot.com/2007/11/introducing-cognitive-dissonance.html.

Chapter 19 Why Do People Believe So Many Different Things about God?

1. As one example, this article for Jehovah's Witnesses explains the alleged danger of reading other material (see "Enemy Tactics"): "Fight the Fine Fight of the Faith," *The Watchtower*, 2004, wol.jw.org/en/wol/d/r1/lp-e/2004126.

2. It's possible that some agnostics would say they are agnostic about whether we can know if any given holy book is true, resulting in their agnosticism about God. I've never met someone who is agnostic at that level (as opposed to rejecting the truth of all holy books and therefore being agnostic about God's existence), but it's theoretically an exception to what I've stated here.

3. "Religion and the Unaffiliated," Pew Research Center, October 9, 2012, www.pewforum.org/2012/10/09/nones-on-the-rise-religion/.

4. Lee and Annette Woofenden, "If There's One God, Why All the Different Religions?," Spiritual Insights for Everyday Life, November 5, 2012, leewoof .org/2012/11/05/if-theres-one-god-why-all-the-different-religions/.

Chapter 20 Do All Religions Worship the Same God?

1. Christine Hauser, "Wheaton College Professor Is Put on Leave after Remarks Supporting Muslims," *New York Times*, December 16, 2015, www.nytimes .com/2015/12/17/us/wheaton-college-professor-larycia-hawkins-muslim-scarf.html ?_r=0.

2. "So Much Arguing, So Little Belief . . .," Planet Think Tanks 2, www.planet thinktanks2.com/forums/viewtopic.php?f=18&t=2241&start=40.

3. "Sikhism 101," Debate.org, www.debate.org/forums/religion/topic/5078/.

4. "Are the Gods of Different Religions the Same?," Quora, January 20, 2013, www.quora.com/Are-the-gods-of-different-religions-the-same-If-not-what-are-the -differences-between-them.

5. "Sikhism 101," Debate.org, www.debate.org/forums/religion/topic/5078/.

Chapter 21 Is What You Believe about God Simply a Matter of Where You Grew Up?

1. *Wikipedia*, s.v., "Islam by Country," en.wikipedia.org/wiki/Islam_by_country #Countries.

2. *Wikipedia*, s.v. "Culture of South America," en.wikipedia.org/wiki/Culture _of_South_America.

3. *Wikipedia*, s.v. "Hinduism by Country," en.wikipedia.org/wiki/Hinduism _by_country.

4. *Wikipedia*, s.v. "Demographics of Atheism," en.wikipedia.org/wiki/Demo graphics_of_atheism.

5. *Wikipedia*, s.v. "Buddhism by Country," en.wikipedia.org/wiki/Buddhism _by_country.

6. "Religious Landscape Study," Pew Research Center, www.pewforum.org /religious-landscape-study/.

7. "Table: Religious Diversity Index Scores by Country," Pew Research Center, April 4, 2014, www.pewforum.org/2014/04/04/religious-diversity-index-scores -by-country/.

8. "Chapter 2: Religious Switching and Intermarriage," Pew Research Center, May 12, 2015, www.pewforum.org/2015/05/12/chapter-2-religious-switching -and-intermarriage/#fnref-23318-16.

9. "Religion as an Accident of Geography," *My Case against God* (blog), September 16, 2007, mycaseagainstgod.blogspot.com/2007/09/religion-as-accident-of -geography.html.

10. As a purely practical point, we should also note that in several countries atheism is the dominant cultural belief. Both belief and lack of belief in God vary with geography, but one of these beliefs must be true—either God exists or he doesn't. This means the relationship between views on God and geography logically can't imply all these views are false.

11. Bob Seidensticker, "Your Religion Is a Reflection of Your Culture—You'd Be Muslim If You Were Born in Pakistan," Patheos, June 8, 2015, www.patheos.com /blogs/crossexamined/2015/06/your-religion-is-a-reflection-of-your-culture-youd -be-muslim-if-you-were-born-in-pakistan/.

12. "'One True Religion': Revelation or Just an Accident of Birth?," *The Atheist Camel* (blog), May 23, 2009, atheistcamel.blogspot.com/2009/05/one-true-religion -revelation-or-just.html.

13. "Given that a Person's Religion . . . ," Quora, September 3, 2015, www.quora .com/Given-that-a-persons-religion-is-most-often-a-simple-accident-of-geography -how-can-religious-people-be-so-convinced-that-their-particular-one-just-happens -to-be-the-only-one-that-is-right-and-the-others-are-all-wrong-at-best-and-down right-evil-at-worst.

Chapter 22 Why Do Christians Sometimes Doubt Their Belief in God?

1. Natasha Crain, "5 Things to Do When You're Struggling with Faith Doubts," June 16, 2014, christianmomthoughts.com/5-things-to-do-when-youre -struggling-with-faith-doubts.

2. This entire book is available for free online at www.garyhabermas.com /books/dealing_with_doubt/dealing_with_doubt.htm.

3. Pastor Bobby Conway has an excellent book on this subject that I highly recommend: *Doubting toward Faith: The Journey to Confident Christianity* (Eugene, OR: Harvest House, 2015).

4. I list several recommended books on my website on the major questions about the Bible's reliability: christianmomthoughts.com/recommended-apologetics -books-on-the-reliability-of-the-bible/.

5. Crain, "5 Things to Do When You're Struggling with Faith Doubts."

Chapter 23 How Do We Know God Hears and Answers Prayers?

1. See page 13 of the study "U.S. Religious Landscape Survey," Pew Forum, www .pewforum.org/files/2008/06/report2religious-landscape-study-key-findings.pdf.

2. Michael Lipka, "Why America's 'Nones' Left Religion Behind," Pew Research Center, August 24, 3016, www.pewresearch.org/fact-tank/2016/08/24 /why-americas-nones-left-religion-behind/.

Chapter 24 How Can We Develop a Relationship with a God We Can't See or Hear?

1. God speaks to us through the Holy Spirit as well (John 14:17; 1 Cor. 3:16). But it's important to remember that the Spirit will never prompt us to do something in conflict with Scripture, so we must have a proper foundation in God's Word to have proper discernment.

2. Ed Stetzer, "The Epidemic of Bible Illiteracy in Our Churches," The Exchange, July 6, 2015, www.christianitytoday.com/edstetzer/2015/july/epidemic -of-bible-illiteracy-in-our-churches.html.

3. Billy Hallowell, "'God Is an Imaginary Friend': Atheist Billboard Ignites Controversy in Colorado," The Blaze, January 25, 2012, www.theblaze.com /news/2012/01/25/god-is-an-imaginary-friend-atheist-billboard-ignites-controversy -in-colorado/.

Chapter 25 What Is the Meaning of Life?

1. Douglas Adams, *The Hitchhiker's Guide to the Galaxy* (New York: Del Rey, 1995).

2. Carl Sagan, *Cosmos* (New York: Random House, 1980), 1.

3. Ibid., 134.

4. Gregory Koukl, *The Story of Reality: How the World Began, How It Ends, and Everything Important that Happens in Between* (Grand Rapids: Zondervan, 2017), 55.

5. Tom Chivers, "I Asked Atheists How They Find Meaning in a Purposeless Universe," BuzzFeed, August 11, 2015, www.buzzfeed.com/tomchivers/when-i -was-a-child-i-spake-as-a-child?utm_term=.idAXqAM0m#.hlkvaRbKO.

Chapter 26 Do We Really Have Free Will?

1. Jerry A. Coyne, "You Don't Have Free Will," *Chronicle of Higher Education*, March 18, 2012, www.chronicle.com/article/jerry-a-coyne-you-dont-have /131165.

2. Anthony Cashmore, "The Lucretian Swerve," *Proceedings of the National Academy of Sciences* 107, no. 10 (January 12, 2010): 4503.

3. Francis Crick, *The Astonishing Hypothesis* (London: Simon & Schuster, 1994), 3.

4. Quoted in *Expelled: No Intelligence Allowed*, directed by Nathan Frankowski, Premise Media, 2008.

Chapter 27 What Should We Do with Our Lives?

1. Moira Welsh, "Flock Sticks with Atheist United Church Minister," *The Star*, September 11, 2016, www.thestar.com/news/gta/2016/09/11/flock-sticks -with-atheist-united-church-minister.html.

2. Gretta Vosper, "Words," April 21, 2017, www.grettavosper.ca/words/.

3. Wendy Thomas Russell, "'It's Not What You Believe but What You Do in Life That Matters': An Explainer," Patheos, August 24, 2015, www.patheos .com/blogs/naturalwonderers/its-not-what-you-believe-but-what-you-do-in-life -that-matters-an-explainer/.

Chapter 28 What Is Our Responsibility to Other People?

1. "Definition of Humanism," American Humanist Association, american humanist.org/what-is-humanism/definition-of-humanism/.

2. Peter Singer, *Practical Ethics* (New York: Cambridge University Press, 2011), 163.

3. "Hunger Statistics," World Vision, www.wvi.org/food-and-livelihood-security /hunger-statistics.

4. Norman Geisler, *Ethics: Alternatives and Issues* (Grand Rapids: Zondervan, 1979), 179.

5. Penn Jillette, "Not Proselytize," November 13, 2009, www.youtube.com /watch?v=owZc3Xq8obk.

6. Natasha Crain, "Is Spiritual Truth a Matter of Opinion? An Open Letter to a Relativist," April 12, 2016, christianmomthoughts.com/is-spiritual-truth -a-matter-of-opinion-an-open-letter-to-a-relativist/.

Chapter 29 How Should We Make Sense of Evil?

1. "Is There Such a Thing as Good and Evil?," Debate.org, www.debate.org /opinions/is-there-such-a-thing-as-good-and-evil.

2. Alvin Plantinga, *God, Freedom, and Evil* (Grand Rapids: Eerdmans, 1989), 30.

3. See chapters 21–24 in *Keeping Your Kids on God's Side* for a discussion of this evidence.

4. "How Does an Atheist Justify Experiencing Moral Outrage?," Quora, www .quora.com/How-does-an-atheist-justify-experiencing-moral-outrage.

Chapter 30 Why Does Biblical Hope Matter?

1. Bertrand Russell, "A Free Man's Worship," in *The Basic Writings of Bertrand Russell*, ed. Robert E. Egner and Lester E. Denonn (New York: Simon & Schuster, 1961), 67.

2. Parts 3 and 4 of *Keeping Your Kids on God's Side* discuss the strong historical evidence for Jesus's resurrection and the reliability of the Bible.

3. Luke Muehlhauser, "Do Atheists Have Less Purpose and Hope?," Common Sense Atheism, July 17, 2009, commonsenseatheism.com/?p=1708.

Natasha Crain is a popular blogger, author, and speaker who is passionate about equipping Christian parents to raise their kids with an understanding of how to make a case for and defend their faith in an increasingly secular world. Her blog, *Christian Mom Thoughts*, attracts more than twenty-five thousand readers each month. The author of *Keeping Your Kids on God's Side*, Natasha has an MBA in marketing and statistics from UCLA and a certificate in Christian apologetics from Biola University. A former marketing executive and adjunct professor, she lives in Southern California with her husband and three children.

Connect with Natasha!

To read Natasha's blog and learn about additional resources for Christian parents, visit ChristianMomThoughts.com.

f @ChristianMomThoughts 🐦 @Natasha_Crain

LIKE THIS BOOK?

Consider sharing it with others!

- Share or mention the book on social media.
  Use the hashtag **#TalkingWithYourKidsAboutGod**.

  - Share this message on **FACEBOOK**:
    "I loved #TalkingWithYourKidsAboutGod by
    @ChristianMomThoughts"

  - Share this message on **TWITTER**:
    "I loved #TalkingWithYourKidsAboutGod
    by @Natasha_Crain"

- Write a book review on your blog or on a retailer site.

- Pick up a copy for friends, family, or strangers—
  anyone who you think would value and be challenged
  by its message!

- Use this book as curriculum for your small group, church
  class, youth group, or Christian school.

- Follow Baker Books on social media and tell us what you like.

  f Facebook.com/ReadBakerBooks

  🐦 @ReadBakerBooks